EXPECTING *the* UNEXPECTED

EXPECTING *the* UNEXPECTED

Teaching Myself—and Others —to Read and Write

DONALD M. MURRAY

BOYNTON/COOK PUBLISHERS
HEINEMANN
Portsmouth, NH

BOYNTON/COOK PUBLISHERS
A Division of
HEINEMANN EDUCATIONAL BOOKS, INC.
70 Court Street, Portsmouth, NH 03801
Offices and agents throughout the world

The following chapters originally appeared in other publications:

Chapter 1: "Writing and Teaching for Surprise," in *College English* 46 (1), January 1984, 8–14. **Chapter 2:** "Reading for Surprise" in *Teachers Networking—the Whole Language Newsletter* 8 (3), February 1988, Richard C. Owen Publishers, Inc. **Chapter 3:** "First Silence, Then Paper" in *fforum—Essays on Theory and Practice in the Teaching of Writing*, ed. by Patricia L. Stock. Copyright © 1983 by Boynton/Cook Publishers, Inc. **Chapter 4:** "The Essential Delay: When Writer's Block Isn't" in *When a Writer Can't Write—Studies in Writer's Block and Other Composing-Process Problems*, ed. by Mike Rose. New York: The Guilford Press, 1985. **Chapter 5:** "Writing Badly to Write Well: Searching for the Instructive Line" in *Sentence Combining: A Rhetorical Perspective*, Southern Illinois University Press, 1984. **Chapter 6:** "Rehearsing, Rehearsing" in *Rhetoric Review*, 1987. **Chapter 7:** "Reading While Writing" in *Only Connect—Uniting Reading and Writing*, ed. by Thomas Newkirk. Copyright © 1986 by Boynton/Cook Publishers, Inc. **Chapter 10:** "The Importance of Bad Writing—And How to Encourage It" in *Conversations in Composition—Proceedings of New Dimensions in Writing: The First Merrimack College Conference on Composition Instruction*, ed. by Albert C. De Ciccio and Michael J. Rossi, Department of English, Merrimack College, North Andover, MA. **Chapter 11:** "What Makes Students Write" in *Writing Now*, a booklet from the conference "Georgia, Write Now," Atlanta, GA, January 4–5, 1985. Copyright © 1986 by Shirley Haley-James, Charles Billiard, and the Georgia Department of Education. **Chapter 16:** "Tricks of the Nonfiction Trade," *The Writer*, 1985. **Chapter 17:** "Newswriting" in *Writing for Many Roles* by Mimi Schwartz. Copyright © 1985 by Boynton/Cook Publishers, Inc. **Chapter 20:** "Getting under the Lightning" in *Writers on Writing*, ed. by Tom Waldrep. Copyright © 1985 by Random House, Inc. **Chapter 21:** "One Writer's Secrets" in *College Composition and Communication* 37 (2), May 1986. **Chapter 22:** "Four Newspaper Columns": "So You Want to Be a Writer," *Boston Globe*, October 1, 1986; "Reflections from a Sick Bed," *Boston Globe*, May 1, 1987; "A Healthy Obsession," *Boston Globe*, July 1, 1987. **Chapter 24:** "Decisions and Revisions: The Planning Strategies of a Publishing Writer" by Carol Berkenkotter and "Response of a Laboratory Rat—or, Being Protocoled" by Donald M. Murray in *College Composition and Communication* 34 (2), May 1983, 156–72.

The following has generously given permission to use material in this book: p. 205–206: From "To Fashion a Text" by Annie Dillard in *Inventing the Truth: The Art and Craft of Memoir*, edited by William Zinsser. Copyright © 1987 by Houghton Mifflin Co.

Library of Congress Cataloging-in-Publication Data

Murray, Donald Morison, 1924–
Expecting the unexpected: teaching myself—and others—to read and write/Donald M. Murray.
p. cm.
ISBN 0-86709-243-2
1. English language—Rhetoric—Study and teaching. I. Title.
PE1404.M878 1989
808'.042'07—dc19 88-8490
CIP

Designed by Wladislaw Finne.
Printed in the United States of America.
10 9 8 7 6 5 4 3 2 1

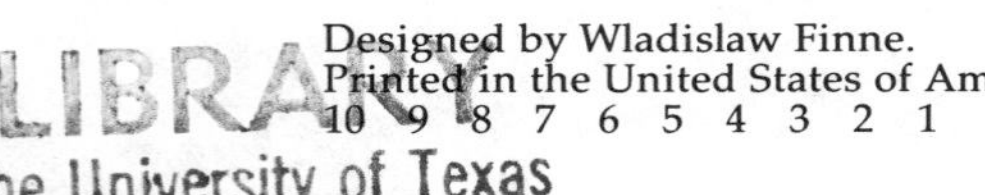

CONTENTS

III. EXPLORING FORM

IV. SITTING TO WRITE

ACKNOWLEDGMENTS

Writing is a lonely act that is never really performed alone. I am grateful to far more than I can name, and it is no cliché to say that my students taught me more than they knew—or perhaps they did know and were kind enough not to tell me.

It was clear as I reread these pieces that there are a number of people to whom I am especially indebted. They know how often and how much I depended on them. They are, in careful alphabetical order: Linda Buchanan Allen, Nancie Atwell, Carol Berkenkotter, Bob Connors, Brock Dethier, Don Graves, Tom Newkirk, Chip Scanlan, John and Tilly Warnock, and Driek Zirinsky.

I am especially grateful for the editing I received from Nancy Sheridan and Toby Gordon. They not only saved me from error but improved my writing.

My wife, Minnie Mae, my daughters, Anne Murray and Hannah Murray Starobin, and now my son-in-law, Michael Starobin, are always my first audience. They sit in the front row and by nods and smiles urge me on.

PREFACE

I was one of those kids who always wanted to get on with it, to stay up late, to leave the house and explore the street, to escape school, to dash through today and get to tomorrow. And now I find myself at a time of looking back, at least as a full-time teacher and a student of my students and the writing process.

And I am surprised. Surprised at having survived a sickly childhood, combat, surgery, the daily automobile close miss; surprised that I who hated school—and teachers—found myself behind the teacher's desk, loved it, and had the chutzpah to write books telling teachers how to teach; surprised I have become a professor emeritus; surprised that I am free to be surprised at my own pages, the secret delight of every writer.

This book, then, is a celebration of surprise. It is one writer/teacher's account of how to expect the unexpected, how, even, to encourage, nurture, and make use of it. Gathered together here are some of the pieces I have written since the publication of my previous collection, *Learning by Teaching* (Boynton/Cook, 1982); this book includes notes on writing I wrote and shared with my students during the writing process; and it presents case histories showing my own writing process at work together with a research article putting those case histories in a larger context.

The entire book, I discovered with surprise, has a constant theme that runs through each selection: it is surprise itself. Looking back, I realize how important it has been for me to seek the unexpected and how revolutionary to search for what so many people fear.

During my last freshman English class I had a visitor from another state who was studying composition teachers at work.

My students were writing in class, and I had time to go through the syllabus and my departures from it with her. Again and again she asked me how this activity or that one had worked before. In each case, I answered that I had never tried it before. Her astonishment and, I suspect, discomfort at this calculated unpredictability in my last class made me realize how vital it was for me to program the encouragement of accident into my teaching plan.

I realized that what I had been doing these past twenty-four years in the classroom is teaching students to expect the unexpected and how to make use of it. I realize, looking back, how radical that was. I suppose I must accept how abnormal those of us are who welcome the unexpected.

I suppose I should have known that. One of the first things I learned on the job is that bosses do not like surprises. They expect you to do what they expect. The unusual solution to a familiar problem terrifies most bosses. People in charge want what they expect.

And for bosses you can substitute editors and teachers. I consult for several publications and see only a few editors—the very best ones—who can accept the unexpected and read it for possibility. Surprise is usually read as failure, and I spend as much time teaching writers how to prepare editors for surprise as I spend trying to convince editors they should stimulate surprise instead of professional predictability.

The academy, throughout history, has been conservative, the defender and advocate of tradition. That is an important part of school. We need to learn the traditions of the past and present, the expectations of society and its members.

But those expectations are rarely met. Time stands still for no scholar or instructor. That is why many middle-aged teachers who teach the traditions of their youth in a traditional manner appear to suffer a permanent dyspepsia. Life will give you a sour stomach if you have a hunger for predictability.

What is certain is change. We must expect unexpectedness. If we are to teach our students responsibility, we must prepare them to make use of change. Writing is ideal for this study; change—surprise—is essential for effective writing. Yet society expects us to teach rhetoric and grammar so that the students will be frozen in whatever propriety is fashionable for the parent.

Writing teachers are radicals—and should be. We seek—hunger for—diversity, difference, contradiction, conflict, evolution, doubt, questions without answers, answers without questions, and we find it, for the world is changing. How we view it is changing, and the forms and language we use to document, communicate, and understand those changes are themselves changing. Our own drafts and our students' drafts surprise us with their unexpected articulateness as well as their insight.

Looking back, I hope that I demonstrated as I wrote with my students, read with my students, listened with my students that surprise is the writer's friend. The unexpected, not the expected, teaches us and allows us, through our writing, to teach.

Surprise should be encouraged and cultivated in the writing classroom. We do it by respecting individual diversity of vision, connection, thought, and voice, by revealing there are few rights and wrongs but many ever-changing options, and by making clear that if we are to survive as individuals and as a society we need to rid ourselves of our learned fear of surprise and embrace the unexpected in our classrooms, on our pages, and in our lives. As a writer and a teacher I expect the unexpected.

I

LISTENING TO THE PAGE

ONE

WRITING AND TEACHING FOR SURPRISE

Rereading this article I am surprised that I like it. I chose this piece from memory as the focus of the book, not daring to read it. But this morning I had to face my own strange words on the page. I circled the text and finally pounced on it. Not too bad, not too bad at all.

Perhaps, with age, I'm discovering that I have no choice, I have to accept myself; perhaps I'm just lowering my standards. I rarely read what I write and when I do I usually feel total despair or a compulsion to revise. I cannot type my own final drafts, or I would change everything. But I like this piece.

Of course I would change it if I had the chance, but my changes would not improve it. The article reads honestly to me, years later. I feel I am reentering the essential writing experience I had when I wrote it. And I think the implications I draw are still significant. Writing should teach the author first. Reading this over, I remember what I learned writing it: the centrality of surprise, how the cart has to precede the horse, the importance of ease in writing, pounceability. And I learn them all again by reading it.

What I didn't realize when I wrote this piece in 1984 was the universal significance of surprise and just how radical it is to teach for surprise. I am correcting that with this book.

My students become writers at that moment when they first write what they do not expect to write. They experience the moment of surprise that motivates writers to haul themselves to their writing desks year after year. Writers value the gun that does *not* hit the target at which it is aimed.

Before they experience surprise students find writing drudgery, something that has to be done after the thinking is over—the dishes that have to be washed after the guests have left. But writing is the banquet itself. As Louise Nevelson said, "My work is a feast for myself."

Writers seek what they do not expect to find. Writers are, like all artists, rationalizers of accident. They find out what they are doing after they have done it.

Students should share in this purposeful unknowing, for writing is not the reporting of what was discovered, but the act of exploration itself. John Galsworthy said, "I sit. I don't intend." E. M. Forster added, "Think before you speak is criticism's motto; speak before you think is creation's." The evidence from writers goes on and on. Speaking of his play, *The Birthday Party*, Harold Pinter said, "The thinking germinated and bred itself. It proceeded according to its own logic. What did I do? I followed the indications, I kept a sharp eye on the clues I found myself dropping."

When you read what I have written it may be the agent that causes surprise in you. But that finished text which gave me the satisfaction of completion is far removed from the moment of surprise when I learned what I did not even know I had to learn. Let me try to take you backstage, no, not even backstage, but far beyond that into that almost always private moment when the writer is alone with language and the words escape intention.

> I am sitting with my daybook on my lapdesk, and my notes at the top of the page—notes I had forgotten until I read them now—say, "Lack of faith—read previous text and feel nausea—physical revulsion." I have come to confront a novel I have been working on for years. Drafts have been completed and abandoned, and there is no hope or anticipation of surprise.
>
> I start again the new first chapter that must precede the chapters already written. I write four lines and strike it through, then start again. It goes well enough, but it is a journeyman's job. The writing seems terribly expected, and as Robert Frost said, "No surprise for the writer, no surprise for the reader." I slog on knowing that the slog can be changed if ever a surprise occurs.
>
> I write, "He could remember when he first became aware of the sadness. He had come back from a swing through the west coast offices and realized he had the usual post-business trip sadness." I can remember the despair at the triteness of that sentence. Then my pen wrote, "'Daddy's wearies,' Lucinda told the children"—the sentence isn't

finished, but I must interrupt, for that phrase that Lucinda uttered was a small surprise, because I had never heard that expression, and it seemed right, revealing of her and their life. The next sentence went ". . . and he set up his paints in the backyard to paint the woods. It was May, but he saw no colors."

That was an enormous surprise. I was inside the skull of a man who would, before the chapter was out, murder his children. I had no hint that this is what he saw, but having received that surprise the text became alive to me.

A few weeks later I was directing a session for teachers on writing in public, and so I went to the board to write in public. These fragments I started writing in such workshops are pulling me with a powerful force toward a book I will attempt on my sabbatical. It is a book about World War II, and I don't know whether it is fiction or autobiography or poetry or history, but the continual force of surprise tells me there is a book to be written. I put down the word "boots" on the board, thinking I will write about the Nazi jackboots or my own paratroop boots, and then see that my hand has written below it "bones," and I am digging a foxhole in that field in France when I realized that I was digging in the buried bones of soldiers from World War I. And so I start to write and, again, it is not what I expect to write.

"I am practicing in the side yard and slowly wind up, look over to first base, then turn to the plate and shoot the tennis ball in on Lou Gehrig. Before it hits the garage door I hear the back bedroom cough next door. It coughs with experience, a cough that sounds as if it comes from an empty room. All spring and summer and fall the room coughs while I play, when I try to sleep at night, when I go out to get my bicycle from the garage in the morning dark for my paper route the room coughs. In winter the window is shut and the storm window went over it, but in the spring the room coughed again."

The man next door, whom I never saw, had been gassed in World War I. That remembered cough, so much louder now that I have experienced war, surprises me. I hope it will surprise and haunt my readers.

Through my daybooks there is a trail of small surprises that led me to give the talk that surprised me enough to draft this article. I had lots of notes about how teachers and students recognize when they are making progress. But

> the material seemed ordinary to me, when this fragment appeared on the page, "Student breakthrough when achieve surprise." And several days later this almost sentence occurred, "When a student is surprised by what he or she is writing then the student becomes a writer central act break-through" and although I did not know what would be the lead sentence of this article I did know it would be this surprise turned on my lathe and shaped for publication.

I'm tempted to go on, to recover for myself the surprises of poetry, fiction, and nonfiction—even the surprises in a grant proposal—that I see on those pages. But I think that the case may be made that the writer's reason for writing is primarily to read what the writer did not expect to write. The carrot on the stick turns out to be a strawberry or a parsnip or a Granny Smith.

Of course there is false surprise, the vision is a mirage; and there are the new surprises that lead palace coups against old surprises and keep the writing in a continual state of disorder. The experienced writer always has the problem of the excess of surprise and must learn how to decide which mermaid is real. These are problems for experience and craft, but first there must be the possibility of surprise. That is the starting point for the effective writer and the effective teacher, and it seems to me there are six elements that help us achieve surprise.

EXPECTATION

The cart does have to come before the horse. We are much more likely to perceive surprise if we expect to see it. Once we have the experience of surprise, then we must remember and build on that moment when language leaves the mind and moves the hand.

The wonderful thing about surprise is that the more you experience surprise the easier it becomes to experience it. Surprise breeds surprise. And you can learn to be patient at your desk waiting for surprise to land.

You can also project surprise onto your students. If you are a writing teacher who writes—who lures and captures surprise—then it becomes easier for you to expect your students to achieve surprise themselves. And once a few students experience surprise in their writing and share it with their peers, surprise becomes epidemic in the classroom.

The more you become knowledgeable about surprise through

your own writing and teaching experience, the more you will learn how to create an environment that will attract and make use of surprise. And your belief that your students can capture surprise on the page will be reinforced.

HABIT

I have the habit of writing. My simple tools are always with me: pen and paper. I try to follow the ancients' counsel *nulla dies sine linea*, never a day without a line. A line, however, may not look like a line to a nonwriter. It may not be a sentence. It is most likely a phrase or a fragment, a word, a list, a diagram. As a writer I must become used to such literary compost.

My habit involves the use of fragments of time, a moment here and a moment there. I treasure those moments, such as this one, when I can write at a swoop. But those few hours are fertilized by what I accomplish writing for a few minutes or even a few seconds in a parked car, in a meeting, waiting for a class to start, during TV, at a lunch counter. I will be surprised by what I write if I'm in the habit of putting words on paper even if I do not have the time to write.

And, in writing this, I realize my habit includes the stimulation I receive from those with whom I can share my early drafts. These people change by circumstance and, to some degree, by the genre in which I'm writing. But they have two elements in common: they write themselves and can accept the draft as a draft, and they make me want to write when I leave them. These are very special colleagues, these test readers. They can be tough, they can be supportive, they can attack and comfort, often at the same time. They are important because they allow me to stand back from my work and gain distance on it, and because, through their faith that I have something worth saying, they can draw me back to my work.

I must, as a teacher, encourage (force?) my students to develop their own writing habits: to write frequently, at least once a day; to write much more than they will complete or publish (maple syrup is the product of boiling thirty or forty gallons of sap to get one of syrup, and in writing there's a great deal more sap that needs to be boiled down); to read writing that doesn't look like writing but which often contains the essential surprise; to make it possible for students to share unfinished writing with myself and the other writers in the class in such a way that the habit of writing will be reinforced.

EASE

When Tilly and John Warnock studied one of my daybooks they were surprised that there was so little evidence of struggle and frustration, that it seemed so easy. I like the martyr pose—writing is so terribly hard for us writers—and was a bit angered at their response. I was surprised at their surprise, and had to look at my daybooks again, and I found they were right.

It takes enormous effort to get to the desk—to shut out the world, to turn off the telephone, to put aside the manuscripts to be read, the letters to be answered, the expense accounts to be filled out, the books and articles to be studied—but I do not write unless the writing comes easily.

I used to force writing, to try to make mashed potatoes pass through a keyhole. But it didn't work. If I am prepared, then the writing will flow. If I'm not prepared, I'd better return to that reflective state where I may play with language, connecting and disconnecting, listening for voice, fooling around, staring out the window, letting my pen, the blind man's cane, tell me where I'm going.

To free my pen I must develop a special kind of ease. It's ease with intention. It's not retirement or indolence but a calculated letting go that is essential if you are going to be effective in battle, while giving the speech, after the kickoff of the big game. There has to be a deadline, and there has to be an achieved calm before the deadline. There is nothing easy about this ease; it is an acquired naturalness.

To be ready for surprise you have to have both discipline and freedom, compulsion and forgiveness, awareness and receptivity, energy and passivity, a strong purpose and a disciplined purposelessness.

And I must make such ease an essential part of my students' curriculum. I must allow them space in which to fool around, to have fun, to aim in one direction and hit a target in another. They must learn not to force writing but to let writing build within them so their pens may have the freedom of saying what their brains did not expect them to say.

RECOGNITION

"You can smell the poem before you can see it," says Denise Levertov, and she is right. We must recognize the aura that precedes surprise the same way I recognize the aura that precedes a migraine. It is the sort of thing that can be learned only through experience. I sense that a surprise is on its way, and I make myself quiet, the page blank and on my knee, the pen uncapped and in my hand.

One of the nice things about surprise is that after you've had one or two or three surprises happen then you become a veteran of surprise and will begin to recognize it.

It may be helpful to categorize some of the types of surprise the writer experiences. There is the surprise of perception that I experienced when the character in my novel saw no color. There is the surprise of recollection when I heard that terrible cough left over from a previous war. There is the surprise of connection when I related my surprise in writing and my students' surprise to their development as writers.

There is the surprise of resolution when we see the solution to a problem we have been circling in our writing. There is the surprise of celebration when we re-create something—a moment, an event, a person, a scene—and can stand back from it. There is the surprise of implication, the surprise of understanding, the surprise of caring when we feel more than we expect to feel, and the surprise of pattern when a whole complex of connections click into place on the page. And there are those especially significant surprises: the surprise of authority—I know what others need to know—and the surprise of voice—I can hear myself on the page.

Our students will recognize surprise when we share our surprise at what we are writing, when we allow members of the class to share their writing and their surprises with us, and when we, as teachers, are surprised by what they are writing. They must see the great range of surprise that is possible when writing becomes exploration.

POUNCEABILITY

"Art gropes," writes John Gardner. "It stalks like a hunter lost in the woods, listening to itself and to everything around it, unsure of itself, waiting to pounce."

The writer, surprised by what is appearing on the page, must cultivate the craft to take advantage of it. The word, the pattern, the fragment, the sentence appears, and the writer must learn how to follow the clue toward meaning.

Again the tension between freedom and discipline. Most of all the craft of making use of surprise is the ability to let the writing flow, to develop the potential of the surprise. Peter Drucker calls it the "zero draft." Calvin Trillin calls it the "vomit-all." I like to call it the "discovery draft." Whatever it is named, the writing has to get ahead of the writer.

But not too far ahead. The writer has to have an easy hand on the reins, but the writer cannot let the reins go. The craft of the sailor is to make use of the wind, of the painter to make use of the brush, of the cabinetmaker to take advantage of the grain. The writer must learn how—through experience—to develop and exploit the surprise that was only a hint, a revealing snap of a twig, a shadow in the bush before the writer pounced.

The writer will never learn to write, for the craft of writing is never learned, only studied. But the teaching writer can share the continual apprenticeship to craft with the writer's students. And they will be motivated together to practice pounceability, lured on by each new surprise. One of the most exciting things about writing is the fact that surprise is much more than idea. Surprise is experience in seeing the vision of the text come clear. Surprise is felt in the working out of the order, direction, proportion, and pace of the text. Surprise is the reward for the line-by-line crafts of revision and editing—the writing keeps saying what we do not expect to hear.

ACCEPTANCE

Surprise, though exciting, may be a discomforting gift. When we are surprised we often do not like what we discover. I am surprised to find I am writing a novel in which the "hero" kills his own children. I do not want to live within his skull, but apparently I must. I do not want to write about World War II, but my trade is paying attention to what appears on the page, not what I want to appear on the page. I do not want to write another poem that forces me to reexperience the death of my daughter, but the poem stands there before me. I do not want to order the writing process, but as I study the writing process through writing about it I must report the order I perceive.

Those are all surprises of subject matter, but there are other surprises that I must learn to expect. This month I intended to write prose and have found poetry coming out of my pen. Poetry upsets my priorities, ruins the writing schedule, makes havoc of my lists, and has absolutely no sympathy for my dismay. Poetry laughs at a writer who had the arrogance of purpose. This month I write poetry.

And that voice on the page is surely not my voice. In the novel it is a convoluted voice that turns back on itself and questions itself. In the textbook it is a bit too clear. In the poem it does not free itself in the way I intended. I think of all the writers I would like to write like. I hear in the distance my own voice, so much better in my imagination than it ever seems on the page. But I must accept my voice as I accept my size thirteen feet, my mother's heavy step, my father's receding hairline, myself surprised in the mirror after the bath.

If acceptance is hard for the writer, it is harder still for the teacher, for education is geared up for sameness. We want our students to perform to the standards of other students, to study what we plan for them to study, and to learn from it what we or our teachers learned.

Yet our students learn, at least in writing, if they experience difference. The curriculum calls for sameness, and we unleash them into an activity that produces difference.

They do not write how we expect them to write or what we expect them to write. We are surprised by what they say and how they say it, and we are made uncomfortable by our surprise. And we can make them uncomfortable. And if we do, the game is lost. We must learn to accept and delight in the difference we find in our students, for surprise is the most significant element in writing. It is the motivating force that makes writers of us and of our students. Surprise is the measure of the importance of writing. We do not write to repeat what others have written but to discover our own surprises, what we have to say and how we can say it.

I have plans for tomorrow's writing, but if I am lucky my writing will surprise me and destroy my plans. I have plans for my students' writing, but if we are lucky we will be surprised at what they write and how—and all our plans will be abandoned as we pursue surprise.

TWO
READING FOR SURPRISE

One of the delights of receiving an invitation to publish is that it gives you an opportunity to pick up loose ends. Richard Owen asked me to do a piece for his Teachers Networking: The Whole Language Newsletter, *which is read primarily by people in the field of reading instruction and research. I saw it as a chance to explore the implications of surprise for reading experts.*

I have no illusions about what I know about reading research, but I hope my ignorance may be a virtue. It may allow me to raise obvious questions that are only obvious after they have been asked. My fantasy is that a researcher, hungry for a new direction, may see my pointing finger and set off on a journey that will instruct us all. How's that for arrogance?

Creaky, cranky, bypassed, emeritussed, I shuffle to my word processor each morning and become the strange, naive boy who delighted in the difference between what he expected to write and what spoke back to him from the page.

His teachers did not delight in surprise and he left high school twice before he flunked out, but he knew long before high school that his secret life of reading and writing would be the quiet center of his world.

A WRITER READS

It was and it is. I do not think what I am going to say. I write dumbly, sometimes from a hint, a clue, a fragment of language, music, a scene half-seen, or from the emptiness that is the writer's best resource. That sentence was not what I expected because I did not expect; I pass from not knowing to knowing by daring to follow language where it will lead.

I read with surprise, scanning back to the text that came before, and match the evolving text to the text that might have been or might yet be. It is not a matter of static decoding, of matching my meaning to another's, but going beyond knowing, learning by drafting.

Of course, I read and reread, write and rewrite. I read as do all effective writers in school and out by constantly passing between the particular and the general. I match the vision of the whole to the implication of the particular, seeing how the line, the phrase, the word, the pause, or the space between words changes the meaning of what I find I have to say. Let me show you what I mean; allow me to reveal an act of dumb writing and reading:

[A note: This method of writing is essentially the same for me when I write familiar, autobiographical essays, textbooks, poetry, memos, fiction, journalism. It may not be the same for others, which is one reason we need extensive research in reading while writing.]

> *I came to my desk knowing I would make a run at writing a column for the* Boston Globe. *It is a column called "Over Sixty" in which I look at the world from the perspective of an ancient. I had looked at the calendar and noticed it would appear on the first day of winter. I started, without notes, writing a nostalgic, gently humorous piece about my childhood winters when:*
>
> "Of course we played war. We knew, in the 1930s, that we were preparing ourselves for the real snow wars we would fight as older boys. In the Battle of the Bulge, cold and scared, I often remembered our Wollaston wars."
>
> *This was not expected. I had no intention of being serious and was not consciously thinking of war until I read these lines as you did.*
>
> "We built huge forts, in memory as big as houses, with enormous ice walls, parapets and steps where you could climb up to launch snowballs at other ice forts or at an attacking enemy. In Belgium, my straight arm arcing a grenade remembered how I learned to make a snowball arc the same way, and today I feel a terrible sadness at the reality of our so serious play."

I did not remember, then write; I wrote, then reading what I had written, remembered.

Another surprise. Reading this I discovered it was true. The text taught me. The text made the connections present and past.

"We learned how to pack snowballs. I can still feel my hands squeezing the water from the snow, half melting the snow from the warmth of my hands, shaping it and making it tight and hard. A well-packed snowball didn't sting, it hurt."

I wrote dumbly, allowing language to re-create experience, which might be followed by meaning.

"And like grown-ups, we learned the temptation of weapons. We learned how to make snowballs, then pour water over them, just right, turning them so they would freeze and become ice balls, manufactured and packed in milk crates, missiles stored against the enemy.

"But those whose heads rang from the well-aimed ice ball learned to retaliate. A piece of coal or a stone hidden in a snowball did more damage than a missile made of ice."

The connections, the flow between past and present—the present reexperienced, then reunderstood by reading—came without pre-thought. It was written, then read.

I had, of course, to decide if I wanted to keep this material and then, if I did, to fit it into the essay so that it would appear natural and also, perhaps, give the piece a depth it did not have before. These paragraphs provide no earth-shaking revelations, but they did give me the opportunity to relive part of my life and to understand it better than I had before. As a writer and a reader, I delight in such small discoveries. These surprises are what give added meaning to my day and draw me back to my desk the next morning.

This complex, fascinating, and significant reading process deserves close attention from reading and writing researchers. We need to know how effective writers read so that we can instruct other students responsibly. This essential reading process has largely been ignored, possibly because of the historic separation of reading and writing research. Now that gulf is being bridged, and the time is right for research in the reading of evolving texts where surprise is encountered, even encouraged, and made to reveal significant meaning.

STUDENTS READ

I don't really understand how I read an evolving text—that's what I hope reading researchers will tell me. But I am not surprised that my reading process is complex; after all, I have been working at my trade for more than a half century. I am surprised, however, at how many of my students—and the students I observe in elementary and secondary classrooms—instinctively read with similar sophistication.

Even remedial students, even students classified as non-readers, can read for surprise and choice when they are writing on a subject they feel strongly about and on which they are an authority. They write what they did not expect to write and are capable of following an unexpected, significant meaning and making use of it in an increasingly successful text.

The writers in each class who are most effective almost always have the ability, no matter how formal their planning activities, to allow language to lead them to unexpected meaning. They allow, even encourage, surprise, then make use of it.

A by-product of reading surprise is increased perception in reading published texts. Students who learn to read surprise in their own drafts see options in the texts of others, both the drafts of fellow students and the final texts of published writers. Those final texts are never quite so final when read by a writer. The student writer sees the road not taken by the published writer as well as the road taken.

The readers who are capable of appreciating the choices made by a writer will read most texts with greater understanding and comprehension—and use what they learn from published writers to read surprise even more effectively when they confront their own unexpected drafts.

HOW SURPRISE IS READ

Sometimes surprise comes in an idea that is not represented in actual words on the page, but usually surprise arrives as an unexpected paragraph, a sentence that turns a corner, a line or phrase that opens a window, a word that carries new insight. At times, it may even be a pause between words, a spacing or pacing that creates a new rhythm, which, in turn, exposes a potential meaning. Other times surprise is the product of error—the exactly wrong word turns out to be the right word, the typo is more correct than what was intended.

Reading for surprise appears to require several skills:

READING WITHOUT INTENT

This may be particularly difficult for the students we classify as the best students. They may be prisoners of purpose. They may, unlike writers, really know what they want to say before they say it; and they may have difficulty in hearing the potential in an unexpected word or line.

Students should learn to respect surprise, to be open to its message. That does not mean that the message is always accepted. It simply means that the unexpected text is read with the same care as the expected one.

READ AHEAD

When a surprise occurs in the text, the student should run with it, creating a mental text that develops the lead provided by the surprise. Sometimes it may even be worthwhile to make notes or to free-write to see where this unexpected lead is taking you.

READ BACKWARDS

The student should also read backwards, scanning through the text before the surprise. Many times a surprise grows out of a train of thought that has been growing unnoticed in the text. A surprise that has been naturally evolving through the text deserves serious consideration. And if it is *not* to be saved and developed, that trail has to be eliminated from the text.

QUESTION FAILURE

Many times a writer will feel despair and be convinced a text is failing because it is not developing in the way the writer expected. Actually the text may be revealing a new and potentially valuable meaning. It may not be a failure, but a success.

READ FOR WHAT ISN'T WRITTEN—YET

Surprises are not always the clear statement of a meaning. Surprises may arrive as a subtle but significant change in the tone of the writer's voice, as a metaphor that isn't quite right, as a line that isn't very wrong but isn't very right. The text may produce clues and hints that, at first, may seem like verbal indigestion but which can, with a reader open to possibility, lead to important new meaning.

READING FOR YOUR OWN SURPRISES

Those who hate reading—and they may be the majority of students, parents, teachers, and administrators—in any school system fear reading. And the greatest cause of fear comes from the school-indoctrinated notion that there is one correct meaning for every text.

Oh, we don't mean *that* we say—and we don't. But still we teach our students to believe there is a single, specific meaning for each word. Take *playground,* for example. It is a happy word for many but not for me.

The playground, for me, was a place of brutality and humiliation. To respect and understand my meaning, you have to get me to talk about my meaning and listen with interest and respect as I tell you of my religious education—"turn the other cheek"—and the brutality of children. But when we make that leap, we leave most of our students behind. They continue during their academic lifetimes and afterwards to think there is always one correct meaning.

What I discover in my reading is not what *you* expect. In fact, it is not what I expect. I reach for a simple, happy word, like playground, and read, to my surprise, a complicated, unhappy word on my page.

Many literate persons, outside of school and in, never allow others to make that leap. They truly believe there is one correct meaning, written in stone, for everything that is written, and when they read a text whose meaning they don't understand or, worse still, when they read something strange, such as poetry, and have a choice of meanings, they feel they have failed.

My delight in writing comes from writing what I do not expect; and yet, when I first taught reading, I thought my students dumb when they did not understand *Lear* as I did. I was growing old—fast—and I had three daughters—one of the reasons I was growing old fast. My students were seventeen or eighteen. I loved the Elizabethan poetry of Shakespeare's language. They wondered why he couldn't write in American.

You don't have to teach *Lear* to college freshman to make the mistakes I did. I could have made them in the first grade or the sixth, but it would be more likely that I would have colleagues who could have helped me if I had been in elementary or middle school. In fact, I learned to teach reading by observing elementary school teachers, not college professors.

Those teachers didn't think their pupils stupid as I thought mine when they didn't read what I read. Worse still, my students thought themselves stupid. I wish I could have that class back. (How many classes we wish we had back!) (How many classes I would *never* want back!!)

That was one of the first classes I taught, and if I had it back I would teach *Lear* today more by listening than lecturing. Whatever text I taught, published or student, in any grade first through doctoral, I would encourage surprise, delighting in our speculations, the wilder the guesses the better. We would laugh and then find unexpected meaning as we explored the meaningful—meaning *full*—accidents in our written and oral responses to the text.

We might come to see that the purpose of literacy is not at first to communicate with others, but with ourselves. We write and read to collect, order, and understand; to make use of experience—the experiences of action and reflection, of speaking and listening; to think, test, and share our thinking.

We would—I hope—learn to read without fear, learn to read surprise and discover its meaning.

THREE
FIRST SILENCE, THEN PAPER

It was my remedial, doubtful, hesitant, insecure students who knew they couldn't write who most sounded like writers. I felt comfortable with them. We shared our fears, our inadequacies, our astonishment at the miracle of writing. I never wanted to go into combat with someone without fear, and I don't want to write with someone who isn't scared: The word is powerful and must be feared.

It was the good students who were strangers to me. I could never understand those who could write without apprehension and with continual satisfaction, even pride, at whatever flowed from the brain. They didn't know the territory.

And school doesn't know the territory of writing. The good students flowered in a world of command and expected response that is counter to the essential conditions for good writing. The longer I taught, the more I felt that the environment for writing was likely to be more important than the content. If we can seek the unexpected, each in our own way, then we will begin to learn to write.

I came to teach at the Wyoming Writing Project in Gillette, and John Warnock told me to shut up, sit down, and write.

I was in the right place. Writing begins when teachers give their students silence and paper—then sit down to write themselves.

But that isn't all there is to teaching writing, a demanding craft that is backwards to most traditional teaching. We have to create an environment in which our students can become authors—authorities—on a subject by writing about it. Then they may learn to write by teaching us their subject, listening to our reaction to it, and revising their text until we are taught.

It isn't easy for me to be a student to my students' writing. I want to be the authority, to initiate learning, to do something—anything—first, to be a good old American take-charge guy. I keep having to reeducate myself to get out of the way, be patient, wait, listen, behave as I was commanded to behave in Wyoming.

This attitude, of course, is what I have to reteach myself day after day, year after year as a writer: to create quiet, to listen, to be ready if the writing comes. I am a writer and a teacher, and those of us who are, each day, both teacher and learner have to teach ourselves what we teach our students. We experience the difficulty of learning at the writing desk what so glibly can be said behind the teacher's desk—"be specific," "show, don't tell," "give examples," "make it flow."

It is our job as writers to create a context in which we can write, and it is our job as teachers of writing to create a context that is as appropriate for writing as the gym is for basketball. To do that I think we must consider seven elements.

SILENCE

Emptiness. Writing begins when I feel the familiar but always terrifying "I have nothing to say." There is no subject, no form, no language. Sometimes as I come to the writing desk I feel trapped in an arctic landscape without landmarks, an aluminum sky with no East or West, South or North. More often I feel the emptiness as a black pit without a bottom and with no light above. No down, no up. Soft furry walls with no handholds. Despair.

That's the starting point for good writing, an emptying out of all we have said and read, thought, seen, felt. The best writing is not a parroting of what others have said—or what we have said—before. It is an exploration of a problem we have not solved with language before. I have circled this question the editor of *fforum* placed before me, "What are the contexts in which effective writing can take place?" I write this text to solve that problem, first of all, for myself. I wonder if I have anything to say; I fear I do not, but I start making notes. I do not look so much at what others—and I—have said before but what I find being said on my own page. The emptiness began to disappear when John Warnock gave me the gift of silence. I sat. I waited. The well began to fill.

We must begin our personal curriculum and our classroom curriculum with John Warnock's gift of silence. How rare it is that we encourage—even allow—our students freedom from busyness, moments of stillness, relief from the teacher's voice—quackity, quackity, quackity.

How rare it is we allow ourselves stillness. I try to start each day with fifteen minutes in which I just stare vacantly out of the window into myself, notebook open, pen uncapped. My vacant staring must be as disturbing to others as a class of students looking out of the window into themselves is to some administrators. It must seem a sign of mental illness, evidence of an acute cranial vacuum, proof you have left the company of those around you and become, in fact, a space shot. When my mother-in-law lived with me she took such staring as a social signal that conversation was needed. When I visit in other homes, or people visit mine, my early morning vacuity (indication to me that I am having my most productive moments of the day) causes them to leap into social action—quackity, quackity, quackity.

We must begin our writing curriculum with quiet, an unexpected and terrifying but productive, essential nothingness.

TERRITORY

Emptiness cannot be maintained. The silence will fill and, if we filter out what is trivial, what we have succeeded at before, what we know, we will see and hear what surprises us. In the writing course the student is surprised at what he or she is in the process of knowing.

Again we have to turn our curriculum away from what is traditional and even may be appropriate in other subjects but is not appropriate for the learning of writing. In most courses our students come to us knowing they are ignorant of the subject matter, and we work hard to convince them of that ignorance. In the writing course our students come to us thinking they have nothing to say, and it is our responsibility to help them discover that they have plenty to say that is worth saying.

The beginning point is, again, a kind of nothingness, a responsible irresponsibility on the part of the teacher. No talk before writing, no assignments, no story-starters, no models, no list of possible topics—nothing that reveals you think the student has nothing worth saying and makes the student dependent on you for subject matter. Students will, of course, plead for a life preserver—a topic, any topic, even what I did on my summer vacation—but if you toss it to them they will not learn how to find and develop their own subjects, the basis of the writing process.

Instead of assignments—our assignments—the student is challenged to find his or her own assignments. We may have to help by drawing out of our students, in class and in conference, what they know. We may have to have our students interview each other, and then tell the class about the subjects on which the person interviewed is an authority. We may have to have our students list the subjects on which they are authorities, including jobs and out-of-class activities. But those are all crutches we use when we cannot stand the silence. It is far more responsible if we have the courage to wait.

TIME

Waiting means time, time for staring out of windows, time for thinking, time for dreaming, time for doodling, time for rehearsing, planning, drafting, restarting, revising, editing.

I seem, to some of my colleagues, prolific, yet most of my writing evolved over years. Some of the things I am writing this year have written roots in my files that go back for ten or twenty years. The psychic roots go deeper. We cannot give our students years within an academic unit that is measured in four to fourteen weeks, but we must find ways to give them as much time as possible. This means fewer assignments, in most courses, with frequent checkpoints along the way to make sure that time is being used.

Students need, as writers need, discipline applied to their time. There should be a firm deadline for the final copy—announced in advance—and then deadlines along the way, perhaps for proposals, research reports, titles, leads, ends, outlines, first, second, third, or even fourth drafts. There may be a quantity demand of a page a day, or five pages a week—pages that may be notes, outlines, drafts, false starts, edits, revisions, as well as final copy.

Time for writing must be fenced off from all other parts of the curriculum. This is not easy, because we have so many pressures on us, and we try to double or triple up. Many teachers are still trying to assign a paper on a reading, correct the first draft for grammar, and say they are teaching literature, writing, and language. Writing should, of course, be used to test our students' knowledge of literature, but that is only one form and a limited, schoolbound form of writing.

We must encourage writing that isn't bound by the limits of someone else's text and isn't restricted to a single form. Students must find their way to a subject worth exploring and find their way to use language to explore it. Dr. Carol

Berkenkotter of Michigan Technological University used me as a laboratory rat in a two-and-one-half-month naturalistic protocol. She discovered that more than 60 percent of my time—sometimes much more—was used for planning. We must give our students a chance to sniff around a potential subject, reminding ourselves of what Denise Levertov said, "You can smell the poem before you see it." We need time for this essential circling, moving closer, backing off, coming at it from a different angle, circling again, trying a new approach.

This circling means that the writing curriculum is failure-centered. If failure is not encouraged, we will only have meaningless little essays plopped out like fast-food patties to our explicit measure.

Good writing is an experiment in meaning that works. The experiment that works is the product of many experiments that fail. The failure is essential, because through trying, failing, trying, failing, we discover what we have to say.

NEED

Out of time and territory need will arise. Too often, as writing teachers, we use words such as "intention" or "purpose" too early with our students, as if such matters could, all of the time, be clarified early on with a formal strategy and specific tactics established before we know what we want to say and to whom we want to say it. The need to write on a subject at the beginning is much less than obvious purpose. It is an itch, a need to wonder about, to consider and reconsider, to mull over, to speculate.

As we give ourselves space and time we find we experience what can only be described as a sort-of-a-sensation, or a pre-sensation, similar to the aura that precedes the migraine.

My mind fills by coming back to clustering specifics. Everything I read, see, overhear begins to relate itself to a particular concern. This concern is certainly not yet a thesis statement or a solution or an answer. It isn't even a hypothesis, a problem, or a question. But as I give it words in my head and on my notebook page it begins to become a vision. I see a shadowy outline of a mountain range I may choose to map. I begin to have questions; I begin to define problems that may be fun to try to solve.

I have begun to be my own audience. I write to read what I have written not so much to find out what I already know but to find out what I am knowing through writing. It is an active process. Dynamic. Kinetic. Exciting. This is what motivates the writer and the writing student: the excitement of learning and that peculiarly wonderful, significant, egocentric experience of hearing the voice you did not know you had.

Writing also satisfies the need to make. Years ago I wrote a story on General Foods and discovered they had created mixes that were too simple and foolproof. They had to back up and, as one executive said, "allow the housewife to put herself into the mix." A strange image, and perhaps a sexist one, but their marketing research revealed the need of making. Writing is a particularly satisfying kind of making, because we can make order out of disorder, meaning out of chaos; we can make something solid out of such powerful and amorphous materials as fear, love, hate, joy, envy, terror.

This brings us to another fundamental need, one we all, as teachers of writing, normally avoid. Beside my own typewriter is a quotation from Graham Greene: "Writing is a form of therapy; sometimes I wonder how all those who do not write, compose or paint can manage to escape the madness, the melancholia, the panic fear which is inherent in the human situation." The need to write above all else comes from the need to reveal, name, describe, order, and attempt to understand what is deepest and darkest in the human experience.

PROCESS

The need demands process. There has to be a way to deal with the volume of information and language that crowds the writer's head and the writer's page. Quantity itself is both a problem and an opportunity—an abundance of information allows us to select and order meaning.

Too often students are forced to write without information or with just a few stray fragments of information they attempt to string together with a weak glue of stereotypes and clichés. It isn't easy to write without information. When students collect an abundance of information, however, they need to make distinctions between pieces of information—to decide what is significant and what is not—and then to follow the flow of the important information toward meaning.

It is of little value to teach skills and techniques, the processes of others, to students who do not put them into use in significant ways. Students who need techniques will develop them and will start to share their tricks of the trade with other students who need them. Then the waiting composition teacher can pounce.

The teacher sees one student making a significant word

choice, and the instructor broadcasts that to the class during the time for a class meeting when the day's writing is done. The instructor sets up pairs and small groups of students, inviting them to share their solutions and their problems. The instructor posts or publishes evolving drafts and outlines and notes to show how members of that particular class are making writing work. The teacher writes in public, on the blackboard, or with an overhead projector, revealing the teacher's own struggle to use language to achieve meaning, and inviting help from the class along the way. The instructor, in conference and in class meeting, shares accounts, techniques, and other tricks of the trade from professional writers at the moment the student defines a problem and seeks solutions. The teacher doesn't correct or suggest one solution but gives the student alternatives so the student will decide which way to turn.

Most important, however, is the testimony from student writers who are writing well. The instructor calls attention to those pieces of writing that are working and invites the student to tell the instructor, and the class, the process that produced the effective writing.

The case histories, first of all, instruct the writer. Usually the student has written by instinct, but when the student is asked to tell what he or she did, the student discovers that the writing was a rational process. It can be described and shared. And, of course, as the student describes the process that produced effective writing to others, the student reinforces that process.

Now students begin to work in a context of shared success. Those who write well are teaching themselves, each other, and the teacher how writing is made effective. They practice different styles of thinking and of working. They write in diverse voices and discover alternative solutions to the same writing problem. They find there is not one way to make writing work but many.

These solutions and skills flow into a coherent process. There are some things that are especially helpful when planning a text, others to help produce a text, still others to make the text clear. These techniques overlap and interact, because writing is a complex intellectual act, but the class discovers that underneath the contradictions there is a rational reason for most writing acts—don't be too critical in the beginning or you won't discover what you have to say, don't be too sloppy at the end or the reader won't be able to figure out what you've said.

It is vital that the process is drawn out of the class experience so the class learns together that each writer is capable of identifying and solving writing problems. Learning will not stop with this class. This class will not be dependent on this teacher; this class will graduate individuals who know, through their own experience, that they can respond, rationally and skillfully, to the demands of the writing tasks they will face in the years ahead.

TEXT

The principal text—and this from the author of writing texts—of the writing course should be the student's own evolving writing.

We have the responsibility to free our students from the tyranny of the printed page. They have been taught there is a right text, and it is printed in a book. They have been taught that the teacher has the code that will reveal the meaning of that text.

Writing is not like that. There is no text; there is a blank page, and then, with luck and work, a messy page. Language is trying to discover its meaning. The writer writes not knowing at first what the writer's own text is meaning, and then has to perceive the potential meaning in the confusion of syntax, misspelling, poor penmanship, and disorganized, searching thought.

Decoding a messy, evolving student text is a frightening challenge for most teachers, because they are untrained for this task. But writing teachers and their students have to learn to read unfinished writing. The use of finished models by far more talented writers is of little help unless the students see their early drafts, their clumsy and awkward sentences, their false starts, their early drafts that document how badly they had to write to write well.

Students publish their drafts in small group and whole class workshops where the writer is asked, "How can we help you?" I prefer to publish only the best drafts from the class to show good writing being made better. The text in the writing course is not what was once written but what is being written.

RESPONSE

The writer needs response when it can do some good, when the writing can be changed; but in school we too often respond only when the writing is finished, when it's too late.

Professionals seek out writers who can help them when it counts. I call Don Graves, Chip Scanlan, or others, for I am blessed with many good writing colleagues—or they call me. We read a paragraph or two over the phone that needs a test reader right now. Not for criticism, not even for confirmation, but mostly for sharing.

Experienced writers need test audiences early on, and it is the challenge of the writing teacher to become the person with whom the student wants to share work that is still searching for meaning. It is also the responsibility of the writing teacher to create a community within the class that makes such sharing contagious. And as the drafts move toward a completed meaning, the writer needs test readers who can become more critical and still be supportive.

Writers need colleagues who share the same struggle to make meaning with words. As we, write—student and professional—we practice a lonely craft, and we need writer friends who can reassure us, remind us of past successes, suggest possible alternatives, give us a human response to a changing text. Sometimes the writer's needs are specific—Will this lead make you read on? Do you understand my definition of photosynthesis? Have I gone off track on page 4?—but most of the time the writer simply needs to hear, by talking at someone else, what the writer, himself or herself, has to say about the text. The writer, after all, every writer, is continually teaching himself or herself to write.

Teachers should not withhold information that will help the student solve a writing problem. The most effective teacher, however, will try by questioning to get the student to solve the problem alone. If that fails, the teacher may offer three or more alternative solutions and remind the student to ignore all of them if a solution of the writer's own comes to mind.

Central to the whole business of response is faith and trust. The teacher must have faith that the student can be the student's own most effective teacher, and must trust that student will find a way through the lonely journey that leads to effective writing. The student will feel that faith and trust. It will goad, support, challenge, comfort the student. And faith and trust given may be returned, especially to teachers who reveal their own lonely journeys as they use language to discover meaning.

These standards are high. The teacher believes you can write far better than you ever believed you could write. There is pressure on the student, and there are standards. At the end of the unit there is a delayed but meaningful evaluation. Students are graded on their final work of their own choice. The grades are based on accomplishment. The students have worked within contexts that allowed them to work well. Now their work is ready for measure. The private act of writing—born of silence—goes public.

FOUR
THE ESSENTIAL DELAY: WHEN WRITER'S BLOCK ISN'T

I learned from my students in many ways. Whenever I discovered that students learned a technique from their major that might help us write more effectively, I invited them to teach it to the class. One computer-science major described a computer programmer form of outline in which you list the furthest opposites in a topic and then narrow the topic within a series of brackets.

I used his technique to help me overcome writer's block and get started on this piece. I had assumed writer's block was all bad, but his method of planning made me consider writer's block a possible virtue since his different way of planning helped me find this essay.

Morison isn't writing. He's a professional writer, published and anthologized, but he's not writing. He goes to his typewriter and jumps up to find more paper. He organizes and reorganizes his notes, makes a third cup of tea, visits the stationery store to buy a new pen, hunts through the library for that one elusive reference. He makes starts and notes and more notes and folders and outlines, but he does not produce a draft.

He wonders if he has writer's block. He clears writing time on his schedule, shuts the door to his study, and watches a tree grow. Slowly. He makes neat work plans, types them up, pins them above his desk, and doesn't follow them. He drafts letters—in his head—telling the editor he cannot deliver the piece. He considers going into real estate, or advertising, or becoming a hit person. He composes suicide notes—in his head—that are witty, ironic, publishable. He grumps at his wife and lies awake at night wondering if there is treatment for writer's block.

But Morison knows he doesn't have writer's block. He's been writing for almost forty years. He is passing through the normal, necessary, always terrifying delay that precedes effective writing.

"Delay is natural to a writer," E. B. White states. "He is like a surfer—he bides his time. Waits for the perfect wave on which to ride in." Virginia Woolf reminds herself in her diary, "As for my next book, I am going to hold myself from it till I have it impending in me: grown heavy in my mind like a ripe pear; pendant, gravid, asking to be cut or it will fall."

To understand writer's block, we have to discover what is not writer's block, what forms of delay are essential for good writing. Again and again we hear our best writers—perhaps whistling in the dark—counseling themselves not to worry as they wait for writing. Ernest Hemingway said, "My writing habits are simple: long periods of thinking, short periods of writing." Franz Kafka had one word over his writing desk: "Wait." Denise Levertov says, "If . . . somewhere in the vicinity there is a poem . . . I don't do anything about it, I wait."

Recently Carol McCabe, a prizewinning journalist, explored this period of waiting. "The time just before I begin to write is the most important time I spend on a piece. By now the piece is there, waiting inside the notebook, tape or transcripts, clip files and photos, like a sculpture, waiting for release from a block of limestone. I just have to figure out how to get it out of there."

"As I begin, I turn on my own switch before the machine's," McCabe continues. "I put myself into a fugue state, a sort of hypnotic trance in which I am sensitive to blips of idea and memory, receptive to the voices of my characters whom I begin to hear as I write."

There is, of course, no certainty for McCabe, Kafka, or any other writer that the waiting will be productive. It may be a pregnancy without issue. Each writer fears that writing will never come, yet the experienced writer knows it may take days, weeks, and months to produce a few hours of text production.

I kept an unscientific account of my writing time for the first forty-three weeks of 1982. I wrote the introductory material for a collection of my articles on writing and teaching, responded to the editing of a collection of pieces on writing journalism, edited a journal article, drafted and revised chapters for two different collections, completed a newspaper editorial, wrote several poems, finished a freshman text and revised it once, worked on a novel. Yet I did formal drafting, revising, or editing for only 206 hours.

I had forty-three weeks, or 301 days, in which to write, yet I averaged far less than an hour a day, less than five hours a week. And my working pace wasn't that even. One week I wrote for more than twenty-two hours, and in ten different weeks I wrote nothing. I had more than adequate time for panic and terror, doubt that I would ever write again, fears of writer's block, and plenty of time for the necessary incubation that precedes writing. My middle name is Morison.

The more I observe the writing patterns of my students, my colleagues, and professional writers; the more I study the testimony of respected writers in published interviews, journals, essays, letters, biographies, and autobiographies; the more I study my own writing processes—the more convinced I become that we not only can state the importance of delay but also can begin to comprehend those conditions or kinds of knowledge the writer waits for. There appear to be five things the writer needs to know—or feel—before writing.

INFORMATION

Amateurs try to write with words; professionals write with information. They collect warehouses full of information, far more than they need, so much information that its sheer abundance makes the need for meaning and order insistent. "One of the marks of the true genius is a quality of abundance," says Catherine Drinker Bowen. "A rich, rollicking abundance, enough to give indigestion to ordinary people." The writer turns over this compost of information in the file, in the notebook, in the head, seeking what Maxine Kumin calls the "informing material" that produces meaning.

The writer also knows it is dangerous to start writing too soon when all the writer has on hand are ideas, concepts, theories, abstractions, and generalizations. Good writers learn to fear the vague and general, to seek the hard-edged and precise. Maxine Kumin says, "What makes good poetry for me is a terrible specificity of detail." "The more particular, the more specific you are, the more universal you are," declares Nancy Hale. Vladimir Nabokov testifies, "As an artist and scholar I prefer the specific detail to the generalization, images to ideas, obscure facts to clear symbols, and the discovered wild fruit to the synthetic jam."

Specifics give off meaning. They connect with each other in

such a way that two plus two equals seven—or eleven. Writers treasure the informing detail, the revealing specific, the organizing fact; and their notebooks are filled with sentences, test paragraphs, diagrams, as they connect and disconnect, order and reorder, building potential significance from their abundant fragments.

INSIGHT

"Whenever the special images and phrases that are always criss-crossing in a poet's mind begin to stream in a common direction, rhythmically and distinctly, he will begin to write a poem," says James Emanuel. That streaming, or insight, is a single vision or dominant meaning that will be tested by the writing of the draft.

The insight is not often a thesis statement; it is less formed than that. It is a figure seen in a fog, a fragile relationship between facts, a sketch, a hint, a feeling, a guess, a question.

Mary Lee Settle says, "I start my work by asking a question and then try to answer it." But it may take a long time of fiddling around with notes, starting and discarding opening paragraphs, searching and researching, and just plain waiting for the key question to appear. Anton Chekhov says, "An artist observes, selects, guesses, and combines." Virginia Woolf speaks in her diaries of "the power of combination." And the writer has to find a way to combine the elements into a single vision before beginning a draft.

One of the most effective forms of insight is a problem that may be solved by the writing. Eugene Ionesco says, "That's what a writer is: someone who sees problems a little more clearly than others." The problem is what motivates the writer, for the best writers do not want to solve those problems they have already solved, to write what they have written before. Joubert says, "To write well, one needs a natural facility and an acquired difficulty." Experienced writers are suspicious of ease, and wait for challenge. As James Wright says, "The writer's real enemy is his own glibness, his own facility; the writer constantly should try to discover what difficulties there truly are inherent in a subject or in his own language and come to terms with these difficulties."

When the writer has achieved this difficulty, or found the question, or defined the problem, the writer may be able to begin the draft. It is important, however, for the writer seeking insight not to expect precision. Exactness comes after the final draft, after revision and rerevision, reading and rereading, editing and reediting. Before the first draft the writer is seeking possibility. As Donald Barthelme says, "At best there is a slender intuition, not much greater than an itch."

ORDER

Barbara Tuchman tells us that "writing blocks . . . generally come from difficulty of organization." John McPhee says, "I want to get the structural problems out of the way first, so I can get to what matters more. After they're solved, the only thing left for me to do is to tell the story as well as possible."

Experienced writers refuse to leave on a trip through a draft without a map. The map may be in the head or on paper, but the writer needs a sense of destination. "A novel is like getting on a train for Louisiana," says Ernest J. Gaines." All you know at the moment is that you're getting on the train, and you're going to Lousiana, but you don't know who you're going to sit behind, or in front of, or beside; you don't know what the weather is going to be when you pass through certain areas of the country; you don't know what's going to happen south; you don't know all these things, but you know you're going to Louisiana."

A significant number of writers wait until they have the ending before they begin. "I don't know how far away the end is—only *what* it is," states John Irving. "I know the last sentence, but I'm very much in the dark concerning how to get to it." Katherine Anne Porter says, "If I didn't know the ending of a story, I wouldn't begin. I always write my last line, my last paragraph, my last page first." Eudora Welty agrees: "I think the end is implicit in the beginning. It must be. If that isn't there in the beginning, you don't know what you're working toward. You should have a sense of a story's shape and form and its destination, all of which is like a flower inside a seed."

An even greater number of writers wait for the lead or first few lines that will set the draft in motion, and they are willing to spend a great deal of time waiting for those lines or worrying them into place. "Leads, like titles, are flashlights that shine down into the story," says John McPhee. "With novels it's the first line that's important," says Elie Wiesel. "If I have that, the novel comes easily. The first line determines the form of the whole novel. The first line sets the tone, the melody, then I have the book."

NEED

Writers often delay beginning a draft until they feel a need to write. This need usually has two parts: the internal need of the writer to speak and the perceived need of readers to listen.

The best writing usually comes from a need that precedes the entire process of writing. The writing comes in a climate of need created by the experiences and obsessions of the writer. The writer has an itch that must be scratched. If the writer does not have that need, then it must be achieved during the waiting period.

We delay writing until we can find the need to write. This is especially true of that writing that comes by assignment or invitation. When the need is initiated outside of the writer, the experienced writer will find a way to discover a personal need that parallels the external need.

Donald Graves writes of the importance of ownership in teaching writing. He argues that the teacher should not take over ownership of the draft, but the student must maintain ownership of what is being written. The struggle for ownership between writer and teacher, or writer and editor, is normal. But the writer must win. The writer must feel as Louise Nevelson does when she says, "My work is a feast for myself."

I almost lost the struggle with the editor of this book while drafting this chapter. When writing the first draft I was too conscious of the editor's suggestions, which I read as instructions. After I completed the draft, the editor responded with a long letter of criticism. I congratulated him for it, since it was perhaps the most impressive editorial response I've ever received. But when I came to rewrite the draft, it was lifeless. I was bored and felt as if I were painting a picture by number. It was *his* draft, not mine. I had to put his letter aside, put away my notes based on his suggestions, put aside my earlier drafts, and start anew.

The writer has to create the illusion that the writing is his, or hers, that only this writer can deliver this message. Such arrogance is essential. I had to internalize the editor's suggestions and make them mine. And, of course, the editor has to have his own illusion. He watches me dance and knows he pipes the tune.

The writer also must have a sense of a need outside of the writer, that there is a reader who has to know what the writer says. In waiting to begin a draft, the writer is also waiting to see a reader, a person who needs what will be written. But we write for ourselves first, and others afterward; we must need to write and need to be read.

VOICE

Morison waiting, staring out the window, pacing the floor, slumped in a chair, is listening, trying to hear the voice that may be able to write the draft. Morison scribbling, crossing out, drafting, crumpling paper into a ball and hurling it near the wastebasket, then writing again and moving his lips as he reads what is written, is listening. Writers know not to write until they can hear the voice that will run through the draft.

An effective piece of writing creates the illusion of a writer speaking to a reader. The language, although written, sounds as if it were spoken. Speech is the glue that holds the piece together. The writing voice provides the intensity that captures the reader; the voice provides the music and grace and surprise that keep the reader interested; the voice communicates the emotion and the mood that make the reader involved.

Each writer, of course, has an individual voice. But the writer learns how to extend that voice so it is appropriate for the particular piece of writing. "The most difficult task for a writer is to get the right 'voice' for his material; by voice I mean the overall impression one has of the creator behind what he creates," says John Fowles. Wright Morris adds, "The language leads, and we continue to follow where it leads."

Morison draws an angry line through the top page of a draft and hurls the stack of paper across the floor. He has written too soon. He forces himself to sit quietly in his Morris chair, to stare into that blurred middle territory between intent and realization, to wait and listen for the essential accumulation of abundant information, for a guess of a potential meaning he may call insight, for an order that may lead him toward that meaning, for a need that makes it necessary for him to write, for the sound of the draft's voice.

This waiting may be the hardest part of writing. "It's a matter of letting go," Walker Percy points out. "You have to work hard, you have to punch a clock, you have to put in your time. But somehow there's a trick of letting go to let the best writing take place." It is essential to let the writing grow within the writer, accepting the doing nothing that is essential for writing. "You have to be willing to waste time," counsels Robert Penn Warren. "When you start a poem, stay with it and suffer through it and just think about nothing, not even the poem. Just *be* there." The writer has to accept the writer's own ridiculousness of working by not working. "I spend a great deal of time simply walking around," says Joyce Carol Oates, "sitting, daydreaming, going through the motions of an ordinary life with—I suspect—an abstracted, dreaming, rather blank expression on my face."

Morison has completed the chapter. It is in the mail. He sits down to write the next book. He is a Puritan; he makes a work schedule on Sunday, and keeps to it on Monday. Not on Tuesday. On Wednesday he reads Simone de Beauvoir: "A day in which I don't write leaves a taste of ashes." He smiles bitterly. The following Monday he forces a draft of the first chapter. It doesn't even come close. He lies awake that night and wonders if he has writer's block. But then he remembers what he has just written the week before. There is an essential delay; he must be patient; he must wait for information, insight, order, need, voice. He must not write to write.

FIVE

WRITING BADLY TO WRITE WELL: SEARCHING FOR THE INSTRUCTIVE LINE

As I indicate in the following article, I thought Don Daiker was joking when he invited me to speak before a conference of sentence combiners. I was challenged, however, by the unexpected opportunity and accepted; then, as the date grew closer, I was terrified—a common sequence. I decided to have fun by establishing a technical problem to solve. My friend, novelist Thomas Williams, once pointed out to me that the writer is often stimulated by solving a technical problem—for example, writing in the present tense or never using a flashback in fiction. The reader shouldn't be aware of these technical challenges most of the time, but it helps drive the writer forward.

I decided to combine sentences, pile up huge train wrecks of clauses, and have fun with the language as well as the content of the piece. I read it to the audience, which I rarely do, because of the complexity of the writing. And they got it. They understood it and laughed with me, not at me.

Not yet in the notebook; in the head:

I want to celebrate first—then analyze, understand, explain?—the instructive line that leads me to the meanings I make—to the meanings I have the need to make—but to celebrate I have to write what I celebrate (well enough to make it a celebration), not to look back afterwards to what someone else has done—some great dead writer who has burned his drafts—but to write writing, following lines searching for a meaning before they really are even lines, to begin to understand how those lines work, as they drag me toward their own meaning, product of my experience and my past thinking but freed—if the line works—from that into becoming what I have not yet thought.

It rarely works clearly—or obviously—but it works. This cleaned up thinking, thinking after I know I am thinking, late pre-thinking but still a kind of thinking—a kind of thinking important for our students to know about—that we think as confusedly as they do, when we are lucky, if our education still allows it (remember that Snodgrass poem "The Examination"), they should see it in action, not because they have to learn it, they *know* it, but because they should be allowed it, because by playing with the line, no, by listening for, no, to the line (((that I know will come if I am quiet and prepared to listen ((it is damn hard to listen for what you do not expect to hear—do not want to hear, even fear of hearing (my mother-in-law always responded to what she expected me to say rather than what I said: "The house is on fire." "Isn't that nice.") but a lot more fun: if I knew what I was going to write, I wouldn't write)) because I have learned to listen before, in other writing, and in listening heard))) it will come and drag me from word through phrase and fragment and line to a meaning that may be tested and made clear by being turned into a sentence.

That is neither beginning nor ending. It is writing writing, writing in the act of writing, not writing written but lines searching for a meaning, a beagle running this way and that through my mind, nose to the ground, tail high, busy, busy, busy.

I thought the invitation a joke. Somebody was impersonating Don Daiker inviting me to a meeting of sentence combiners, a rabbi invited to a Nazi rally. But I called back. It was Don Daiker and he was serious. We want you because you are not a true believer. Such an invitation; such chutzpah to accept. Of course I would address the rally.

And would I suggest a title? Well, the sentence might be appropriate, the sentence seen from the inside, trying to tug the writer along on the search for meaning: "Following Language Toward Meaning." Language, not sentence, some instinct gave me room. Glad I did. I want to deal with something less and more than a sentence: the line.

Poets talk about the line, not the sentence or the verse. Modern poets, anyway. Valery's line given. Of course the line has a validity in poetry, modern poetry anyway. Line breaks, that sort of stuff. The line is the basic unit, comes as a fragment. My poems are prose I suppose first but as Charlie Simic says,

"Last fall I did a lot of poems. Not really poems, but something that looked like poems." I write stuff that looks like poetry. But isn't. It has lines, but they don't break the right way, they are prosey (prosy?), too much like sentences. The poems are in the fragments. Pieces of pottery lying around from which a poem may be built. Chunks of language (Frank O'Hare jammed up against me as we rode in the backseat of a car in San Francisco, talking about chunks. Didn't find out what he meant really. Glad I didn't, freed me up to think about chunks my own way), space debris drifting by, thoughts, no, almost thoughts, not yet thoughts, images, chunks, stuff when meditating, something to catch your eye or ear but never looked at head on, a state of half seeing, half listening, recording. If you pay too much attention, you'll miss it. To find the right language, at least the beginning of the right language, you have to train yourself to inattention ("Donald, stop staring out the window."), not to listen too well.

Many teachers complain that their students can't write sentences. I complain that many of my students write sentences. Too early. Following form, forgetting meaning. Following language toward correctness. For its own sake. Sentences that are like prison sentences. They don't unlease meaning, they contain meaning, compress meaning, squeeze the meaning out of language and leave me with the juiceless skins and pulp, enough of that, but then I too have those who don't write sentences when they should, well, to hell with that now. Now I am in praise of bad sentences, stuff that isn't ready to be sentences and wouldn't be helped by becoming sentences. Now. At this time. Premature births. But births. Living.

We don't know enough about how to write badly—and why. Syntax often breaks down when we approach a new and interesting meaning, something we have thought before or are afraid of thinking or sabotages what we had thought before and, God forbid, said at an academic meeting or, worse still, had published. I am surprised when they take me seriously when I guess and write what I don't yet know. But I don't have to take myself as seriously. I must make sure I'm not glib and professional—at least at the wrong times. Polished, the meaning all rounded and shaped and shining until it is no meaning at all.

Ed Corbett told my wife he was astonished that I spoke extemporaneously and that all my sentences parsed. My reactions were immediate. I would never speak again. Someone was keeping score. It isn't true, it can't be true. Maybe it is. I mean, Ed Corbett, if anyone knows such a thing, Ed Corbett does. Wow. Great. Terrible. That's what worries me most about speaking. It comes out so neatly, and the audience likes that, naturally, and you get warm and wiggle all over when they respond but it's too neat, parsed, all contained.

Well, isn't writing? Yes, but, I hope, I think, there is a difference. Speaking involves a lot of tricks you can't get away with in writing. Writing can be examined, read back, studied. But it is a worry that the meaning will be made too clear, that sentences will eliminate doubt and questioning and contradictions. Perhaps we will succeed, think of that, and our students will think clearly all the time. What's the definition of a demigod, a dictator, a nonthinker? One who thinks clearly all the time. We need to teach unclear thinking. Perry—and others—Elbow looping away madly, Macrorie, others, are aware that the young often think too clearly, see everything in black and white, precisely, every effect having its cause. What if we give them the language patterns into which they can fit these prematurely clear thoughts.

Well, certainly my students . . . I know. Perhaps we need a grammar of bad writing or unfinished writing, a codification of those ways . . . Whoops. Well, at least we need to find out how we write the nonsentences that made meaning-full sentences possible. Now, you're talking. Is this like jazz improvisation? Sort of. Probably yes. There's experience and tradition but the need to push the edges, to go beyond, to fail. I've got to fail more in my writing. You say: "You've made it in this piece." Good.

I accept the assignment. And my mind knows it is going to have to work on that. I don't think. My head does better if it is left alone. It will make its own connections, become aware when something is said or read that may fit. But some stuff surfaces in the daybooks. Often it is diagrams but not in this case. It isn't often free writing written down. Free writing isn't free enough, at least for me. It takes over or perhaps my professionalism takes over and it begins to shape, encompass, enclose, tighten up, screw down, compress, refine, limit. A lot of what follows are fragments, drafts for titles, one-line drafts of the talk that may become a chapter. Such title fragments are typical of my planning for writing. They seem to lead me. Perhaps they are abstractions for free writing or free thinking. Signposts pointing toward meaning. Tracks. Clues.

Perhaps more. Lines. A kind of shorthand which allows me to see where I may go. Not sentences. Not even uncombined sentences. Not yet.

What do I see in them, hear in them? Voice and dance. I listen to what they say and how they say it, watch to see how they move.

Connections. Attractions and resistances. Tension. Especially tension, forces that are working against each other but not escaping each other. Marriages of ideas. Ideas I've had but haven't forced together yet. Ideas that can't escape each other but are uncomfortable with each other in an interesting way. Forces that react with each other to create something that is more—or different—than they are alone. At least when it works. It works when it is on the edge of not working but still does, sort of, at least.

How can we define the line?

The line is a word or a series of words that points the writer toward a potential meaning.

Note that the line has one reader: the writer. The line need only communicate to the writer, and therefore the line is often made up of code words that have private meanings that appear general, vague, or cliché to other readers but which are loaded with precise meanings for the writer.

Calvin Trillin says, "I do a kind of pre-draft—what I call a 'vomit-out.' . . . It degenerates fairly quickly, and by page four or five sometimes the sentences aren't complete. . . . I have an absolute terror of anybody seeing it. It's a very embarrassing document. I tear it up at the end of the week." Fair enough for Trillin. He's not a teacher. He's a stylist, writes for the *New Yorker*, makes me sick he writes so good, so easily, so trippingly on the tongue. But if he were my teacher I'd need to see those "vomit-out" drafts; I'd need to learn to write as badly as he does and then learn to work from there to the pieces that are published, the examples of what looks like effortless craft.

These are random selections. They were written in bunches or alone, spread out in:

THE DAYBOOKS 24–32, OCTOBER 6, 1982–OCTOBER 11, 1983:

uncombining sentences
how sentences lead to meaning
following language to meaning
language leads to meaning
chunks, sentences and paragraphs
learning to follow language
breakdown of syntax
how combining and uncombining lead to new meaning
teaching on the student's text
need for rebellious sentences
let your sentences rebel
sentences that make their own meaning
how sentences find their meaning
let sentences lead you to meaning
incorrect sentences may lead to meaning
sentences that don't work may think
sentences reflect thought already thunk
people don't think in sentences
need sentences that betray thought, cause vision, surprise, anger, twist and turn toward their own meaning not mine
find ways to study language in search of meaning so students will be able to write uncorrect sentences which
William Carlos Williams:

> "I am that he whose mind is scattered
> aimlessly."

celebrate the prose line—the sentence
line—the sentence—leads to meaning
grows its own laws out of its own need to make meaning
must consider the line before the sentence—the fragment
ends of lines
how a sentence makes meaning
the magic of the line
the prose line
a celebration of the prose line
energizing line
inspiring line
insightful line
fragment to sentence
the teaching line
the instructive line
the instructing line
the suggestive line
finding the instructive line

seeking the instructive line
hunting for the instructive line
hearing the instructive line
        listening
        lying in wait
            3 stages
                given line
                following, leading line
                in (something) sentence
celebrate the prose line
        less and more than a sentence
a celebration of the prose line
adventures with the prose line
following the prose line toward meaning
from word to phrase to sentence to meaning
from word to phrase to line to meaning
from word to line to meaning
how line leads to meaning
how the prose line leads to meaning
how the prose line may lead to meaning.

A year of fragments. How does the prose line teach (instruct) me? It is a way of thinking, not thought then writing, not even thinking in language within my head ((often I think in pictures (images) and in patterns (designs)) but thinking by seeing what I have written.

But since here my research and my thinking are *about* the line, I must use the line.

Let's share a line trying to find its meaning. This was not written before. It is being written now. The line that beckons me—the dead will not stay put in their graves—has passed by before, a fragment of feeling from my autobiography, a fragment that has anger in it and guilt at the anger. I don't particularly want to deal with it, but it is attaching itself to me. And it may be poetry. I don't want to write poetry here and now, but again I seem to have no choice.

the dead will not stay put in their graves
the dead will not in the grave
the dead will not stay
underground
out of sight

where they who have deserted me
belong

the dead will not stay put
in their graves
underground and out of sight
I expected memories and of course
a certain sadness
but not this
ghosts would be better than
this
not knowing
if the dead are dead or I am alive

My father, trailing wires, that box still strapped to his chest still smiles. Without his glasses, I cannot still read his eyes, get behind the smile. Tear the mask. Am I him now, bearded, smiling, just as masked to my children—my wife, my students, friends? He would tell anyone, it seemed, too much of himself, selling himself instead of his damned ladies hosiery. And now I am open, too, but what can anyone see in this openness. Am I what they see or do they see what they need to see.

I play all the parts
to (my) children the father
to the wife a husband
to parents son
to students teacher
neighbors neighbor

I play every part
to my children the father
to my wife the husband
to parents son
students teacher
neighbors neighbor
and to my friends the
   mirror
they need to see
   themselves
as they need to be seen
until at night I take off
the masks the costumes
speak no lines

This trails off. Perhaps it will draw me back. Perhaps not. No matter. It looked liked poetry, became prose, then poetry again, but it was really no genre yet. It was pre-genre, pre-form, and all the courses we teach that demand form before meaning (always virtuous, always justifiable, always neater than the writing experience). Yes, often correct, appropriate. I *teach* nonfiction (although I write fiction and poetry and nonfiction), but we run the danger of closing down thinking, exploration, and discovery if we pay too much attention to genre at the wrong time. The line will lead us to the form. And should. And our students must have the experience of writing what they do not expect to write. That is the essential writing experience, and if you do not feel that firsthand, you cannot understand writing.

The line is more open than the sentence. It is still searching for the meaning that it does not yet have. It may be important for the student writer to discover there is a legitimate presentence with which to work, play, sketch possible meanings.

Writing fast is a component of free writing but it must be separated from free writing. Writing fast is one important way to draft because it frees the writer from notes, research, outline, pre-thinking and encourages language to race ahead of the writer seeking a precise meaning. This is not free writing for there is a goal, the subject of the piece being written. All the planning, rehearsal, research is there—in fact, all those activities prime the writer and make meaning-searching language possible. I have gone to sleep knowing not what I will say but what I will say about—the topic or the point of view or the feeling felt or sort of half thoughts not dragged from the subconscious but disturbed a bit to make them, to stimulate them, like the farmer who loosened his tomato plants "to scare them" and make them hurry up their producing, and then I wake up knowing I will be writing and what I will be writing about but still not allowing sentences, just protecting the feeling of the writing from language, only half listening to TV and half reading the newspaper and really not writing so I can go downstairs and allow the language to come in such a way it will surprise me and tell me, because of its speed, I'm like Faulkner said, a writer is "like a man building a chicken coop in a high wind. He grabs onto any board he can and nails it down fast" so I will be able to step back from my chicken coop and see what I have built. This speed is most apparent when I am dictating and we have all had the same experience speaking in class, rare, but enough, and we hear ourselves saying what we did not expect to say, better than we expected to say, and that is one reason I dictate to get the speed to force my writing beyond my thinking although I'm not dictating this but it comes out in sentences too often and so I'll push myself like this with the word processor, trying to get ahead of syntax so I will write what I do not expect to write and all my education and experience and publishing, all my professional glibness, gets out of the way and I do not do it often enough.

You *do* have to write badly to write well. Of course. Badly in the sense of neatness and completeness, for effective thinking isn't neat and complete. This word processor thinks neat and complete. It is dumb, everything is programmed. It follows orders, everything is a simple matter of yes or no. We think by leaps, by inference and intuition, by hunch, guess and accident, especially accident. When I studied and did not learn watercoloring, the teacher said we had to rationalize our accidents. We needed material that would cause accidents and we had to have the experience to increase our accidents. Yes, writing is like that. We have to be able to have productive accidents and to be able to perceive in the mess what is worthy of rationalization, what has to be thought about. Writers are a very special kind of reader; they have to be able to do a special kind of reading, reading what isn't there yet, what may be developed and then shaped and polished with sentences into something that others can read not like this but a nice meaning that may, unfortunately, seem more than this jumble but be, in fact, less because of all the polishing. Yes, I like Linda Flower's writer-based and reader-based prose but I guess what we have, what I teach, what I force is often too much reader-based prose when the writing I most admire that stretches me because it stretched the writer is writer-based prose, writing that continues to search for a meaning after it leaves the writer's desk and can we tolerate it then in our composition classes? Well I don't at least not for a grade at the end and I guess I shouldn't but then perhaps I'm cheating my students if I don't do something to let them loose. We all have students who write too well, don't we, who are uptight, imprisoned in themselves or write with too much ease, parsing their way toward suitable meanings, what was it Joubert said, "To write well, one needs a natural facility and an acquired difficulty." Yes, that sort of thing, language fitting together with an instructive roughness, no polish yet.

I am drawn back to that haunting line—the dead will not

stay put in their graves—which has, within it, an interesting tension that may describe a feeling that many of us have at times. There is, in the line, strong feeling, perhaps anger, and there is a surprise in the action and reaction between the words. We usually think that the dead stay in their graves but here's a line telling us they do not and, more than that, the line has an opinion about it. Not an Easter-like celebration—they are risen—or pleasure, or fear, but a kind of impatience that they are not behaving properly. It will be interesting to see where that line may take me this time.

the dead will not stay dead

Grandma sits up
half lying the way she was propped
against her pillows
she's been watching
disapproving

Mother is curled away from me
or is it father
from whom she turns
this enormous woman
always child to her mother
sucks her thumb

Father still smiles
he's still the deacon
usher at funerals
floorwalker salesman
hidden behind the well-pressed suit
starched collar moustache
smile

Lee waves
she seems as surprised
as we were that she went first
but does not seem unhappy waiting
she was always the sunny one
and she still tries to comfort us

Look. I did not want to write about that, to confront the ghosts, to feel the loss, to share it, to expose it to myself, to others, the bad writing, the uncomfortable feelings, is it self-pity, and am I exploiting my family, embarrassing readers? I don't want to expose myself to myself and, in fact, I expected to write a line that would begin a story or an essay on this subject, to stand at a distance from it, but I must write where language takes me. I must be open to the night dreams and daydreams, the thoughts that wander behind my own protective, salesman's smile, hiding what I am thinking from others but not myself.

There are things in the lines that surprise and intrigue me. Mother turning away, for example, curled up as a baby as I once saw her during her dying, when I became parent to my parents and they children to me. But then another line comes to me out of nowhere. No, not a line, a picture of the baby of close friends. My wife and I had dropped by their home the day before and visited for a few minutes, delighting in their joy at their little girl.

Caitlin is seven months old
and she stands wobbley legged
looks back over her shoulder
black-eyed woman already

we talk of how fast she learns
to stand explore judge
charm to be herself in a world
that tries to make her fit

(I am stunned at what Caitlin knows)

(what Caitlin knows
she has come so recently from death
born into living)

(what Caitlin knows
so recently arrived
from Death)

(what Caitlin knows
of Death from where she came
she will not tell
but celebrates her living)

(touching tasting
reaching out)

WHAT CAITLIN KNOWS

at seven months
and standing wobble
legged
looking back over her
shoulder

WHAT CAITLIN KNOWS

at seven months
standing wobble legged

looking back over her
shoulder

woman already

how fast she learns
we say watching her
crawl
touch taste search reject

and charm

forgetting how much
knowing
she brings from Death
which can't be darkness
if she smiles
remembering

woman already

how fast she learns
we say as she crawls

beyond the rug to
recapture
the yellow plastic ring

forgetting the knowing

she brings from Death
(we should remember
what she does smiling)

I must stop and not follow language where it takes me. Not this morning. I have a paper to write. I look at the clock. For the first time in twenty years of teaching I have written right through a student conference. The line has concentrated all my attention on that moment and its meaning. I have gone from death to birth and perhaps beyond. It felt good and it was exciting—following the line. But I don't know whether I have written well or not. Don't care. That is unimportant. But I have followed a line toward an unexpected meaning and it's happened right here (it's all here) and I hope the reader—the listener—can feel just a bit of the excitement I felt when I intended to write prose and found that the line was leading me to poetry, or something that might become poetry, and that when I wrote of death I found myself moving from those ghosts that haunt me to Caitlin Fisher and to the experience yesterday afternoon when I sat on the floor and enjoyed her and enjoyed her parents' and my wife's and my own enjoyment of her. And my language pulled me toward an understanding that surprises me. It may not be a great thought for someone else, but it wasn't so much a thought for me as a perception, an understanding, an experience, a realization that she came—so full of life, so happy—from where my Lee is and where we all go, and somehow the feeling that it can't be so bad if Caitlin arrived so full of happiness.

What is the instructive line? What is it in a line that leads me on, that teaches me that meaning may lie ahead? Well, it's not something that I think about normally; it's something I do. If you think about hitting a curve, you won't. And so I don't think about it. But if the batter becomes a coach? Alright, I have to think about it. To make money I am led to arrogance. I presume to teach, to find out what I do, and then, no matter how embarrassing, or unacademic and unprofound and unintellectual, to expose it, to reveal what is simple and obvious to others. And then to be surprised, for it isn't, apparently, quite so obvious—and perhaps not so simple.

- I listen to the line. In fact, I hear it rather than see it. I only write it down so I can hear it again. First the line is played. I listen for:
  - —The beat, the pace, the rhythm.
  - —The flow.
  - —The emphasis, or the lack of emphasis, or the relationship between what is emphasized and what isn't emphasized.
  - —The intensity, the caring, the mood, the feeling, the concern that is carried by the music of my language.
- I watch for the point of view, the angle of vision from which my language is making me see the subject, the distance I am standing from it. And, yes, my point of view does, in part, mean opinion. What do I think about the subject? What is my emotional attitude toward it?
- I am aware of what isn't appearing on the page that I expected to appear. It is always interesting what the line does not contain or does not point to, or is not interested in.
- I look to see what the line does include, with what it connects. The line is what makes the leaps we call thinking possible. The line is the leaping. It is the leap, it is the jump from one thing to another that gathers in from all our experience that leads us to discover what we did not know we knew. I try not to be frightened by what connects in a line, to accept what is brought up by my writing, whether I like the look of it or not.
- I pay attention to how I feel and if I am embarrassed or uncomfortable, if I have any strong feeling, I pay attention. The line connects as well as disconnects. It creates tension and challenge and contradiction.
- The line also produces analogy and examples and metaphor, especially metaphor. I pay close attention to metaphor.
- Alliteration. The line loves to lead by luring—watch out for alliteration. Don't let the reader see how helpful alliteration was in leading you on. Of course, being led on doesn't mean you end up where you should be.

- The wrong word is often as instructive as the right word, even more so sometimes, and typos are wonderful, and slips of the tongue and pen and word processor, errors, mistakes, are treasured, delighted in, studied.

It's marvelous when writing is pushed beyond meaning, beyond syntax, rule, and principle, when the whole business just breaks down. That's one of the nice things about the word processor for me. It allows me to write worser than I usually write so I can examine the mess and, perhaps, discover that language had, through failure, pushed things together in an interesting way.

WHAT CAITLIN KNOWS

at seven months
standing wobble legged
looking back over her shoulder
woman already

how fast she learns
we say as she pursues
on hands and knees
the ball beyond the rug

forgetting the knowing
she brings from Death
Nothing
Dark
before

she will live
Caitlin will live
learning what she knows

WHAT CAITLIN KNOWS

at seven months
standing wobble legged
glancing over her shoulder
woman already

how fast she learns
we say as she fits
the yellow ring
over the red spike

forgetting the knowing
she brings from before
Caitlin will live
learning what she knows

In our desire to be responsible and to make our students write correctly there is a danger that they will misunderstand and think they have to write correctly from the beginning. But language will not be a tool of thinking unless our students are able to allow language to run free and stumble and fall. Caitlin turned from her proud parents standing by the couch and fell. Her father said, "She has to do a lot of falling." And writers have to do a lot of falling if they are to write anything worth reading.

Yes, I have students who don't seem to be able to write a sentence, and I seem to have more of them this semester. I have to work to make sure that when they finish their final drafts they have used the traditions of language to discipline their thinking and to make that thinking clear to others.

But I have other students who write too well too soon, and I have to help them—and I think I too often fail them—to get beyond their correctness, their teacher-induced, parent-induced, society-induced, genetic-induced desire to be correct, as if language could be contained by rules. The whole spectrum of students I work with—from remedial through graduate students to professional journalists—want correctness before meaning, before voice. And that can't be. If writers are to find the instructive line they must realize it is not only permissible to write badly, it is essential. We have to let language lead us to meaning. We have to write lines that may become sentences.

A call for research. We need to understand how writing can be made incorrect in a productive way. How do writers write badly to write well? What instructs them in their journal notes, in their mind before there are notes, and between the notes, in their early drafts, what allows them to see what we cannot see?

We have a vast inventory of drafts and notebook entries from writers living and dead that can help us in this research. But technology may be making that resource an endangered species, for on the video display terminal, bad writing is written (one of the values of the word processor is that it encourages productive bad writing) but then it is zapped and it flies to Saturn or beyond. Perhaps we can build research word processors that will save the bad writing—"Donate some of your k's to saving bad writing"—so interesting bad writing can be studied. If it is studied and understood, perhaps we can learn to teach our students to write badly so they can write well.

I have tried to do my part in this article, writing badly in a way that may be instructive to me, to you, to our students. My way of writing badly may not be yours or your students'. There is no one way to write badly any more than there is one way to write effectively. And remember that if this were written the way I usually write these days, most of what appears here would not appear, for I would have done what you may think I should have done and pushed the writer's favorite key: DELETE.

SIX
REHEARSING REHEARSING

When I first started publishing in our field I was scared of the reader—and in a sense, I still am. The reader will find me out. The reader will expose my ignorance.

That happened but not enough to worry about it. Instead the reader, no matter how authoritatively I wrote, no matter how much I used voice and rhetoric to impress and exclude, the reader read the meaning the reader needed to hear.

I was infuriated. Didn't they understand? Didn't they read my text carefully? Why couldn't they get my reading of my text? But their readings were so different, so autobiographical, so eccentric, so amusing, so instructive to me that I began to delight in them and even began to write texts, as the one which follows, that were designed to let the reader in. Since I was talking about rehearsing, I planned to end up, as I did, with the title as the last line.

The writer rehearses
A writer rehearses
A writer rehearsing

hearse: "A vehicle for conveying a dead person to a church or cemetery." To rehearse is to go back and forth to the cemetery. *Herse*—Middle English *herse*, harrow-shaped triangular frame for holding candles and placed over the bier at the funeral service, from Old French, from Latin *hirpex*, harrow, rake. Rehearse from Middle English *rehercen*, from Old French *rehercer*, to repeat, originally "to harrow again"

No
To rehearse, to rehear
To listen
Rehearsing is listening.

In a play rehearsal you listen to others and yourself. In writing you listen to yourself.

Yes, I hear what I am saying before I see it.

The writer hears—oops, sexist singular coming up—writers hear what they are going to say before they know it.

Jayne Anne Phillips: "It's like being led by a whisper."

To write, students have to learn to hear well.

Writers hear what others do not hear.

Writers hear earlier than nonwriters.

Writers hear what they are going to say before they hear it. Planning to write includes the skills of collecting; of ordering, of forming, of structuring; of seeing a need in the self or in the reader, or in both; but most of all in hearing. Writers do not proceed until they hear the voice. And experienced writers hear early. What do they hear?

From what do they hear?

Fragments
Words
Word play
Code words
Specifics
Connecting specifics
Revealing specifics
Igniting specifics
Notes
Sentences
Phrases
Paragraphs
Chunks

From where do they hear these things?

Inside their heads—talking to themselves, listening to themselves

Talking out loud to themselves

Talking to others and listening to themselves

Writing in daybook—log—journal—predrafts—what they think are drafts and aren't

Go back:

Writers hear what they are going to say before they know it. Before writers start that crucial first draft they have usually rehearsed what they are going to say over and over again, because they have to hear what they have to say to know what they have to say.

Hearing is a way of knowing for the writer. The writer, in writing, uses language to find out what the writer already knows and also uses language to teach himself or herself what may be known. How? How may it be known? By making language, and then hearing what it has to say.

[Know. Biggest problem for academics. They think writers know what they know. They don't. Dumbly they write—dumb, not able to speak—they can speak by writing and that is an end to the dumbness of silence, of ignorance. They discover how much they know about what they didn't think they knew. Academic world deals with the knowing without and that's OK but there is knowing within, unknowing unknowing, unknown knowing that is only uncovered by writing—word play, fragments, free writing, noodling around. You get smart by writing what you don't know so you may *know.* May.*]*

Writing requires a strange form of planning and making. It takes patience and time. It takes room (play room, room in which to play, room in which to tumble around in and make mistakes. You have to make yourself write badly, not trying to write badly but letting it be made so it can be heard).

What does hearing tell the writer about meaning?

INTENSITY

Rehearsal is vital to the writing process because it allows the writer to mobilize the language that will make a draft with a strong voice possible.

Rehearsal reveals voice, and voice reveals meaning—to the writer and then to the reader.

DISTANCE

An effective pedagogy of composition will introduce the student to the range of distances from which the writer can view the subject.

The writer must move in close enough so that the reader will care about the subject, yet stand back far enough so the reader will understand the significance of the subject.

[Trying out sentences as I say them. Not thinking sentences but saying sentences and hearing them, then thinking about them?]
[Dictating to hear during *speaking. But same when I write with pen, typewriter, or word processor. The writing is heard, then seen.]*

Am I revealing meaning, or the hearing of meaning? Perhaps. The categories are a prison. I could go on—intended to go on—to genre, flow, point of view, fullness, direction, music, density, all sorts of stuff. Too restrictive, I won't.

Sometimes the rehearsal is so fast that there is a dance of meaning in the head and on the page. Hearing is a way of knowing. You have to write with your ear. Wallace Stevens said, "The tongue is an eye." The ear is an eye; the ear is a magnet. Writing is a sort of dumb act, a babble, word play, a random flow of particles in space bumping into each other. The ear picks up the collisions that are purposeful. Free writing? Perhaps. But it's too fast to be written down. What is written down is but a small part of what is happening, and it can control and limit that part. I dictate to hear what I'm saying. Right now I hear "right now," but I don't know what's going to follow right now. Right now the words pour out of me and are not heard in the inner ear, but are heard on the rebound. Tough to be an academic writer. No way to let it out. The fear of ridicule. But you have to say before you know. You may even have to say what doesn't look right but can't be understood by looking, only by hearing, reading your text aloud, hearing the intensity of the words, their relationships.

Okay, break planning down:

- Collecting
- Focusing
- Ordering
- Designing

All these things are done most of all by language. Therefore we hear what is significant, what has meaning. Early on, a newspaperman, yes, man then, I would place stars beside the significant fragment or specific in my reporter's notebook. It wasn't just facts or what was said, although it could be. It might be a pause, or what wasn't said, or a contradiction, or a connection with something else. Hey, there is a kind of music in reporting, notes come from documents and observations and quotations—all sorts of places—and then the notes begin to have a certain melody or theme. The great lake of notes sink, and rising above it three birds. Hey, I'll mix a metaphor any day to get a meaning. Hey, where do metaphors come in? Pretty important, I'd say. Was it Frost saying one thing and meaning another? Yeah. That's what I'm thinking about, talking about. Those things which language allows to give off meanings that are beyond the meanings.

Harrow. There's something important in that, to fertilize the field, that same old field, with new experience. I've got a small farm, just a few acres of writing process, of an obsession with how writing is made. And I keep growing new crops on it—a freshman text, a reader, I hope a handbook, some articles, talks like this. How do I do it? I keep putting new experiences into the field, fertilizing it (watch where that's going). And then harrow, turning it over, cutting through or destroying what I've said, not reading the first edition of *A Writer Teaches Writing* to write the second edition, setting the knives into the ground and letting them cut right across that old text to see what new text might be grown. Rehearsing, reharrowing, rehearing. My wife, who plants in nonmetaphorical earth, is able to read the tiniest crack in the spring, a touch of green invisible to me. All spring and summer she is able to predict from experience and instinct and feeling and caring and knowing what will live and die and produce. She is rehearsing her garden. Yeah. That's what the writer does, sees and hears in small what others cannot see and hear.

The student writer must see the rehearsal of experienced writers, hear it. There has to be talk about writing and reading about what may be written, and the reading of notes and fragments and bad writing. How often in conference and workshop the writer writes what seems to be terrible writing, or the teacher reads it. Aloud. The text is, indeed, bad, but from the text we hear a meaning that the writer could not himself or herself hear. If we force the writer to read the text aloud (forget the shame, pass over the apologies, push aside the embarrassment), then the writer in the act of reading to a teacher, a classmate, a workshop will hear a meaning that was not in the writer's mind but was in the writer's language. That's what we have to be able to hear, the meaning that is in the language.

The music. Music? Yes, music. The music of language reveals the meaning. I will write and write and write to hear what appears and appears and appears so I will know to what my words return and return and return. My words will beat the dance to which I will learn to make my meaning.

Or

Let me talk about the way a word—hearing—becomes active, aggressive, going after what it wants to hear, what it expects to hear. It is a hunter who has only an eye for the buck (that's awful—don't go back, move on). Listen, a soft word, listen. When I am listening I am quiet, quietly alert, quiet alert. There is no silence when you listen, only silence when you speak. Hey, where did that come from? Damned if I know, but I'll take it. It was unprepared, unrehearsed, off-the-wall, out-of-space. But perhaps I'm getting somewhere.

There is no silence when you listen, only silence when you speak. To find out what you may be going to say you have to stand back from writing, because when you are talking you cannot hear. I can feel the power of that text taking me somewhere. It has that flow that is so important to rehearsal. Momentum. Energy. The force that makes language press on in a specific direction carrying you with it, and sweeping up evidence from your reading and your experience. It is exciting, for at last the block is broken, I have a text moving forcefully toward meaning. My voice is authoritative, direct, commanding. But, of course, there is something wrong in what I have heard—I have either not heard well or not heard the right direction or simply heard words that sound good but don't make sense. It seems to me that there is a kind of sense in that sentence, "There is no silence when you listen, only silence when you speak." But as I wrote about it, moving from that point, I realized, of course, that I was saying that you should not write so you can hear. That sounds good in a way, but the sentence I am using came to me while I was writing.

[And yet.

There is no silence when you listen, only silence when you speak.

Turn the ground over again.

In silence we hear what we have to say, what there is to say. Silence is the absence of noise. In silence we can hear ourselves, ourselves talking, ourselves saying. Speaking creates a kind of loud or concentrated silence, a speaking silence. This isn't making sense. Good. I have too much of sense, there's little to learn from sense but there may be a lot to learn from nonsense. We have to be able to hear ourselves and shut those other voices out. Critics. Editors. Teachers who are done with their learning and make sense, have it all ordered, who know what they know.]

Ah. The effective rehearsist (isn't that wonderfully awful?) has to be able to hear while talking. The mouth produces a stream of words that may or may not contain meaning. It is the listening ear (Hey, I did a piece on the listening eye, why can't I have a listening ear, or a seeing ear?) that discovers meaning,

meaning that is to be explored, potential meaning, meaning that will be tested by the text. (Did I get that secondhand from Linda Flower?)

A phone call. Now I do not hear the flow of language about rehearsing. Flow. A river. It is time to go to ground. To eat lunch at the landing watching the tide go out or come in. Time to read and think and drift, time to return to revise and edit a finished text, rehearsing how it should be changed, rehearsing what is to be added, cut, reordered to fit the voice of the text. How do they rehearse plays that have been in performance or rehearsals after tryouts? There's a whole new category of pieces about postrehearsal. Rehearsal is a part of rewriting. Carol showed how much of my revision is planning—rehearsal—and editing is too, I expect. And then there is the kind of hearing you have to do *during* writing, hearing the text and bringing the text parallel to the heard or established voice. Hearing, no listening, to discover what may be said, what is said, what was said. Voice—hearing voice—all through the process. And after, the reader's voice. How do we encourage the reader to hear our way. Or is that impossible, even unethical. What—how—does the reader hear? Another paper, another article.

There is no silence when you listen, only silence when you speak.

There is only silence when you listen.

There is no silence when you hear, only silence when you listen.

Out of silence comes a text.

To speak, the writer has to dare silence, be quiet, wait so that the word, the phrase, the line—not yet the sentence, the paragraph, the page—that is unexpected, that has not yet been heard, may . . . The rustle of a dead leaf, the branch lightly brushing bark, the careful step, and where there was no meaning the shadow of meaning is seen—and gone. It is enough, for the writer's prey is what may be made out of nothing. Writers hear what has not yet been said and by their saying allow the music that exposes meaning.

Too poetic? God, I hate that hunting metaphor. Why do I keep coming back to that? I do not hunt. Well, not for deer. But I do sit in the loud silence of the woods, trained to hear the small, revealing sound.

And so I come to the title of my talk:

"Seeing with Your Voice"

SEVEN
READING WHILE WRITING

This article tries to reveal and examine the writer's reading process as well as the writer's writing process. Of course, it is my own peculiar process—that's all I've got to work with—but I hope it will invite each reader to become aware of how he or she reads.

In recent years there has been an attempt to bring the study of writing and reading back together. I am an optimist about most things, but my optimism is well controlled on this issue. I remember only a few years ago how those who studied writing—or wrote—were treated by scholars of literature or reading. And recently I chaired a Conference on College Composition and Communication committee which explored the poor treatment of young composition scholars by college and university English departments.

I do hope that readers and writers can become colleagues, but the reading instruction and critical literature industries are vast and entrenched. They may not understand how different writing what isn't yet written is from reading what is written. Those of us who look forward to our unwritten texts are in a different world than those who look back to the written texts of others. Writing and reading instruction should each have an important place in the academy, but will they ever be colleagues, open and equal partners? That will be difficult.

Still they are involved. Readers can read without writing but writers cannot write without reading, and I do believe we have a great deal to teach each other if we can talk—and listen—with respect to what is being said.

The writer writing. The writer reading. The writer hearing from the page what the writer does not expect to hear. The writer hearing (reading through the ear?) the line passing through the mouth before it is thought, read, accepted, known. The line changing as it is read. The purpose of the line adapted to the expectation of the reader *or* the text, the need of the reader *or* the text. The writer surprised by the given line, learning to read surprise, possibility, unexpectedness. The writer learning to accept surprise, possibility, unexpectedness. The writer reading what is there, what may be there, what isn't there until it is placed there by the reading. The writer reading other writers, hearing what their texts did not intend, did not need to say, did not need to know. Writing by reading, writing in the ear a text that belongs to neither writer. The writer learning, stealing, adapting, accepting, using, seeking to hear in the line passing out through the mouth, passing through the eye, something that is not there until the act of writing/reading, reading/writing.

One evening after a day's writing, numb from my own words, the writing going on, refusing to stop, we went to the mall to eat, too full of writing to eat well. Afterwards, we allowed ourselves to be drawn into the anonymous current of mall walkers. I resisted the too-bright bookstore with the light glinting off the plastic book covers; this week's talk show best seller, last month's nonseller reduced. Then I saw Jayne Anne Phillips' *Machine Dreams* and took it down automatically, as if to weigh it. A peck of words, a half peck?

It opened itself to the first page. Journalism gave me an obsession with leads—first words, the first line, sentence, paragraph, page that establishes the authority, voice, direction, pace, meaning, music of the book. My own leads direct me toward my own discoveries, and I am both fearful and respectful of leads. I have learned that few books survive a poor first page (but that many books don't live up to a good one). In bookstores I am a taster of first lines, just a quick sip, cupped on the tongue, tasted, tested.

I can still feel—not remember but refeel—the physical impact—not intellectual but physical—of the first page of *Machine Dreams*. I felt the same way when I opened the door of the coal furnace and was pushed back by the red heat, white at the center. I didn't read the page so much as receive it. The experience *of* the text was more powerful than the experience reported *in* the text.

I couldn't handle such a book right then. I wanted to escape writing and I forced the book shut, pushed it up and into its place on the shelf. I wanted casual reading while writing. I wanted reading that wouldn't intrude on my own writing. We drifted out of that mall and into another and passed another shining bookstore where, as if sleepwalking, I went in and bought *Machine Dreams*.

Let's look at that first paragraph, but don't get your critical scalpels out. I think this is a fine lead to a significant piece of work by an important writer. This novel is, in my opinion, a major, significant work, but that isn't what we're dealing with here. What I'm trying to explore is the impact of that text on one writer who is writing while reading.

> It's strange what you don't forget. We had a neighbor called Mrs. Thomas. I remember reaching up a long way to pull the heavy telephone—a box phone with a speaking horn on a cord—onto the floor with me. Telephone numbers were two digits then. I called 7, 0, and said, "Tommie, I'm sick. I want you to come over." I can still hear that child's voice, with the feeling it's coming from inside me, just as clearly, just as surely as you're standing there. I was three years old. I saw my hands on the phone box, and my shoes, and the scratchy brown fabric of the dress I was wearing. I wasn't very strong and had pneumonia twice by the time I was five. Mother had lost a child before me to diphtheria and whooping cough, and stillborn twins before him. She kept me dressed in layers of woolens all winter, leggings and undershirts. She soaked clean rags in goose grease and made me wear them around my neck. Tommie would help her and they'd melt down the grease in a big black pot, throw in the rags, and stir them with a stick while I sat waiting, bundled in blankets. They lay the rags on the sill to cool, then wrapped me up while the fumes were still so strong our eyes teared. I stood between the two women as they worked over me, their hands big and quick, and saw nothing but their broad dark skirts.

(Having written—read—my second draft to this point, I drove to a nearby town to get a newspaper and a cup of coffee [and, yes, a doughnut]. I needed to step away from her text and my text to read without a written text, to half remember, to dream the text that may be written or read. Driving, I am free to read, to write, to image [imagine] a text. I am purposely purposeless, and by allowing my thoughts to drift I have, by the time I return, read several interesting unwritten texts, texts I wouldn't yet want to record. My reading away from the text told me that there really was a text of this article to be written. I had caught a glimpse of a misty middle section and an even more unclear final one, and that was all I wanted right now. I would not want to read too clearly at this time. I might prevent surprise. I return to the previously written text.)

READING OFF THE PAGE

When I read—scanned—Jayne Anne Phillips' opening paragraph for the first time, I received at least three texts from that text, almost simultaneously, overlays, each ignited by her text.

> It is an August afternoon, just after lunch. The air is heavy, humid, and the sunlight is so bright it hurts my eyes when it glints through the broad maple leaves. I have escaped the dark, cool house to sit on the granite curb and play in the wonderful, black stinking tar I watched a crew of sweating men cook and spread that morning. I press my feet into the heat of the tar that almost burns and roll small, satisfying mashed potato balls of tar with my fingers. I do not hear the truck but see its green snout with M for Mack on it, growing larger, larger, larger and the great wheel, a swollen tire of the trucks in the funny papers, growing larger and larger. All silent, even when the truck shakes the curb and veers away so close I can see the great greasy naked drive chain passing almost over me and feel my grandmother yanking me back.

That is what I read in her text, that is what her text said to me. I read her words and passed back to that moment and then forward through a sickly childhood and teenage years marked by fever and delirium. The worst vision in the delirium was the great cartoon wheel growing larger and larger. I can dream it today, and I see it standing in that mall store. And I read another text of my own in her text.

> My grandmother, strength of my childhood, is on the floor and her arm has a bruise the size of a muffin and it is growing as I stare at it, and she tells me, who is not allowed to use the telephone, to use it to call Dr. Bartlett. And I do, and he comes in his Packard, and I let him in the front door. He puts a splint on Grandma's arm, and before he leaves he tells me what I knew, that I am grown up, growing up at least. I learned that the fear of something happening to Grandmother was greater than the happening. I could do what I had to do.

And still another text.

> I sneak into the pantry which is filled with the purple smell of grapes cooking and reach up to see in the great crockery bowl when the flood of molten jelly pours over me and across the floor into the kitchen where Grandma is screaming. And I hear those screams, hers and mine, today and that dreadful feeling at what can never be undone.

Behind those paragraphs stand the ghosts of hundreds of other paragraphs waiting to be read before they are written. This reading off the text, away from the page or through it, is a tribute to the writer and her text. When I attend a poetry reading, for example, a test of its success for me is how much I write in my daybook, fragments of what may become poems. They are not the poems being read and not the poems I would have written without the reading. They are something in between, created in the air between the poem floating toward me and my lines floating toward it. In reading how often I stare into that middle distance, remembering, imagining, reading a text that is neither the author's nor mine. These imagined texts are in a very real sense readings of the original text. They would not occur without that text.

Having crept this far out on thin ice, let us speak for a moment with respect for noncomprehension, for encouraging our students not only to understand the text they are reading, but to allow that text to spark other texts, ghost texts (bastard texts?) that are born because of the communion between the written text and the experience of the reader. The writer reading the writer's own pages or the pages of another writer is often reading an unexpected text that has only minimal relationship to the text on the page, but would not exist without that text. Perhaps these texts are fathered by a traveling man, but once they are read, conceived, they can be written down and revised into their own reality, and then read with care as well as with stimulating uncare.

READING WITHIN THE PAGE

Writers do not only read off the page, however, they read within the page, bringing their own experience with their craft to illuminate the hidden craft of the writer. I am impressed by how quickly Phillips drew me into the whirlpool of her story. One sentence, just six words—"It's strange what you don't forget"—and she has connected with me, has prepared my mind for the remembering that will accept and reinforce her story. She has begun a dialogue with me. I ask what is strange that she can't forget, and she begins to tell me. In effective writing, the writer involves the reader in the creation of the full text.

Immediately after that we have a switch—or a refinement—of point of view. As a writer I am impressed by her smooth move, which puts me within the narrator's (the rememberer's) experience, reaching up a long way to pull the phone down. At the same time Phillips has begun to hint at a time and place: years ago in a rural area. And in the same sentence I have been drawn back into the narrator's mind and then put within her childhood. I become the child.

And yet I am moving back and forth within the experience of remembering. I am remembering simpler, older telephone numbering systems with the narrator. I am also feeling the importance of the experience: I am sick and in need of help.

Now there is another nice twist that I can appreciate the way an old basketball player appreciates a head fake to the right and a move to the left. Phillips' narrator stands apart from herself, and we hear her grown-up narrative voice, with a touch of dialect (West Virginia?) hearing her own childhood voice. And I read on and off the page simultaneously, bringing depth and density to her text. I am projected into my own life, where I so often these days see myself both young and old, experiencing life through a series of double and triple exposures, seeming to be, for example, father, son, self, all at the same time. I want to discover how Phillips can spark that reaction. The good writer is always forcing the reader to contribute to the text. What is published is only half—or less—of the text of the book.

I notice that Phillips uses the second person for the second time and gets away with it. That is something the young writer rarely gets away with and I wonder how she makes it work.

I'm also intrigued by the double narrative Phillips establishes. The writer is telling me a story, and in that story a character is telling me a story. She is establishing a technique that will be used again and again in different ways as she allows the people in her book to reveal themselves to the reader.

We are only a third of the way down the paragraph and the narrator takes us back through the opening scene, seeing it again, hearing it again, filling it in with detail, making it more a believable reality. Phillips uses the technique of the oral storyteller, who moves forward and then back and then forward again, making sure that the listener understands. One of the greatest problems for the writer is moving back and forth in time, and I'm impressed how Phillips moves me to the time when the narrator was three, and then forward to when the narrator was five, and then back to before the narrator was born—in two sentences. Only a writer who has seen his or her own prose become twisted and tangled in problems of time can appreciate how gracefully this writer moves back and forth in time.

The writer reading this paragraph appreciates that intangible voice which is the most important element in writing. In a matter of lines the author has established that her strong voice, heard previously in her stories and poems, will be adapted to the book. The text, in other words, will possess its own voice. And then within that voice we will hear the voices of the characters themselves. Speech in this paragraph is not real, it is better than real. It gives the illusion—the authoritative, believable illusion—of real speech.

And finally, in this one paragraph, the author plunges me back into childhood, and I experience the childhood of the narrator, and I must read on to discover what happens to this child. This is not suspense, but inspired curiosity. The writer has instilled in me a need to know what will come next.

How conscious am I of this kind of detail while I read? Very conscious. But not an articulated consciousness all of the time. And yet when I read a good writer—Jayne Anne Phillips, William Kennedy, Toni Morrison, John McPhee, Robert Caro, Anne Tyler, Raymond Carver, and so many others—I find myself laughing out loud with sheer delight when a move is made that I know can't be made or I hear myself say "Go, go, go," as I become cheerleader to a text that is working.

I've been reading and writing for more than half a century, and I do not often need to articulate what my teachers, my editors, and my own writing have taught me. I must, however, pay particular tribute to Mortimer B. Howell, who taught me the difference a word can make in that critical year before World War II. I still have his marked-up copy of Hardy's *Return of the Native*. It took us weeks to get off Egdon Heath we so carefully attended to the text. And after the war I studied with Dr. Sylvester Bingham of the University of New Hampshire, who so carefully analyzed a text that a classmate of mine who later went into the CIA said our course was the best training he had for military intelligence. My reading of craft may now be instinctive, but it was taught and learned from those two instructors, and many others.

I also believe that in my continual reading I am storing away far more than I am aware of, and that those texts off and within the page are stored in the brain, waiting to be recovered during the act of writing. What seems spontaneous to me is probably high-order plagiarism.

WRITING WHILE READING

The writer, of course, never stops writing. The writer goes to the writing desk for an hour or two, or sometimes a heroic third hour a morning, but continues to write all day and night away from the desk. Many writers believe the most important writing takes place away from the desk, and most writers try to live a life—mostly unsuccessful—that protects the writer from those interferences that invade the secret territory in which writing is taking place. Those who live with writers must grow accustomed to the blank stare, the unhearing ear, the sudden "Huh?" or "What did you say?" or even a bark, "Can't you see I'm writing?" when the writer is apparently staring out a window, watching television, walking down the street, eating a meal, or reading. The writer reading your novel is reading his or her own. I pay close attention to Phillips' lead, but standing around within my peripheral vision are all the other leads I have written, the lead to my own novel, the lead to the chapter I am trying to discover. It is as if all previous lovers, wives, husbands, friends, and family have shown up at the same party. I do not want to measure my love against a present new one, but . . .

A kind of comparison does take place. My lead competes with Phillips' lead. And so writers become very careful about what they read while writing. These are writers whose voices distract or force imitation. Few writers are defeated by this competition, even when they should be. The better the material writers read, the more it stimulates their own writing. I publicly denounce competition and intellectually do not believe in it, but secretly I practice it. And Phillips has defeated me in head-on competition. But it does not matter. She is better than I am. So what? I am writing my book, she is writing hers.

This paper could stop here, and perhaps it should, for I am less sure about what comes next, less sure about the relationship between her text and mine. I hope there is none. I do not want to imitate her text, and if I were conscious of doing this in any way I would do something else. But this paper is about the relationship of reading and writing, and as I write, I read. We cannot separate the two acts, and so I must try to show you something about one kind of reading I do of my own texts.

I shall reread the opening paragraph of a novel I am working on after having read and analyzed Phillip's opening paragraph. I am in no way conscious of imitating her, but I am certainly conscious of being inspired by her to make my own text better.

I read the following two paragraphs quickly without a pen in hand, forcing myself just to absorb the text and not to make any changes in it. I wanted to hear the text, see what was shown to me by the text, to attempt to be a reader seeing the text for the first time, and then I go to work.

(2)
1. ~~It is dark but I am awake and I must not allow myself to drift into the morning sleep of nightmares remembered.~~

(2) (2) to (2) as (2)
I ~~will~~ rise ^ ~~and~~ steal the early morning from the day ^ I ~~first~~ learned

(2)
~~the importance of early morning during~~ those four summers in Maine before I

(3) (3) (2)
(2) ~~now-then~~ leaning my (3)
was 12., ~~when~~ I ^ ~~would~~ slide out of bed and, barefoot, ~~allow~~ ~~the~~ weight ~~to~~
(3): ~~then-now~~

(3) (2)
~~rest~~ on one foot, then the other, sneak~~ing~~ down the outer edges of the stairs

(3)
boards do (2)
so they ^ ~~would~~ not squeak.

(5) from a boy's knowledge,
(4) from summer camp, from Boy Scouts, ^
In the Army, I was taught ~~the~~ v tricks v I already knew ^ and combat seemed,
(5) such (5) as

at first, hide-and-go-seek without the mothers calling us in just as the game got good.

lifting up (2)
(2) ed ~~leaning down~~ on the handle to keep it quiet
I ~~learned to~~ open/the front door, ^ ~~ever so slowly~~ and race~~d~~ across

(4) then,
(2) into (3) I felt it ^ name it now.
the dunes until I entered ^ the great loneliness of the beach. ^ If I sail

east I will see nothing but the mountain waves until Portugal. The sand

(4) (4)
stretches so far south the houses on the headlands shrink ~~to miniatures~~ and

(4)
even the great resort hotels to the north grow tiny. ~~enough to fit inside a~~

(3)
(3) overhanging green blue
~~dollhouse livingroom~~. The Atlantic, an ~~always differing shade of blackgreen~~,

(2)
(4) always south to
is ~~ever~~ on my right as I run north and on my left as I run ^ home. My feet

(5) I
hurt from the ice cold sand at the tide's edge, ~~as~~ my toes ^ dig in and toss a

(3)
Going out,
comet's trail of sand behind me. ~~At first~~, the morning sun is so pale I have

no shadow to race, and I look back to see the Robinson Crusoe trail of

(2), dark brown, hard and level,
footsteps, the only marks on the waveswept sand ^ . I run again, then stop to

take inventory of driftwood, mussel shell, boat splinter, bottle without a

(4) (4)
note, seaweed, crab shell, sneaker, and, one morning, my first dead body, a

(3)
purple, (5)
woman, naked, ^ scarlet, swollen, her tongue so large it cannot fit back into

her mouth.

Having read Phillips' lead, mine does not seem immediate enough. It seems to stand back a bit, to instruct the reader, to get in the way. I'd like my lead, in its own way, to be as immediate as hers. I uncap my pen and make the changes marked by the number 2 for the second reading. There are few delights to compare to the joy of taking a sharp pen to your own text, a text that you feel needs work, but that is capable of working. As Bernard Malamud says, "I work with language. I love the flowers of afterthought."

I strike the first paragraph and move closer to the real text. The prose becomes more immediate and active, and that's the main contribution of that reading. I have made the text cleaner, cutting out what might get between the reader and the text. In a sense, I am eliminating myself, the writer, even though this is a book in the first person in which the narrator, the writer, is simultaneously telling and experiencing the story.

I stand back from the text overnight and then read it again, making the changes marked with 3. I begin the third reading by putting in, "now then," and taking it out; putting in "then now" and taking it out. Whenever such changes are seen on a text we must realize that they are but one or two of the dozens of readings that may take place consciously and possibly unconsciously by a writer who is paying close attention to the text. The changes of this reading continue to make the text more immediate, until we come to the insert and the line "I felt it, name it now," where that line seems to me to deepen the book and put it into a more effective context. I wasn't conscious of moving back in time the way Phillips did, but perhaps I was inspired by her. The other changes are simply efforts to make the text honest.

Readings four and five are the writer fussing, reading what should be put in, reading what should be taken out.

Now the text reads:

> I rise to steal the early morning from the day as I learned those four summers in Maine before I was 12. I slide out of bed and, barefoot, leaning my weight on one foot, then the other, sneak down the outer edges of the stairs so the boards do not squeak. In the Army I was taught such tricks as I already knew from summer camp, from Boy Scouts, from a boy's knowledge, and combat seemed, at first, hide-and-go-seek without the mothers calling us in just as the game got good. I open the front door, lifting up on the handle to keep it quiet and race across the dunes until I enter into the great loneliness of the beach. I felt it then, name it now. If I sail east I will see nothing but the mountain waves until Portugal. The sand stretches so far south the houses on the headlands shrink, and even the great resort hotels to the north grow tiny. The Atlantic, an ever-changing greenblue, is always on my right as I run north, and my left as I run south to home. My feet hurt from the ice-cold sand at the tide's edge. I dig my toes in and toss

> a comet's trail of sand behind me. Going out, the morning sun is so pale I have no shadow to race, and I look back to see the Robinson Crusoe trail of footsteps, the only marks on the waveswept sand, dark brown, hard and level. I run again, then stop to take inventory of driftwood, mussel shell, boat splinter, bottle without a note, seawood, crab shell, sneaker, and, one morning, my first dead body, a woman naked, purple scarlet, swollen, her tongue so large it cannot fit back into her mouth.

There was, of course, before I had read Phillips, a similarity in the technical problems we both faced, and that may have been one reason I was struck by her book. I am trying in my novel to achieve the kind of time within time that she is establishing. I am concerned with the multiple levels of experience we live in middle age, experiencing and reexperiencing life simultaneously, and I am particularly concerned in the novel with how the images of war in this military nation create particular realities for all of us, but especially for veterans.

While I write my first drafts and my later drafts, my early notes and my revisions, my plans and my final edits, I am reading the text I intended to write, the text I am writing, and the text I hope yet to write, a kind of triple vision or triple reading that is made possible by all the other readings of my own texts and the texts of others that have come before, the few texts I remember (with a memory that is distorted by the need of the moment), and all the texts that I have forgotten but that are somehow there.

RESEARCHING WRITING/READING

My own revelations, perhaps better called confessions, are merely the speculations of one writer, and they should be suspect. They are not conventional research findings. Perhaps this whole subject cannot be explored by our traditional research techniques but, in any case, I am not a researcher. I am a writer and a writing teacher, who looks within to try to understand my subject matter. I realize better than my critics how eccentric this may be, but I hope it can be a starting place for more authoritative research into how we read while writing and write while reading. I think this relationship is the most significant research frontier in our profession at the present time, and I would like to pose some obvious questions that apparently haven't been obvious as we have attempted to keep our discipline divided into separate camps of reading and writing.

- How does the writer, other than by direct modeling, make use of other texts in creating his or her own texts?
- In what ways does the experience of writing increase the act of reading?
- How does the writer cause the reader to write a text while reading?
- How can this off-the-page or ghost text be described?
- What is the relationship of this ghost text to the written text?
- Does the writer create a ghost text that is different from the written text the writer produces?
- How does the writer read to see the possibility of an entire text in fragments of writing—code words, phrases, lines, sentences, paragraphs, notes?
- Does the writer create a pre-text in the mind that is read during the act of writing? If so, how can it be described?
- What are the different ways the writer reads the unfinished text of another and the unfinished text of his or her own?
- What are the reading skills the writer needs at different stages of the writing process?
- What are the reading roles a writer may play at different stages of the writing process?
- How does the text control or direct both its reading and its writing?
- How much of the text is heard and seen?
- How does the reader's voice affect the reading of the text?
- How much does the personal experience—and feelings and opinions—of the writer/reader affect the writing and reading experience?
- How can the interaction of reading and writing during both the reading act and the writing act be described?
- How do different writing and reading tasks change the description of the writing/reading interaction?

These are a few of the questions to which I would like answers. Wouldn't we all? The implications of those questions are, for me, that we need new research methods so that we can attempt to capture the complex idiosyncratic nature of the reading/writing interaction. Today we recognize that it is impossible to separate reading from writing. Every writer reads at the moment of writing. It has appeared possible for the reader to read without writing, but I wonder if that is really possible. Does the reader while reading actually write a text that is quite different from the one written?

I hope that this conference, which is part of a national trend toward increased examination of the integration of reading and writing, will play a role in sponsoring a new, integrated reading/writing research that will focus primarily on the reading/writing interaction.

TEACHING READING/WRITING

When I first became a teacher of writing at the University of New Hampshire, I was told that I could never become an associate or full professor because I was a writer. I didn't realize the theological importance of those ranks, and so that didn't bother me. I was also told that I could not serve on committees, and I am forever sorry they broke their word on that one. I was also told that writing courses couldn't count for major credit. I wasn't surprised. When I attended this school American literature courses couldn't be counted for literature credit.

I naturally responded to such snobbery with a reverse snobbery of my own and succeeded in being as petty and pompous as any of my colleagues on the other side of the aisle. But things changed, and we have moved closer and closer together. The writers in the department got promoted; we serve on committees—unfortunately—and we believe in the interaction of reading and writing.

In recent years my own conference teaching has changed so much that I see myself as a reading teacher as much as a writing teacher. My students make the first appraisal of their texts, because I must know how they read their own text. I monitor their reading and try to help them read more effectively, for they cannot write better unless they read better. That is only one of the ways we can bring the teaching of writing and reading closer together. Some others may be:

- To encourage and take seriously the texts students write in their heads while reading, especially if those texts seem eccentric to us and do not match the text we have created (written in our own heads) while reading the same pages. Am I speaking in favor of noncomprehension? Perhaps, at times, as a higher comprehension on the part of the teacher.
- To work with our students, in conference and in workshop, to develop the skills of reading fragments that may inspire

a text and to read an unfinished text so that it evolves into increased purpose and meaning.

- To give our students more experience in reading the early drafts and evolving texts of publishing writers within and outside the classroom.
- To encourage increased writing of parallel texts within writing classes, texts that are not so much about what has been written by another but texts which allow the student to approximate the writing experience of the writer.
- To listen to our students (and to published writers?) as they tell us how reading affects their writing and writing affects their reading.
- To design courses in which reading and writing share equal emphasis. This should not mean a return to the traditional freshman English course in which the student was assigned an essay and expected to produce a formulaic response in writing to that essay. In such a course both honest writing and reading, as I practiced it as student and instructor, was often not tolerated. I am imagining classes in which reading and writing texts evolve in a contrapuntal interaction in the way I speculate that writers work.

I know that I am always reading while writing and writing while reading and that if we encourage and study this challenging, complex relationship we will be blessed with a problem we can never solve. We can, however, learn much that is significant in the attempt, and that is what we want, after all, isn't it? Not answers so much as important questions, and there are few questions more important than: What is the relationship of reading and writing?

EIGHT
REVISION AS VISIBLE CRAFT

Back in the olden days when we wrote with typewriter and pen or pencil, it was possible to trace the history of a text through its drafts. Revision was visible. Today most of us write on word processors, and our false attempts, early drafts, and revisions are dispatched to some mysterious elephant graveyard by a punch of a key, never to be seen again. Here is what revision by a professional writer looks like.

This piece was written to describe revision by revealing it, but I couldn't get it published—the editors didn't think it would interest writers. I still used it, however, as a class handout. Like most of my handouts, it demonstrates a technique on a text which discusses the technique so that I may get a double whack at the student.

The word processor ~~makes~~ hides the craft of editing. ~~easier - and invisible.~~ ~~but~~ The skills of cutting, adding, moving with all their infinite variations, are ~~done~~ accomplished ~~by machine, and~~ in electronic secrecy while the text remains forever virginal and young, never showing the scars of its evolution.

~~Sometimes~~ I wonder if ~~the~~ computer makes editing ~~electronic process~~ is too easy. ~~It seems~~ Editing becomes so antiseptic and remote~~, and~~ that I feel nostalgic for the days of a more intimate relationship with my texts. Crossed out lines, some with dots under them to restore them to life, words inserted above and below lines, ~~other~~ words transposed with a special weaving line, sentences and paragraphs circled and moved by arrow, chunks of text slashed out, all ~~the~~ evidence of A ~~the~~ writer at work. I can feel the scissors in my hand cutting the text, ~~into new order and the~~ smell ~~of~~ the glue, heal ~~or~~ the (click ~~of~~ staple) ~~as~~ pieces of text INTO PLACE, ~~are forced together.~~ I ~~used to~~ loved the grand messiness of my creations.

I am nostalgic, but I won't return. The computer is easier. But I WORRY ~~wonder~~ that ~~if~~ writers who have not edited by hand, cut and pasted, will learn ~~know~~ the ~~same~~ craft I ~~have~~ learned in an EARLIER ~~other time,~~ GENERATION.

***

The final satisfaction for the writer is not publication, that long after the fact anticlimax, but the final editing when the writer ~~practices the craft of precision,~~ interacts ~~ing~~ with the text so that it becomes ~~is~~ accurate, clear, and so natural it appears spontaneous. Here is the PHYSICAL joy of working within language, shaping, fitting, joining – cabinetmaking.

I ALWAYS radiscovee ~~There is~~ excitement ~~, even joy,~~ in this final, intimate exercise of skill. I AM WRITING MORE THAN I KNEW. ~~for~~ meaning still surprises: there is discovery, the reason popping out from behind the action; unexpected music, rhythm and melody which emphasize; the explosion of word against word in phrase; the sentence which runs clear, instructing writer and reader; the paragraph in which the firmly packed information delivers ~~provides~~ new insight. There is pleasure in ~~the~~ sure, practiced skill. And ~~there is~~ sadness for the ~~as this~~ relationship OF WRITING AND TEXT is finished. ~~and~~ the text NOW goes forth to ~~make new~~ relate ~~ionships with~~ to other readers. ~~The text is now on its own, never to belong to the writer – if it ever did.~~ The child has grown AND SHOULD LEAVE home, become A FAMILIAR STRANGER.

***

What isn't done, is done; what is left out, ~~is there.~~ Acts of omission, like sins of omission, shape and create. It is a measure of the craftsperson to leave alone. All that not doing takes skill, judgment, discipline. And it should count as work done in the Puritan ~~readers mind~~ as much as all the bustling doing that justifies our time.

***

Respect for the text is fundamental to the craft of effective editing. It is the text itself that makes most ~~of the~~ decisions of what works and what needs work. All the elements in writing come together in the text, each ~~one~~ interacting with each other. It is the challenge of the editor to help the text contain all these tensions ~~and focus them so they work together to clarify an evolving meaning.~~

~~At each moment of crisis or decision it is wise to allow the text time to consider how it can solve its own problems. Solving any problem in isolation from the interaction of the elements of the text usually creates greater problems than the original one.~~

***

~~The writer is reader, and those~~ writers who are most effective in achieving readers are either instinctively Everyman, or they ~~are able to~~ become their reader. They have the talent of empathy, ~~of~~ entering ~~into~~ the ~~skin, sympathetically,~~ of ~~those to whom they are writing.~~ ~~The calculating writer, looking down on an audience, is usually revealed by the text, exposed as one who does not respect or understand the reader, but simply wants to manipulate. That writer is not to be trusted.~~

***

~~During the act of~~ editing the writer must ~~be able to~~ move in close, intervening with the text in the most intimate manner, and then ~~be able to~~ step back ~~and see~~ it whole. The writer must ~~be able to see~~ the effect of change, ~~and often to discuss a meaning or effect that~~ the writer ~~does not want. It may reveal the writer, contradict the writer, make the writer uncomfortable, but it may not be able to be changed. Writing is exposure, and not saying may reveal as much as saying.~~

This ability to participate and observe at the same time is the artist's advantage and curse. The writer is lost in life and a scholar of life simultaneously. Writers have no choice about this. They are committed, they care; they are detached, they judge.

***

Threads of meaning ~~woven~~ through the text ~~can help~~ the reader ~~by providing~~ moments of familiarity ~~as the reader moves~~ forward through unfamiliarity. They prepare the reader for the surprises ahead ~~and comfort the reader,~~ giving the reader something to hold on to as the reader's world is changed by the reading.

***

The act of writing is egocentric, and the writer must ~~admit~~ a sense of self, what is ~~right~~ for this writer. Editors, past and present, teachers, others writers, other readers, readers of ~~the~~ early drafts, authorities in the field - all those people who have shaped and judged us gather around the writing desk, telling ~~us~~ what to say and how to say it. We have to preserve our loneliness. No one wants our individuality until it has become familiar. We have to create our own audience, our own readers, our own need. The final resolution is what is right for this text ~~that~~ is ours. What is it in the text that reveals us - the usness in us - and ~~can not~~ be changed.

***

As we edit we must be aware of the point of view, from ~~where is~~ which the subject ~~being seen;~~ is observed. Where are reader and writer standing overlooking the subject, what can be seen or known from that position and what can not? ~~and therefore can not be kept in the text.~~

***

On what foundation does the weight of the text rest? Where does it get its authority? Is it built on assumptions that are true? Are these assumptions shared by reader and writer? Where is the documentation, especially the implied documentation that does not appear in footnote or bibliography, citation, or reference? What in the reader's experience will make them give us the authority to say what we are saying? ~~so that we will connect with the shock of recognition?~~

***

The text ~~will~~ should be heard by each reader. Have we put in the heard quality into the text, ~~the voice,~~ the music of story or persuasion or explanation or entertainment? Is there a single, appropriate voice underlying the text? ~~a voice that is~~ ~~to message, and which can be heard by the reader?~~ (~~Are there productive ways of playing off that voice, having other voices speak, of improvising on the theme, of deepening and extending the voice?~~)

***

I had a writing professor who argued that punctuation ~~is all a matter of~~ was simply breathing. Perhaps. We should see punctuation not just as a matter of rule, but as a matter of clarification, of pacing, of rhythm, of beat, of creating pattern that will make ~~the~~ meaning both clear and interesting.

***

Writers speak of polishing the text, but I don't ~~like~~ use that phrase. The highly polished text seems slick and glib to me. The text should flow inevitably toward its conclusion. But it doesn't need to flow smoothly, it needs to sweep forward in an interesting and inevitable way, swirling around or over obstacles, carrying meaning on its surface, narrowing through the rapids and then flooding on the plain carrying the reader along on the discovery of meaning.

Sometimes I speak to myself of roughing the text, of giving it interesting obstacles, of making it more clumsy or awkward or difficult. I want to make sure that it is natural, handmade, not machinemade, that the text is not so finished that it doesn't allow the reader to enter it and participate in the making of meaning, ~~-- the~~ even a reader's own meaning which may ~~not be mine.~~ contradict my own.

***

~~Even when you are not writing a story, you're writing narrative, the story of an argument, the story of an explanation, the story of an idea. The writing gets its energy from the dramatic interaction of concepts or facts or observations. The skillful ~~writer~~ EDITOR allows the writing to reveal itself to the reader, to ~~reveal~~ INVOLVE THE READER IN the interaction between the parts of the text that drive the writing forward.~~

***

The editing writer keeps the text rising towards a climax in one continuous line or, more likely, in a series of ascending peaks. When the climax is reached, the writer finishes off the text as soon as possible.

***

The satisfaction of cutting never fades. The quick line runs through the unnecessary text and the meaning comes clear. There is the feeling of surgery about it. Precise, essential, cruel, kind: what is needed ~~is~~ done.

***

Generalities are easy but it is hard to find the right specific. But what satisfaction when you do - the revealing detail, fact, quotation, statistic.

***

~~The~~ energy ~~of verbs,~~ active verbs loaded with meaning, GIVING OFF

***

Variety. The delight of interesting change. Sentences stretched with clauses, sentences that contain complexity and contradiction. Short sentences for emphasis. The wonder of rediscovering the power of the subject-verb-object sentence.

***

And always accuracy, each detail checked and rechecked. ~~And~~ more important, honesty: ~~the~~ EACH fact i~~s~~N ~~appropriate~~ PROPER context.

***

The ~~always~~ unexpected right word. It is always new in context - and inevitable once it is on the page.

* * *

Sometimes I laugh out loud when one word collides with another and the phrase gives off more meaning than I can predict. Two plus two equals seventeen.

* * *

NINE

CASE HISTORY: FINDING AND CLARIFYING MEANING

"The Silence of Veterans" had a difficult birth. I documented these difficulties in a "case history" to share with my students; I wrote it not to say to them "look what I did" but "look what you can do." I hope you will also discover how much you can learn by studying your own writing and the writing of your students as they learn by compiling their own case histories.

As I reread the first draft of "silence," I see a writer meandering over a vast territory, trying to find his way. The writer, who is writing a novel that has its roots in his combat experience, keeps discovering new implications in what he is saying. As I read the last draft, published by its side, I see a meaning found, clarified, developed, not, perhaps, eternal Truth but, in Robert Frost's words, "a momentary stay against confusion."

Professional golfers, tennis players, baseball pitchers—and, I suppose, great lovers—keep a record of what they did when everything went well. When it doesn't, they compare what they are doing to what they did when they were successful. Writers should develop their own form of such instant replay.

It is invaluable to have a record on paper—and in your head—of how you wrote when the writing worked. The time of day; the lack of interruptions, or the form of interruptions; the amount of preparation and planning; your attitude toward the task and its audience; your tools; the pace and time and feeling of the drafting; the way you read and revised the draft; how you edited it. It is the small, revealing details of such an account that usually reveal the significant clues to success or failure.

The autobiography of a writing task will not only help the

writer in trouble but help the writer to grow and develop. And if writers can bring themselves to trust each other and share their accounts of when the writing went well, they will teach each other and extend each writer's repertoire.

My essay, "The Silence of Veterans," obviously has roots that grow back through my childhood to my ancestors. It may seem unusual to have a story with such distant beginnings, but most stories, even the most objective news stories or scholarly reports, grow out of who we are, our individual visions of the world, our own interpretations of our investigations, our personal theories of what makes the world work. The most objective researchers are still asking their questions and seeing their own answers.

The writer must look honestly at himself or herself to understand and make use of what is appearing on the page. In my compulsion to write about World War II, I discovered and have had to live with my own irrational pride at having been trained to kill and having survived, luck translated into virtue. I do not like what I see, but unless I confront what I discover about myself I will not be able to understand and confront what I observe in others. In this sense all writing is autobiographical, no matter the genre or the distance achieved in perspective and voice.

An important part of my writing pattern is *immersion*. I have an image of a submerged log that lies below the surface of my consciousness. It emerges for a moment, is examined, and then sinks out of sight, but not out of thought. The war was always there, below the surface, but in writing spontaneously on blackboards in front of teachers at workshops the war kept surfacing, and I have begun to observe that log a bit more carefully.

This piece flows from recent history: a few years ago, two women students of mine told me during the assault on Granada that they wouldn't date men who weren't willing to serve their country. This alerted me to those signals of a reemerging militarism, after a brief pause for guilt about the Vietnam War. I made no formal notes, but the log kept rising one way or another whenever I wrote freely or worked on fragments of a novel called *A Military History of the Twentieth Century*.

I've now been writing the *Globe* "Over Sixty" column for six months and find I'm responding well to the demand of a deadline. On September 26, 1986, for some reason I was aware that my October 1 column would soon be printed, and I turned back in my mind to the notes I'd made here and there about the possible November column. Without reading those notes I made a quick notation in a matter of seconds and went on to other writing tasks. That note contained what is essential for me, a catalyst and at least a sense of the appropriate voice.

I call the catalyst the *line,* because so many poets talk of the line given. It is rarely a sentence; it is sometimes a word, often a code word or words loaded with personal meaning. Reye's syndrome is a medical term to most people; to me it is the disease that killed a twenty-year-old daughter. Our language is filled with code words that have special meanings for us. We can't just give those words to our readers and expect them to understand the meaning. Most jargon, for example, consists of code words and phrases. While a few people may share these codes on a football field or in a laboratory, as writers we have to translate the code. Still, the code words are important. On September 26 I scribbled in my daybook, "My father missed his war and he didn't want me to miss mine." Then I inserted after "his war," "the month of Veterans Day," and then inserted above that "what I still call Armistice day." And then I added, "the one to end all wars."

That word "Armistice" made me feel I had a start. There was *tension* for me, and I need the sort of tension between words that gives off the energy that will drive my writing forward. For me there was a tension between Armistice Day and Veterans Day, an irony and a difference. To explain what I felt between those words would take more than a column.

In addition to tension there was an *image,* or images. I usually see an idea, even for an academic paper. In this case I had a quick series of images: unfurling flags being carried in a parade; veterans in uniforms of the Grand Old Army of the Republic, the Spanish American War, the Great War, my war, their (the Vietnam veterans) war. Sometimes the image is used in the piece, sometimes it is not, the same way that the line may or may not be used. These are starting points.

And I will not start writing until I hear or sense the voice of the text. I have trained myself so that I only need a tiny fragment of voice to which I can tune a piece of writing. I don't have to articulate the voice, but I will try in this case. It is my voice, of course, the voice of a man sixty-two years old, a Boston boy, of Scottish descent, who listened to sermons and who's been trained as a journalist. We all have many voices within our voice, and I heard in that screwed up and never polished or revised nonsentence a nostalgic, historical tone with a sharp edge of irony, a voice that could be distant and close, sad and angry. But I didn't tell myself what the voice was this way, I heard it and I used it.

On Thursday, October 2nd, [1986], following an artificial discipline I've established for myself, I set a timer and tried to get thirty minutes done on the *Globe* column. I glanced at that sentence in my daybook—"My father missed his war and he didn't want me to miss mine"—and then started dictating. In thirty minutes I had about half the text. The timer binged, and I went on to other things. At this stage my biggest problem is *faith*. It is hard for me to have confidence in what I have written. I often feel, as I felt on the second, an exciting fullness of myself as I write. I think this is really rolling, and then in a page or two or three I crash. It's all bull dung; it's hopeless; I'm hopeless. I've learned to defer such judgments to another day.

The next morning I set the timer and drafted the rest of the piece myself. Dictating is marvelously helpful, because it allows me to write at greater speed, and *fast writing* is extremely important for me. I type much more slowly than my wife—and much, much, much more inaccurately—but with my own typing or my dictating I try to slam through the text, trying not to worry about standards, or correctness, or talent, or brilliance. I'm just trying to follow the text.

Speed is vital, because it suppresses my critical sense. I simply can't be critical at top speed. And in my case that's good. The discipline is there; it needs to be freed. Speed causes the accidents of language and thought: the unexpected evidence, the surprising connection, the weaving of thought and language that may produce a workable, revisable text.

Voice is important. I want to put the heard quality of writing into the page so that it will be heard by the reader. Dictating helps me to hear the text. But when I write with pen or typewriter or word processor I hear the text more than I see it. I listen to how I am speaking. I am conscious of the music—the melodies, the pace, the rhythm—of the evolving text.

There's a spooky quality to my fast writing. The material has been absorbed through immersion, and a text has been ignited by a catalyst. Sometimes I mark down a few words or images in a list, rarely as many as five, and sometimes number them in a different order. In this case I didn't need to know that I would move from my father's training of me to the church to the school to the victory parade. I had an instinctive, chronological trail through the material, and I didn't need to put it down on paper. In fact, I wanted it to be natural and not calculated. I'm generally rather relaxed about this, because I have a head that seems to work easily at creating structures of thought as I write. I think someone once called this kind of thinking associative. Sounds good to me.

Many effective writers speak of the importance of knowing where you *may* end. I emphasize the may because it's not a contract. It's a direction or a potential destination. And the trip may be over before you get where you're going. But you wouldn't get there unless you had a destination. In this case I had a feeling I'd end up with this year's Veterans Day. I didn't know what I'd say or do about it, but I thought that's the direction in which I was headed, and I didn't need to write that down either. Often, however, I scribble down the same kind of fragmentary note for an ending as I do for a lead, before I start to write.

The next morning another half hour at the word processor, and I had cut and shaped the piece into its present form. I took out paragraphs and sentences and details that didn't seem to move the argument forward. I made some words stronger and rearranged others for emphasis—an emphasis closely related to music. I heard the piece and edited it so that it could be heard more clearly.

During the writing there are many elements to which I am attending instinctively. The instinct is the product of years of training, reading, editing (by others, by myself), and writing, writing, writing. Some of the things to which I pay instinctive attention include:

- *Voice.* Worth repeating. I am always listening to the text and trying to speak in a way that is appropriate for me, appropriate to the audience, and appropriate to the subject. I want the writing to flow easily, gracefully, naturally.
- *Specifics.* I prefer the generalizations to occur in the reader's mind. I want to cause those generalizations of thought or feeling, or both, through the stimulation of revealing specifics, concrete details that make the reader see, hear, feel, think. And I am aware that the reader is more likely to read the specific than the general—it is more lively—and is more likely to believe the specific than the general—it has the illusion of authority and may even, if the writer is honest, have the reality of authority.
- *Directness.* I don't want to write *about* the subject. This is one of the worst faults of the ineffective writer. Such a writer circles the subject, telling the reader about it, discussing it, always standing between the reader and the subject, explaining, explaining, explaining. I want to get

out of the way, to be Orwell's pane of glass through which the subject is seen.

- *Respect.* I intend to respect the reader's intelligence. The reader may not know the subject, but the reader is not the twelve-year-old to whom some writers write down. They haven't met with twelve-year-olds. I've worked with twelve-year-olds and written for twelve-year-olds, and they are a tough, intelligent audience who deserve the same respect from the writer as any other reader.
- *Adjectives and Adverbs.* I always feel a tiny sense of failure when using one.
- *Nouns.* I like to write with nouns filled to capacity with meaning.
- *Verbs.* I feel that I write with verbs—simple, active verbs—that provide the energy for the sentence.
- *The Clause.* Watch 'em, especially the dependent ones.
- *The Sentence.* The backbone of our language is the subject-verb-object sentence.
- *The Fragment.* Is a felony when it doesn't work, the English minor sentence when it does.
- *The Dash.* Is a comma raised two decibels and used for emphasis. This is one of my personal heresies, and I delight in it.
- *The Paragraph.* It should present, develop, and document a single idea and carry enough information to satisfy the reader's hunger.
- *Emphasis.* We can't have meaning without emphasis. We emphasize, in a sense, by everything we do. I am particularly aware of emphasizing by brevity, using shorter words, sentences, or paragraphs for the most complicated or important ideas. I'm also interested in emphasis by location—for example, placing important information at the edges of the paragraph, especially at the end. The same thing is true for the beginning and the end of a piece of writing.
- *The First Person.* All writing is in the first person; we admit it when the reader will believe what is being said because of the personal authority of the speaker.
- *Context.* Everything in a piece of writing exists in a local context that evolves as the reader reads. I want that context to be honest. I want everything in the piece to be in context. There are also contexts of writer and reader and subject, and I want to be honest to those contexts so that I do not take my information out of context or imply an inappropriate context.

- *Prejudice.* I want to know myself well enough to know my prejudices, to know the assumptions upon which the piece of writing is built so that I can correct them or confess them to the reader.
- *Pace.* I want to pace the piece of writing so that there is an energy that pushes the reader along, but that also allows the reader to absorb one point before moving on to the next.
- *Evidence.* I want to give the reader fair and sufficient documentation so that the reader will believe. I want to vary the documentation so that it is appropriate to the point being made.
- *Threads.* I want to weave my writing with threads of meaning that reoccur again and again through the piece, holding it all together and creating a pattern of meaning that is attractive and convincing to the reader.
- *Surprise.* Someone once said that a good style was a series of tiny surprises, and I'm influenced by this. I don't want so many surprises that the reader is disconcerted, but I want little surprises, turns of phrases, metaphors, analogies, unexpected words that have an interesting spin on them, that are not quite what the reader expects. I want to play with metaphor, with analogy, with language, touching up a cliché, having fun with jargon, inflating or deflating my diction, balancing humor with a clause of seriousness, and seriousness with a clause of humor.
- *Discovery.* I write to discover what I have to say in the hope that what I discover will be significant. I don't want to just report what I have discovered but, whenever possible, to take the reader along. I want to write, in a sense, the narrative of thought, inviting the readers to think with me, to enter into the text with me, so they can make their own meanings from our shared text.

It is up to you, of course, to decide how well I have done what I have tried to do. Please remember, however, that my way is not your way, and should not be. We should take pleasure in diversity. Our importance lies in our difference, and you should not hold me to your standards but only to my own standards. And you should not accept my standards, but merely consider them to see if what I'm trying to do and how I'm trying to do it has value for you. I've tried to share my account of this writing so that you may begin to see the value in creating your own account, your own record of what you did and felt and thought when your writing went well.

I wrote the above account to my students after completing the draft. Later, I shared with them more of the story of this piece of writing:

There are few jobs more satisfying than having the opportunity to cut and reshape a piece of writing. It's a physical job, the article grows and changes under my hands. I must listen to it, respect it, help it find its own shape.

It is especially helpful when you have readers who make you feel you have something to say and who are able to suggest ways you may have to say it better. I was unblessed by the *Providence Journal* editorial writers with whom I shared the draft during a coaching session. They did not like the piece, said that they knew war from movies and books as well as I did—apparently missing the point that I was talking about *my* war—and seemed to feel I was unfairly antiwar, which I certainly hope I was.

I was stunned, angered, and momentarily paralyzed by their response, but I was blessed by the responses of others with whom I shared the first draft, inviting them to edit, question, attack, support, to tell me what worked for them and what needed work. I showed the draft to twenty-eight freshmen, fourteen graduate students, Minnie Mae, and Chip Scanlan. All of them were helpful.

I cut, reordered, and added. The draft is on the left and the final version I submitted for publication on the right so you can compare the changes and second-guess them if you wish.

DRAFT	**FINAL**
	THE SILENCE OF VETERANS
The month of Veterans Day—that I still call Armistice Day for the war to end all wars—brings a holiday I do not celebrate. There are too many memories, especially the memories I do not remember. They are there, silent, waiting to be summoned up, but I do not want to disturb them.	The month of Veterans Day—that I still call Armistice Day for the war to end all wars—brings a holiday I do not celebrate. There are too many memories, especially the memories I do not remember. They are there, silent, waiting to be summoned up, but I do not want to disturb them.

My father missed his war. His father had died, and he was the eldest son, and he could not march over there. He remembered how much he admired the drummer boys in Fall River who were his age and who marched off to the Spanish American War. He felt he had missed something important on the road to manliness when he couldn't enlist in 1917, and he communicated this sense of loss or anxiety to me. He would sing old army songs to me; he loved cranking up Sousa on the Victrola; when we went on Sunday afternoon walks we often marched—hup, two, three, four.

I was brought up on a muscular, male, military religion. The church organ made noises like a marching band, and sometimes there were even real trumpets imported, sometimes even bagpipes. There was "The Battle Hymn of the Republic," and I dreamt of

My father missed his war. He felt he had lost something important on the road to manliness when he couldn't enlist in 1917, and he communicated his sense of anxiety to me. He would sing "Tenting tonight, tenting tonight, tenting on the old campground" as a lullaby; crank up Sousa on the Victrola; march on Sunday afternoon walks—hup, two, three, four.

I was brought up on a muscular, male, military religion. The pipe organ made noises like a marching band during "The Battle Hymn of the Republic," and I dreamt of enlisting with the Onward Christian Soldiers marching as to war.

y grandmother told me
stories she had heard
ancient men, one who
my name who had
ht at Waterloo. But the
es were secondhand,
I tried to find veterans
would tell me what it
like, really like, how
derful it was to be

heroic, how manly, how close you felt to your comrades, how exciting the taste of victory.

At school, we had Memorial Day and Armistice Day assemblies, in which veterans—or politicians wearing veterans' uniforms—talked about patriotism. But I wanted to know what it was really like, and they didn't tell me.

One Sunday School teacher would bring in helmets, gas masks, bayonets, rifles, and let us fondle the Christian implements of war. But he told us Bible stories transplanted to the trenches. Russell McPhee's brother went to Panama in the army, and we would wear his pith helmet and touch, oh so gently, his razor-sharp machete. And he hadn't really been to war, just to the jungle.

The veterans I questioned reacted badly to my inquisition. It turned out they had gotten all the way to Fort Banks in Winthrop, where they cooked beans, or they had been in the trenches and they wouldn't talk about it.

The silence of the veterans irritated me, and I searched the history books. Most of them didn't really put me there, but I found a few pictures of trench warfare that should have warned me

heroic, how manly, how close you felt to your comrades, how exciting the taste of victory.

We had Memorial Day and Armistice Day assemblies in school, at which politicians wearing veterans' uniforms talked vaguely about patriotism. One Sunday School teacher brought in helmets, gas masks, bayonets, rifles, and let us fondle the implements of war, but he turned our questions about life in the trenches into unsatisfying moralistic generalities.

The veterans I questioned reacted badly to my inquisition. It turned out they had gotten all the way to Fort Banks in Winthrop, where they cooked beans, or they had been in the trenches and they wouldn't talk about it.

The silence of the veterans irritated me, and I searched history books. I found a few pictures of trench warfare that should have warned me that combat wasn't all barners unfurled and that combat wasn't all banners furled and trumpets sounding, but I must admit that these photos made war even more dangerous, more exciting, more terrible, more thrilling. I really would be tested, and I would come home a man.

The day after Pearl Harbor I volunteered for the Marines, but the sergeant whipped off my glasses and said, "Read that sign." I said, "What sign?" And he said, "Next." I volunteered for the Navy, for the Coast Guard, for the Army, but nobody wanted Four-Eyes. And then, when I had started college—a huge step forward for a kid who had flunked out of high school—I was drafted.

Being drafted wasn't enough. I wanted to be a hero. When I was in the service I volunteered for the paratroops. Four-Eyes knew what to do now; I had a quart of Four Roses in my blouse, and I passed the eye exam with 20–20 vision. I didn't make it to hero, but an adequate number of Germans shot at me, and I came home with the 82nd to march in the official victory parade in New York City.

I know that many Vietnam veterans wanted a victory parade, and I try to understand that. But I found the parade a farce. As the bands played and the

trumpets sounding, but I must admit that these photos made war even more dangerous, more exciting, more terrible, more thrilling. I really would be tested, and I would come home a man.

The day after Pearl Harbor I volunteered for the Marines, but the sergeant whipped off my glasses and said, "Read that sign." I said, "What sign?" And he said, "Next." When I was drafted, I still wanted to be a hero and volunteered for the paratroops. My eyesight was still a problem but I knew what to do now. I handed a quart of whiskey to the eye doctor and developed 20–20 vision.

I didn't make it to hero, but an adequate number of Germans shot at me, and I felt the special companionship of combat; the concentration of all the senses when confronted with terror; the guilty, erotic, thrill of survival when you walked away and left the dead behind.

confetti rained down and the politicians smirked and waggled their fingers at us, all I could see in my mind's eye were the images of war, heads without bodies, bodies without heads. I kept imagining a Hallowe'en parade of the crippled and the maimed, of the skeletons of the young who would never grow old.

The average age in our division when we went overseas was 19 for enlisted men and 21 for officers. I believed in the war, and was glad we had won. More than that, I was surprised I had survived, and I did not want to look back at who had not survived or at the accidents of survival. I began to understand why those men who had come home from the trenches did not want to talk to me and tell me what it was like. The more they had experienced the less they were able to talk about it.

Now I had my own secrets, and I've developed my own war stories, neatly polished, that can be turned this way or that way to make a point. Stories get better through the years, but not more truthful. The big problem is that they make a point, and in combat, at least for this infantry private, there rarely was a point. Combat is a course in Surrealism.

Now I have my own secrets. The man next to you, taking a crap, doesn't do a movie dance of death, he simply disappears in a direct hit from a German 88. I only feel his passage like a burly ghost. The dead lieutenant sits at attention in his jeep balanced neatly on top of a telephone pole after he hit a landmine. I had been with him minutes before. Digging a foxhole I

The man next to you, taking a crap, didn't do a movie dance of death, he disappeared from a direct hit from an 88. I only felt his passage like a burly ghost The lieutenant in his jeep perched neatly on top of a telephone pole after he hit a landmine. The Easter morning when I reached down for my K-ration and put my finger in the mouth of the dead priest. The feel of the jeep steering wheel as we bumped forward, driving over the bodies of Americans I knew, who had been killed when they were ordered by an American Colonel to attack another American outfit.

realize the bones in my hand are human—heroes from the war to end all wars. I almost kill my buddy I am so angry at his luck; he will go home to Chicago without his feet, but alive. I will go back on post.

Forty-two years later I still wake to see Jim sitting against a tree waiting patiently for Graves Registration. He was always kind and patient. He holds his head neatly in his lap. Easter morning I reach down for my K-ration and put my finger in the mouth of the dead priest on whose cold body I unknowingly sit in the dark shadows of the church. I still feel the sudden twists of the jeep steering wheel as we bump forward, driving over the bodies of Americans I knew who had been killed when they were ordered by an American colonel to attack another American battalion.

How do you talk about war to people who have only seen movies and read history books? How do you share the fact that combat is a time of constipation and diarrhea with no in between, and you wore the same underwear from December through March? That's what people, who want their own war, ought to know. And yet writing about combat makes it sound in some way heroic,

How do you make people who have only seen movies and read books smell combat? How do you share the truth of the front lines, that war is a time of constipation and diarrhea with no in between, and that you wore the same underwear from December through March? That's what people, who want their own war as I so desperately did, ought to know.

Writing about it still

certainly not dull. Yet it is important that the young who are the raw material of combat, realize that war is ultimately boring in a particularly terrible way: what man can do to destroy other men becomes ordinary, as routine as going to the office, day after day, to turn on the gas ovens in the concentration camp.

Yet, the silent veterans do not let the next generations know what it was like, because they can not allow themselves to probe too deeply into memory beyond those few neat little stories. And so the people who talk of war are men—and women—like my father who didn't go to war and politicians who are thrilled by bands and awed by the toys of war.

On Armistice Day I will not attend a parade, observe the placing of a wreath, listen to a politician. I will go through the day lonely for those who are not here, and will be struck at unexpected moments by images from the past. And I will protect myself by performing the ordinary

makes it sound in some way heroic, certainly not dull. Yet the young who will be the raw material of combat need to know that war is ultimately boring in a particularly terrible way. What man can do to destroy man becomes ordinary, as routine as going to the office day after day. I learned to carry my rifle as casually as a briefcase, and other men yawned as they turned on the ovens at Auschwitz again and again.

I envy the pacifist but cannot enlist. We failed to disarm in the Thirties—as we are failing in the Eighties—and the time came when we had to stop the Nazis and contain the Japanese, but all wars are a failure of will and intelligence, and we seem to forget the price. The actors in our "action" movies wash off the ketchup blood and go home. The silent veterans do not let the young know that few go home from combat, and those who do are afraid to remember.

In writing this I have remembered too much. On Armistice Day I will not attend a parade, observe the placing of a wreath, listen to a politician. But if more veterans had the courage to remember and speak, there might be fewer wars, at least fewer boys hoping, as I did, for my own war.

chores of my living and not
speak—or allow myself to
think—of the realities of
war.

But I wish we could
speak. Perhaps if we did,
there would be fewer wars,
at least fewer boys hoping,
as I did, for my own war.

I hope it has been helpful to see how one professional works. Remember, it is just one professional and just one writing task. There are significant differences between writers and between writing tasks. But I think it is important to see how writing is made.

I had, as I mentioned, many valuable responses to the text, and I had a copy of the text in my daybook that I had marked up. I worked with that beside me, but only referred to it sporadically. I had absorbed most of the criticisms and knew them without referring to the text. Mostly I worked consciously within the text, letting the text make the decisions for me—what works and what needs work.

The final version is about a page and a quarter shorter, but it includes quite a bit of new material. I was working with pace, proportion, honesty, accuracy, voice. I hated to see the parade go, but it had to go. I felt that the editing was a process of deepening, diving into the subject and into myself, and that in turn gave me not only new material but the ending.

The final version took me about two hours to write, half an hour more than it did to produce and edit the previous draft.

II

LEARNING BY SHARING

TEN

THE IMPORTANCE OF BAD WRITING—AND HOW TO ENCOURAGE IT

I never intended to become the apostle of bad writing, but I have found myself in a political climate that discourages intellectual exploration—the daring to be wrong that is essential to good writing.

Our political leaders, administrators, too often our colleagues, parents, students all seem obsessed with safeness, caution, correctness, propriety. They say they are emphasizing writing but, in fact, they diminish it, hoping to return to the good old days when correctness ruled meaning, when a few were rewarded for their formality in writing and the majority—myself included—were cast out. Am I writing autobiography instead of scholarship? You betcha.

I have traveled around the country this past year, and I am worried about the state of writing instruction in our schools. But my concerns differ from most. I find a disturbing increase in good writing—writing that is neat, proper, nice.

> *Autumn is my favorite season of the year. . . .*
>
> *I certainly agree with Henry David Thoreau, a man of today if there ever was one, who said . . .*

I find few surprises in student papers, less that is unpredictable, few topics that are threatening, hardly any papers that combine genres and structures in a manner which exposes an unexpected meaning, few accidents of syntax and diction that work although the books say they won't. Instead of excellent writing—or challenging failures packed with potential—we see, well, "good" writing, supermarket white bread instead of home-baked, satisfying, dark bread.

Comes fall, comes school, comes the end of summer when I worked with grown-ups who thought I was one and go back to school, a playpen world. Treat me like I got diapers, I got diapers. . . .

When my mother died I found an unexpected coldness in me. I found her. I did all that had to be done, you know, calls and stuff. I even lifted her to the bed. I was old, right then, just like that, and there's no warmth yet. It's always cold. I'm cold. My father was proper broken up not me. . . .

We don't need Thoreaus. He was a troublemaker. He was one of those grandstand quarterbacks who always know what to do but couldn't with people rushing in at them.

Instead of such "badly written" drafts that are ready to explode with significance, I read careful essays that are error conscious as well as error free. I have inflicted upon me the same sort of bland competent mediocrity achieved by our fast-food chains and our fast newspaper chains. Sometimes, while listening to student drafts written to formula (on whole-class assignments) I find myself quietly chanting the language ahead of the student. These young people are able to achieve the clichés we expect in the plodding prose of college presidents.

There is no surprise for writer or reader, and therefore no challenge, no difficulty, no thinking. Composition becomes a trivial subject, a matter of etiquette, writing that is traditional, imitative, standard, noncritical, nonthreatening. Our students are not using language, they are being used by it.

Of course society is pleased by bland writing. They would be delighted with correct writing, actually believing that writing should and can be contained in a prison of formal rules. Most people believe writers know what they are going to say before they say it. They do not know that writing is a thinking skill. They think style can be bought like the lift heel or the hair color that try to make you tall and young. Some—and they include eager-to-please English teachers—even believe that the aim of education in English is to enable students to fill out job applications, when we all know that few jobs are ever filled on the basis of a job application.

But if society is not disturbed, we should be. We need—and the nation needs, even if it does not know it—a curriculum that causes students to write badly in a significant way. We should want our students to attempt the leaps and suffer the failures of form and voice that produce good writing. We must allow—no, encourage—our students to make use of language to explore the inner and outer worlds each is driven to explore.

And when students have found their own territory, they must search it with the language—and the language skills—they have, not what we wish they had. Once they start grappling—on the page—with the meanings they need to discover, we can help them see how the traditions of form and language help clarify thinking.

What they produce, at first, will *not* often be traditional, expected writing, but quite often—more often than you will expect if you haven't done this—the surprising, insightful, thought-provoking and emotion-evolving writing that grows from the nourishing compost of failure.

Our responsibility is to unteach our students, who have been taught language arts and English year after year, until they know too much about rules and principles—what can't be done—and too little about the exciting dangers of language. They don't know the experience of spinning out of control when they hit an unexpected verb, of becoming gloriously lost in a wandering sentence or being unable to find their way out of a paragraph maze or a quarter-thunk thought.

How sad it would be—and is—to have a student never have the stomach-grabbing terror and sudden beautiful insight as an unexpected text whips through a series of Peter Elbow loops. Think of a student writing papers so short, so neat, so correct that there is never the flow of unexpected meaning, never a play of words, never a tangent luring the student away from the outline toward an unsuspected meaning.

Of course unteaching is as disturbing—and frightening—for the instructor as the student. Class, workshop, and conference become unpredictable, uncomfortable, terrifying, discordant, contradictory, confusing, but you will never have excellent writing unless you have wonderfully rich and profound failures. To have meaningful texts we have to keep finding ways to write differently than we have written before.

If we study literature, listen to music, visit art and photography exhibitions, we will begin to understand that excellent writing comes from the distortion of tradition. What delights us about the arts is that we have an expectation of color or line or sound or language, and the artist goes beyond that expectation. The writer makes us hear what isn't said; the artist draws negative space; the writer who is more than good distorts tradition and meaning, twisting the world and the language around in such a way that we see and hear and feel and think in ways we haven't before facing this page.

We need to design courses, assign reading, and, most of all, create a climate in which our students both experience and appreciate the creative imbalance and insightful disproportion that go beyond the reader's expectation. Purposeful distortion attracts, holds, educates the reader; yet we do not make distortion a significant part of the curriculum or seize that moment on student drafts when accidental distortion that illuminates occurs and may be recognized and rationalized.

Let's look, for example, at the elements in a successful story. Character, action, place, theme, and voice are not dealt out in equal proportion but developed disproportionately, with one or more elements emphasized at the expense of others. There is a richness and a strangeness to the writing that becomes part of our experience, so that we think and behave as if we experienced the page—which we did.

To encourage and produce bad writing, we must build our courses on a carefully constructed foundation which is designed for our students and makes use of our own teaching strengths. This curriculum might include the following five elements:

Demand. English *is* often boring. We do not demand enough of our students. We give them topics, bland assignments, fill-in-the-blanks strategies. We patronize them by deciding in advance what students can do and, therefore, trivialize our curriculum. When students are trying to do so much that it can't yet be done with the structures and the voices they have, they begin to understand what writing can do to teach the writer. Only then will they begin to feel the need for the traditions—the tools—of effective composition.

Climate. To receive really bad writing—not just disinterested, lazy writing—the teacher has to establish a climate in which teacher and classmates alike listen to drafts with respect for what the student is trying to do. The reader should delight in hints of meaning: the unexpected word that isn't right but may point toward a meaning, the almost revealing phrase, the sentence that loops toward significance before it collapses, the paragraph that holds so much potential that it is swollen out of shape, the voice that says more than the words it is using so badly at the moment, the very intensity of the writer's need which draws the reader to the text and the writer to the revision. The classroom should be filled with laughter, sharing, support, listening, and a contagious enthusiasm for what is being attempted and accomplished in writing.

Failure. Outlaw error and you outlaw real writing. The students who know the rules will play the teacher-pleasing game of delivering the expected, what has sat in long-term memory ready to be dressed up in the costume of correctness. The students who do not know the rules will drop out and sit on the sidelines, bored by what the emphasis on rightness has produced in the "good" students' papers. There will be no thinking with language, no exploration, no discovery, for those intellectual activities bring with them an essential messiness in which the rules are ignored or challenged until they prove their worth. Recently I attended an exhibition of Picasso's sketchbooks. At first his work was academic, full of skill, controlled by skill, and then he broke free of his own accomplishment. How often, how delightfully, how easily he failed. His learning was there in his failures, and the sketchbooks were an invitation to play the game of art. "Come on in. Join me. Have fun and you, too, may discover your own world. See, it is easy to screw up a vision, to draw the wrong line, to smear, to do too much. Try it." The teacher who wants bad writing must cultivate failure so that students will learn how writers mine their failures for the meanings we find so gracefully, so easily laid out on the published page.

Demonstration. The teacher must become Picasso and demonstrate what it means to use language to explore experience for significant meaning. The teacher should write with the students and in front of the students: printing copies of notes and outlines, writing beginnings that are spectacular failures—hilarious, ridiculous, dreadful—on the board or overhead projector, reading rough drafts out loud, giving copies of later drafts to students and asking their help in revising and editing. Never write down—I've found no need to do that with elementary school students, high school or college students, or professionals—since I've always been able to produce a pleasing surplus of failure while trying to do my best. The students have been taught it is terrible to fail; you have to show them how and why failure is productive—and demonstrate you can survive these essential failures.

Activities. Games are the best way to help students learn how to write badly. These activities should never be corrected or graded. They are always classroom or homework activities which are supplemental to the continual writing the students are doing as they use form and language to search for meaning in the important materials of their lives. But these activities make it possible for the students to see how they can use writing to explore their worlds.

I'll suggest some games, but it is always more helpful to have each class make up their own and adapt your suggestions to their own needs.

1. Write about what you don't know anything about. Or follow Grace Paley's advice: "We write about what we don't know about what we know."
2. Lie. Make up the research. Empathize. Imagine. You may find the facts after you've found the truth.
3. Choose an uncomfortable distance. Get too close to the subject, or too far away.
4. Use an inappropriate genre. Write a poem as a memo, and a memo as a poem.
5. Reverse the order. Construct a flimsy structure. Be illogical. Move against the natural sequence of thought, travel, or time.
6. Create an imbalance of the proportions of the piece. Have too much description or too little; too much exposition or no exposition; all dialogue or no dialogue.
7. Distort the pace of the piece of writing. Write in a musical form that is inappropriate, change the beat.
8. Look at the subject from an unexpected point of view. Tell the love story from the point of view of the gossip, and the story of the scientific breakthrough from the point of view of the janitor who cleans the laboratory.
9. Write at a pace that is uncomfortable for you: too fast or too slow.
10. Write with your left hand if you're right-handed. (Artists will do that when they feel they are too skilled at their drawing, or they may attach their pen to a yard-long stick.) Interview artists, musicians, scientists, craftspersons, creative people to see what they do to protect themselves against their skills.
11. Ghostwrite. Write from someone else's point of view in their voice, not yours.
12. Write with words that are not your own. Use a false voice.
13. Write for an audience with which you are unfamiliar. Write for young children, or retired people, experts or amateurs, people who are emotionally involved in the subject or those who couldn't care less.
14. Require a ridiculous length of yourself. Tell the history of the world in one paragraph. Write fifty pages on sitting in a chair.
15. Write for an eccentric publication. Write about Christianity for a skin magazine and the swinging life for a Baptist newspaper.
16. If you know a foreign language, write in that, then translate. If you don't, write in an oral language you know that is

more informal or more formal than your normal writing language.

17. If you write easily, make the writing hard, work with tension, anxiety, and pathological care; if writing is hard for you, free-write, stream your consciousness, loop, flow.
18. If you write in short chunks of time, tie yourself in your chair, as John McPhee used to when he was a beginning writer, and write for a whole day. If you write only in long periods, set a timer and write in fifteen-minute chunks during the day.
19. Change your purpose. If you write to persuade, write to entertain. If you write to entertain, write to inform.
20. If you're a morning writer, write late at night, between yawns, when your guard is down and your eyes unfocused. If you're a night writer, write in the morning before you get out of bed, before your guard is up, between yawns, when your eyes won't focus.
21. Take the best piece of writing you've done (or a good piece of writing by one of your favorite authors) and work it over to make it really bad, fascinatingly dreadful, brilliantly awful.

Be responsible. Learn how to encourage really bad writing in your students and in your self: the awful, the clumsy, the illogical, the awkward, the different, the weird, the mixed-up, the incoherent, the messy, the distorted in which new meanings may hide. Be a Peter Elbow who enjoys and delights in bad writing and knows what to do with it. Share the strange satisfaction of receiving bad writing with your students until they, too, delight in the poor writing from which good writing grows. Then, perhaps, your students will learn to produce writing that is joyfully, significantly worse than anything you've ever seen.

ELEVEN
WHAT MAKES STUDENTS WRITE

Many of my articles were also spoken, and sometimes it is hard to separate the content of a piece from my memory of the conditions under which it was presented. This article was first given as a talk at Georgia State in Atlanta. I spoke in a basketball court that was paired with another court hidden behind a huge curtain—plonk, plunk, plonk. The crowd coming to hear me kept growing, and as it grew wider and wider on the bleachers, they kept moving the podium back, until it stood in center court. When I finally began speaking, I had a long crowd stretching far to the left and right and an enormous vacant space between me and the first row, so vast I could not read the faces of my listeners. I never had realized how much I depended on that reading to pace and develop my talk.

The audience was wonderful and Georgia friendly. Later my hosts asked me to produce a text from my notes and I did, but I couldn't work in the plonk, plunk, plonk from the other court.

I've pretty much given up being an educational circuit rider. It becomes a demanding career in itself, with its own culture, problems, challenges, crafts, and amusing stories. And for a shy kid who hid in the closet rather than come out to meet the company, it was a rewarding and potentially addictive career. At first you are delighted that people take you so seriously, and then you realize, with horror, that some take you more seriously than you take yourself. That gives one pause.

In my case, I began to feel that my speaking often contradicted my message. My philosophy for teaching writing can be summed up simply: write and look to yourself, pay attention to what you feel, what you say, how you say it, how you create a situation that makes your best writing possible. Do the same for your students. Respect them as individuals, delight in their difference, observe and listen to them as you have observed and listened to yourself. Help them on their individual ways by teaching them to teach themselves. Make yourself unnecessary so you can turn to the next wave of insecure, overtaught students coming to your class.

And I find myself giving this message of individuality and difference to hundreds of people. I believe the real authority is the teacher writer and the student writer, each listening to themselves together. Yet I contradict that, inevitably, by standing on the platform, a speaking statue, placed in a position of authority.

I do, however, have the arrogance to tell others how to teach in my written texts. I try to invite readers to enter my text and make it their own, but I am guilty of arrogance as charged. At least when I write, I do not have to see myself up there talking as if I knew what is right for you when all I really know is what is right for me—and that keeps changing.

Yes, I'd like to have you read my articles and books, alone, with skeptical eye. They should not think for you, but, if they work, I hope they will inspire challenge, doubt, question, adaptation, theft—thinking of your own.

Writing programs are usually based on the goals we all want our students to achieve—meaningful and vigorous prose which demonstrates their ability to use language effectively. We may be more likely to achieve these goals, however, if we construct a curriculum from the forces that produce clear, thoughtful writing. Three of the most powerful of these forces are difficulty, discovery, and demand.

DIFFICULTY

Students are most likely to write—especially those students who are least likely to write—when they confront a personal problem that may be solved by writing. Writing must have a purpose for us to take it seriously, and the universal purpose that writing may serve is our fundamental need to understand our world.

It is logical to give our most elementary or remedial students the simplest assignment. We ask them to write about small matters of utter trivia and then help them with assignments that further limit exploration or thought; we sometimes even give them story starters or word lists, as if we could present them with our language. All this seems logical and it is certainly traditional, a repetition of what has failed with these students in previous grades. The problem is that it doesn't work.

It doesn't work because it trivializes the act of writing. Writing begins in terror, in loneliness, in despair. It begins even for the experienced writer—*especially* for the experienced writer—in the feeling that there is nothing to write.

We should encourage, if not extend, this despair, allowing our students to understand that it is normal and probably essential. It allows us, even forces us, to confront major questions, and we may begin to become writers when we look critically at our feelings on the death of a parent or a child, on our own fear at entering the operating room, at the way at which we have hurt and been hurt, at what we have done and not done, at the events and the people who have shaped our lives. In other words, we need—in specific terms—to write of love and hate and loss and hurt. As the poet Alan Dugan says, "I'm still doing business at the same old stand—love, work, war, death, what the world is like outside this window tonight."

Of course, the student will struggle in writing about such things. The student will not sit down and produce a nice, neat, little text; the student will produce drafts that half work, or a quarter work, or do not work at all. The student will fail to focus on the subject at first, to limit it, to order it, to develop it, to make it clear. The student's voice will falter, will grow weak and fade and recover and grow weak once more. The writing will be uneven, erratic, and quite possibly exciting, because the student will discover that language and rhetoric are not dry matters of precise rules but are living processes, lenses that can illuminate the world, catching quick glimpses of potential meaning, of understanding, of clarification.

By writing badly—as all writers must write—the student begins to hold the world in place, just a small piece of the world and just for a moment, but the student will make connections and discover context and meaning.

DISCOVERY

What we have been talking about is the discovery of meaning, not a meaning that is known by the teacher and assigned but a meaning that is *not* known by teacher or student. The single most powerful motivating force for the writer is the confidence, confirmed by experience, that the pen—or the word processor—will lead the writer into territory the writer needs to explore and the act of writing will reveal meanings the writer has not foreseen.

Writing is not thinking reported, it *is* thinking; many times it is such a sophisticated and subconscious kind of thinking, we don't even call it thinking. But it happens, right here in the head and on the page. Head makes a guess and page tries to understand. Page tells head what is confusing, and head tries to understand. Head tries again and page says "Better, but. . . ." Page waits, and head becomes angry at this aggressive patience. Head gives up and turns the job over to mouth. Mouth dumbly speaks, and hand writes it down while ear listens. Ear tells head there is something there, a word perhaps, unexpected, "dumbly" speaks, or a bit of music or an unusual angle of vision, not much but something, and page nods. Head shakes back and forth in puzzlement. Yeah, something has happened. That dumb mouth has unknowingly said something and now it has to be made clear and tested. Head goes to work and page purrs.

Students need a problem to solve—a meaning they need to make—and the space in which *not* to write about it. Time for staring out the window, daydreaming, thinking and not thinking, allowing the brain to collect and connect, fitting and discarding fragments of information that may construct a meaning—and may not. And time to write: to make notes, to doodle, to draw designs, to outline, to rehearse lines and paragraphs, usually leads, often ends. And time to produce drafts that are just that—drafts. Experiments in meaning. Sentence fragments that may become sentences; essay fragments that may become essays.

We are motivated to write when we communicate to ourselves. Others come later or not at all. It is satisfying to share, to entertain, to explain, to persuade, to reach an audience, but it is a great, private joy to hear yourself, to be quiet and to listen to the music of your own meaning wrestling itself free of confusion, to see a page on which your hint of potential meaning stands free of you, rooted in its own understanding.

Students will write if we give them understanding and support as they stumble toward discovery. How do we know how to do that? By experiencing the process of discovery ourselves. You cannot teach what you do not know. If language has never taken you by the hand and led you off the road of reason into the woods and introduced you to surprise, you cannot encourage it or recognize it. But if you write on your page what you do not expect to write, then you can entice your students to write what they do not yet know instead of imprisoning them in what they know.

DEMAND

If we are to motivate writing by taking our students and their writing seriously, then we may delay demand but not eliminate it. In fact, demand itself is a motivating force. We know this on the football field but ignore it in the classroom, patronizing our students because we do not believe in their potential. Writing should be hard. We are asking of writing nothing less than an understanding of the world in which we live.

We must demand quantity so that there may be quality. We must have deadlines—a week is about maximum—for writing. That writing may be notes and outlines and fragments and rough drafts at first, but there must be arbitrary road marks that say, for example, "A Subject Is Found by Now," "A Test Draft for Peer Evaluation Is Ready by Now," "A Final Draft Is Completed by Now." Inspiration is the product of freedom *and* discipline. There must be time for out-window-staring, doodle making, rerehearsal, failure and experiment, but there must also be a time when there is no time.

And since we have allowed our students to find their own questions and their own answers, their own messages, their own forms and their own language, we must help them to find their own way to make their thoughts clear. Working to make a meaning come clear that they need to know, they will discover the traditions of our trade. They will find that the writers who have gone before have refined a craft that is available to them. They will make use of an energy-giving verb, a noun that captures meaning, a sentence that connects, a paragraph that develops, a comma that gives pause, a period that completes.

We have made writing too easy. We have emphasized the mechanics of meaning while ignoring the development of meaning. We have written off both our best and worst students by failing to introduce both groups into the hard work of using language to find meaning in a world where meaning is hidden and where the meaning found is more often discomforting than comforting. But that's our trade, teaching people to think. As Hemingway said, "Prose is architecture not interior decorating," and our students will write when they find writing is hard but worthwhile, a way of constructing meanings that will help them live and understand.

What makes students write? Difficulty, discovery, and demand.

TWELVE

LISTENING TO WRITERS

Much of my understanding of the writing process has come from exploring different genres. The same thing is true of my teaching. Although I have primarily been a university teacher, I have taught freshmen and graduate students, writing students and nonwriting students, student teachers and practicing teachers.

Off campus, I've worked in primary classrooms where the furniture is dreadfully small. I've not only worked with students across the grade levels, I've taught people in government agencies and on hospital nursing staffs; I've taught computer company writers, business writers, and, most of all, professionals on newspapers across North America.

When Tom Newkirk joined our faculty I told him there was little difference between working with writers in the fourth grade and with professionals on a nationally recognized newspaper. He didn't believe me and, being Tom Newkirk, he told me he didn't believe me. But he does now that he has worked with writers on all levels. We all keep returning to the basic issues in our craft: honesty, accuracy, clarity, development, order, voice.

And in teaching, it is the same problem: How do we best help individual writers learn most effectively how to teach themselves? When do we intervene, stand back, speak, be silent, encourage, point out, draw out, listen, question, respond, criticize, praise?

This article was written for presentation at a seminar of newspaper writing coaches, those who work with working writers to help them improve their writing. But I think what is being discussed relates to those who teach first grade all the way through to those who teach last grade.

Editors who want to improve writing must learn to commit an unnatural act: listening.

You can't order good writing like a Big Mac. Editors may command good writing, but the next edition proves that commanding good writing doesn't produce good writing any more than style books guarantee style.

The best writing always surprises. It surprises the writer, surprises the editor, surprises the reader. An individual voice rises off the page and speaks. Such voices appear almost accidental. They are so natural they seem spontaneous but the accidents keep happening to the same writers, the ones whose individual talents are honed by practice and supported by editors who know how to cultivate surprise.

Good writing can be encouraged. It can be drawn out of writers by an editor who turns writers into colleagues, supports and stimulates them, and, above all, listens to writers so well that they discover what they didn't know they knew about their story and its writing.

WHAT WRITERS KNOW

Too many editors have the easy belief that the writers on their staff are illiterate, lazy, rebellious, and perverse. But if you work with writers in city rooms, you find that writers are embarrassingly eager to please. They may adopt the cynical pose—I did when I was reporter—but they are as eager as a puppy to get a pat on the head. Editors who receive bad writing must realize that they are receiving what their writers think they want. Writing is not a dumb act: it is an intellectual craft, and writers make editorial decisions based on their beliefs of what the editor expects.

When my colleague Jane Harrigan first joined the editor's guild, she was surprised to discover that other editors had forgotten that writers knew what they were doing. Their stories—especially many of the real turkeys—were carefully crafted to give the editor what the writer thought the paper wanted. Writers not only know what they are doing but why they are doing it.

The effective editor, such as Harrigan, doesn't put writers down but tries to find out why writers are producing such stories. Since writers are performing a purposeful act, the editor must not just say the story is wrong but discover the principle the writer is following so the reason behind a string of ineffective stories can be discussed and changed. Writers usually think they are writing instinctively, but they are not, and they must learn through unthreatening questioning what rules, theories, and principles they are unconsciously following if their writing is to improve.

- "I'm interested in how you organize your stories. Do you have a system you follow most of the time?"
- "You are one of the best storytellers in the city room. Yesterday, you broke me up with your account of Mayor Bragg at the hearing, but I never hear your speaking voice in your stories. You have a professional voice that is very, well, wire service. Do you do that on purpose?"
- "What are the writing rules you find most helpful?"
- "What did you learn at the *Daily Globe* before we hired you? What were the things you found hardest to learn on your first job?"
- "OK, I know you've got to get your stories through me. Let's make sure we're on the same track. When you sit down and write, what do you hear me saying?"
- "If you had to edit this story, how would you go about it?"
- "If you were going to write a memo to the staff today about the principles of good newspaper writing on this paper, what kinds of things would you say?"

Each draft is, after all, the product of a series of writing-process decisions. There are roads not taken and taken. Most writers are full of rules, principles, and commands that they have understood or misunderstood from their journalism teachers or their editors. Their heads are filled with absolutes—"Never use a quote lead," "Always include an attribution to each quote"—that not only control their drafts but also tell the writer to obey a rule instead of attempting the experiment in style or meaning that may produce good writing. Editors' commands too often keep writers from making the thoughtful decisions that will produce stories that make the reader think and care.

Writing that makes a difference, that attracts readers, that tells a truth that hasn't been told before, that reveals and probes, is always a product of risk. Yet the usual city-room climate outlaws risk. There is often a greater penalty for breaking a small stylistic rule than the reward for producing an exceptional story.

That climate can be reversed if the editor stops behaving as top sergeant, treating reporters as troops on latrine duty, and makes writers colleagues. Writers who are treated as recruits, especially those who are twenty years older than the editor, will behave as recruits. I spent three years, much of it in combat, working my way steadily up to Pfc. I learned to play the army game, once even letting General Patton drive into an ambush after he chewed two of us out for telling him to take the left fork when he was determined to turn right. I saluted and said, "Yessir," listening gleefully for the cheery sound of German small arms fire. He roared back a few minutes later and went left. He didn't return my salute, but his driver gave me a wink.

Many stories are written badly on a Patton-like command. If the new city editor wants a Big Mac, he'll get a Big Mac. The boot-camp approach to writing relieves the writer of any serious responsibility for producing a good story. The writer always has an out. I delivered what was ordered. A consulting, listening editor will put the responsibility for the writing in the paper back where it belongs—on the writer.

THE INDIVIDUAL CONFERENCE

The most efficient way to do this is not with memos, publisher's lunches, a retreat to the country club, or a city room meeting with an editor standing on a desk addressing the staff, but with individual conversations, called conferences, that will slowly and solidly change the climate of the newsroom.

The editor first has to recover from white space fear and realize that there is an efficient machine in place that will produce routine stories in a routine way. It's a machine that hums on the editor's day off as well as the day on. The Big Macs will flow majestically through the word processing system, and therefore the editor can begin to try to encourage a story a week, and then perhaps a story a day, that is special.

It takes time to earn writers' trust. Writers have been invited to do something different before and have suffered criticism, sometimes public ridicule. The writer will be, and should be, suspicious of yesterday's top sergeant who suddenly becomes a teddy bear.

It is difficult to deinstitutionalize a writing staff. We all know of the drunk who tries to get arrested so he can return to the comfort of the jail, the mental patient who is afraid of a world without walls. The military city room is safe and predictable; the troops know what is expected; they salute, click heels, and deliver. You can't expect a writing staff to accept unaccustomed responsibility without a certain amount of justifiable anxiety. The resistance will be real, but it can be overcome.

We get many an interview by flattery. It is an ego trip to have a reporter come to you and say that you are the authority. The same thing happens when an editor consults seriously with a writer. Remember the shock you would have felt if an editor sat down to listen to you. Writers may be apprehensive, but if the editor says, "I need your help. I need your ideas on what stories should be written and how they should be written," even the most surly old-timer is likely to start beaming like a small boy at confirmation.

The editor can start slowly to establish this new policy of listening by going to an individual writer to ask an honest question—and going to the writer is always more effective than summoning the writer to the editor's desk. The editor might begin with a question:

- "Got an idea for a story we ought to be writing and aren't?"
- "You've done a good job every time we've dumped this story on you, but how do you think it can be done differently?"
- "I wasn't at the hearing. How do you think it should be covered?"
- "What surprised you when you were covering the story?"
- "If you didn't know how we write a story like this, how would you write it?"

There's no magic question. The editor should merely ask a question that implies respect for the writer's experience, a willingness to listen, and a question that can't be answered with yes, no, or a grunt. We all know how to ask such questions of our sources. We should ask them of our colleagues.

It may be helpful in the beginning to have a conference pattern or design in mind. I don't follow my basic design all the time, but it is the pattern I return to when I find my conferences not working as well as they should:

- *The writer speaks first.*
    - —Because the writer knows the subject better than the editor. The writer, not the editor, was out reporting.
    - —Because the writer knows the history of the draft better than the editor. The writer made many editorial decisions. The product is the result of that rational intellectual process which can be recalled and reconsidered. Both the editor and the writer need to understand what decisions have been made and why.
- *The editor reads the text.*
    - —The editor needs to know what the writer thought he

or she was doing to understand the text and how it can be improved.
—The editor also, of course, reads as a reader, seeing if the reader would know what the writer was doing.

- *The editor responds to the text.*
  —The response is usually most effective in the form of a question, which returns the fundamental responsibility for the quality of the text to the writer.
- *The writer responds to the editor's response.*
  —The dialogue on how the text can be improved begins.

The conference is the beginning of a professional conversation that should go on as long as the writer and the editor are working together. As the writer's opinions are solicited, the writer will begin to have more opinions. This doesn't mean that each suggestion has to be followed. Some stories will work out, some will not. But the editor will accept the failure with good humor, putting the experience in context, "Well, *we* booted that one [with the emphasis on *we*], but I'm glad *we* tried it. What do you think *we* learned that could help *us* next time?" The editor wants to establish an atmosphere in which risk taking is encouraged, for the best stories are either A or F, a home run or a strikeout, because all exceptional writing is experimental.

Writing will not improve on a newspaper without failure. In any creative activity, in the laboratory or at the canvas, it is the failure that instructs. We learn how to do things differently by trying, failing, and getting a glimmer of what may work the next time, or the time after that.

We should be more forgiving of ourselves. I know of no reader who has cancelled a subscription to a newspaper "because I didn't like the use of the first person in that feature on the second front," or "I expect all my business stories to be told at a distance. You did a close-up on Thursday, and I will never read the paper again." You will hear editors who invoke the reader to support the most traditional principles of journalism, but few readers, if any, are really aware of what we are doing and how we are doing it. What they want is information, information they cannot get from TV, radio, magazines, books, or their bookie, delivered in a way that is interesting and efficient. In other words, they want good writing.

TALKING *WITH* WRITERS

Some editors will sit down with a writer once a month or once a year and talk with the writer for an hour or more. Some special projects demand this sort of attention, but most city-room conversations should not be fifty-minute sessions with a psychoanalyst. I've timed such effective writing conversations; an amazing number are ninety seconds long, but some are three minutes, or five, or seven. Once trust is earned, an editor and writer can speak in a shorthand most of the time.

"They were really nuts at the city council meeting today."
"Oh?"
"I think we just ought to quote those idiots, perhaps a lead that says, 'Listen to what your city council has said today.' Then the quotes."
"Just a jumble of quotes?"
"You got it."
"Well, let me see it. It won't take twenty minutes for you to turn it into a traditional story if it doesn't work."

One of the most significant benefits of an emphasis on writing will be an increase in the quality of reporting. That reporter covering city hall who became a writer has been paying more attention to what is said and how it is said. Why? Because you can't write nothing. Writers are interested in facts—the best building block of writing—but they are also interested in the context of those facts: how a source is speaking and why; what isn't being said; what ought to be said; what revealing detail of manner or behavior, caught out of the corner of the eye, may illuminate the story.

Go back to the best stories you have published and the award-winning reprinted stories you admire and imagine the research that made it possible to write the article. Note what Joan Didion or John McPhee had to ask or look up or observe or sense or feel or investigate to produce an outstanding story. Nobody can write nothing. All writing—the poem and the novel as well as the legislative report or the profile—depends on accurate, revealing information.

The more I coach writers, the more I realize I am coaching readers. Few of us read our own stories well. We read with undeserved confidence or undeserved despair; we read what we hope is on the page or not on the page; we read what we intended or what we feel we failed to accomplish. To write well, reporters have to read what readers will read.

Editors believe they are good at this and they often are. A

writer turns in a story and the editor sees what is there and isn't there. Usually the editor displays this critical skill story after story. The problems of each draft may be solved, but the writer continues to read his or her own story badly.

The trick is to train writers to read their own stories so the editor doesn't have to display repeatedly his or her critical skills. It may help to suggest that the writer role-play a specific reader, someone the writer knows, and read the story through that person's eyes. More important, the editor, by calm questioning, not a formal interrogation, gets the writer to see all the stories he or she writes from a reader's point of view.

- "Is there anything else a reader might need to know?"
- "Or want to know? Get a kick out of?"
- "Imagine you are an intelligent reader who has never attended a city council meeting. Are there things that you'd have to have explained?"
- "I've read the first three stories in the series and you have read them, but what does the reader need to know who starts with the fourth story?"
- "What might make a reader think about what this story means?"
- "Is there any way to make the reader feel this story? Care about it?"
- "If you were a reader, are there places where you are being fed too much—or too little?"
- "If you were listening to this story, are there places where your mind would wander?"
- "What pieces of specific information would you find yourself telling someone else after reading this story? If not, have you got any tidbits in your notebook you can feed the reader?"
- "What voice do you hear when you read the story? Is it consistent? Does it fit the story, carry the meaning? Would you like to listen to it?"
- "What questions would the reader have about this story? Are they answered? In the order the reader would answer them?"

As their reading improves, writers will discover they report more effectively, see more perceptively, question more incisively, listen with greater understanding, accumulate more revealing information. Writers must have an inventory packed with significant information from which to draw if they want to write well. In the conference, the editor can reinforce the reporting that produced good writing and, in so doing, help the writer realize the kind of information it is important to have in the notebook before sitting down to write:

- "That detail on who the mayor called first really helps. What other specifics would you like to know?"
- "You did a great job of letting me hear what the jury was muttering to each other when you sat on the front row rather than at the press desk. Where are you going to sit when you cover the school board meeting?"
- "What details do our readers need to know to understand the long-lasting hazards from this chemical spill?"
- "I'd like to have our readers see the new police chief, get to know him. How do you think we can do that?"

THE LISTENING VOICE

There is a danger, of course, that a conference will become THE CONFERENCE, when the writer must defend himself or herself before an inquisition by the editor. The conference is most effective if the tone is conversational, good humored and professional, and if each conference is merely part of a continuing professional concern.

The conference doesn't just take place at one time in the writing process. It may occur when the editor needs story ideas, when an assignment is given, all through the reporting and writing process, even after the story is published.

- "Got an idea for a story we ought to be covering and aren't?"
- "What surprised you recently?"
- "What's worrying the people you're hanging out with?"
- "What's a story you'd like to write?"
- "You got the press conference. How do you think we ought to handle it?"
- "You've done this story before. How can we do a better job of it this time?"
- "You know those guys at city council. How do you think we can show the reader what's really going on?"
- "Before you go out on your interviews, what do you think the key question is?"
- "What do you think is the biggest problem we have in covering this story? How do you think we can solve it?"
- "What do you think we need to get to make this story really work?"
- "Before you write can you give me the story in one sentence?"

- "Now that you've done the reporting, what's different than you expected?"
- "I've been sitting here on my duff while you've been out reporting. What do I need to know?"
- "If you don't mind, I'd like to see your lead. I just want to make sure I'm selling the story you're writing."
- "Mind if I see your lead?"
- "This is a tricky story. Would you be willing to try four or five different leads so we can make sure we're going down the same road?"
- "How can I help you?"
- "Now that you've got the story done, what did you discover in writing it?"
- "What should I look for in reading the draft?"
- "Before I edit this I'd like to know what you think worked and needs work."
- "What kind of a reader do you want me to be? How can I help you with this story?"
- "We've got time for another run at this story. What do you think we can do to make it work better?"
- "That was a tough one and we did it. How can I be more help next time?"
- "Now that we've got the story in the paper, what should we do the next time we get a story like this?"
- "That was a fine job. What did we do that made it so good?"
- "That story really worked. What do I need to know about how it was reported and written so I can help someone else?"
- "What can I do to become a better editor for you?"

The range of responses is enormous. They vary from editor to editor, from writer to writer, from writing task to writing task, from inexperience with the task to experience. The response should always be human. It involves the personal as well as the professional.

Each writer-editor relationship is so different that it sounds difficult for the editor to control it, but that's just the point: the effective editor doesn't try to control it. The basic agenda for each relationship is established by the writer in response to questions from the editor or from the implied invitation for the writer to speak first. The writer constantly initiates the renewal of the relationship, and the editor responds in a way that is natural to the editor. There is no one editing personality, but it is the duty of the editor to respond to the writer in such a way that the writer continues to direct his or her own development.

Once you've established a basic pattern for conferring, then you can develop variations on conference style. When the writer and the editor know and trust each other, they can confer on the telephone when their schedules don't coincide. They can also confer over the tube, sending questions and answers back and forth, approximating the tone they have established in oral conferences. Sometimes editors and writers can confer about pieces of writing they like in the paper, in magazines, in books, even comparing what works and what needs work as well as what has application to the paper in television shows and in movies. One of the most effective conference variations is the editing conference, when writer and editor sit side by side at the video tube. The editor may suggest problems and the writer attempts to solve them, or the editor may make changes in the copy, explaining why he or she is making the changes, while the writer looks on and responds. The attitude is the same: "I'd like *us* to play around with this. I don't know whether I can make it work better, but let me try to show you what's on my mind."

When I do this as a writing coach I have several simple rules:

- The text belongs to the writer. I'm not back on my old job of rewrite.
- All writing is experimental. We don't know what works until we try it. Failure is normal and instructive. From failures we see ways to achieve success.
- Fooling around with language is fun. We are playing a game of voice and meaning, and we can't afford to take it too seriously.
- I rarely make one suggestion. I point out several alternatives, usually three. This might be the lead, or that, or something back there. I wonder what would happen if this were cut, or made longer, or tightened up. I keep revealing the possibilities of the text, so that the person I'm working with will learn to see and take advantage of those possibilities.

The conference allows the editor to keep putting the writer's work into context. Writers need to recognize how their work is contributing to the paper. Writers also need to know how a particular story fits into their overall development as writers. In providing this context the editor would be advised to use questions—"I'm fascinated by how you're coming along. How do you see your work helping the paper?" or "You wouldn't have done this story this way three months ago. How do you feel you're changing as a writer?"

In all the conferences, I try to avoid generalized praise or generalized criticism. "This stinks." "It's great." I know which of those I would rather receive, but I don't know what to do with either of them. Both praise and criticism are most effective when they relate to a specific issue—how complicated facts were made clear, how the documentation was provided to the reader, how the reader's questions were answered.

The editor should remember that every conference trains writers for the most important conferences of all. Those are the conferences writers must hold with themselves during the writing process. The most available editor can only hold a few conferences with an individual writer, but writers are talking to themselves all the time. And the editor's conferences provide a model for constructive self-criticism that will make it possible for writers to identify and solve writing problems to make the evolving draft better than the last one.

The conference should take place in conditions that make the writer comfortable. It's usually constructive to go to the writer rather than to summon the writer to the editor's desk. Many times it's helpful to share a cup of coffee or to sit down in a neutral territory. The editor should always be aware of who's overhearing the conference. Many times writers will learn more from the tone and content of a conference that they have overheard than they'll learn from their own when their work is on the line. On the other hand, people can be humiliated or will be inhibited from conferring honestly when a colleague is within earshot.

If you have to make a choice between having a conference with a good writer or a poor one, pick the best writer. This seems contradictory, but one of the biggest mistakes we make in the city room is to give all our attention to the writers with the least promise. They do need help, but the payoff is less certain. They include a high percentage of people who should never have been in the business or who are overwhelmed by personal problems the editor cannot solve. They need attention and support, but the chance for spectacular improvement is slight. It takes a long time and a lot of effort.

We tend to forget the best writers, but they deserve our attention. We should remember that they are best because they are eager to do well. They start each story at zero point, full of anxiety and fear as they attempt to achieve unrealistically high standards. They care about their writing, and they need to know that you care.

The good writers are the people who can make the paper better. They need attention or you will lose them. Some actually leave the paper or the profession, but others are lost in the city room as they lower their standards to what they think you want, and soon have the habit of poor writing ingrained in them. We have carefully taught many of our worst writers to write badly. They are the pros, the hacks, the journeypersons who are just peforming a job.

When some of our best former students leave papers or the newspaper business, their editors will call us saying that such and such a person was the best writer on the paper, why did he or she leave? We ask if they ever told the person that, and they haven't. They have been too busy editing the copy of the worst writers, while the writers with real potential are ignored. They feel unwanted. In your eyes they are writing the best stories in the paper; in their own eyes they are not living up to their own extraordinary standards, and your silence seems to be criticism or disinterest. Empathy is one of the reporter's most important skills, and the ability to put yourself into another's skin is vital for the effective editor. The editor must understand where the writer is in the writing process and in his or her own evolution as a writer to comprehend the significance of what the writer is saying and doing. The best training for editing is writing.

I'm amazed at how quickly a writer becomes an editor and forgets his or her own struggles in reporting and writing. I think it helps if the editor goes out and does a story once in a while. But I think it is even more important for the editor to be writing every day. It is not so important what the editor is writing as it is for the editor to be in the writing act. Perhaps the editor is working on the history of the *Friendship* sloop, a memoir of Vietnam, a family history, an essay on abortion, a novel, a poem, a screenplay—something that can be worked at in small chunks of time, fifteen minutes or half an hour before work or at the beginning of work. This short spurt will help the editor be a writer. It also may help the editor to stretch and expand his or her knowledge of the writing process. But most important, it will allow the editor to understand what the writer is saying in conference and why he or she is saying it. The best preparation for listening to a writer is to be writing yourself.

Writing cannot be taught in the abstract. Perhaps it cannot

be taught at all. But it can be learned by those who have effective listeners. The act of listening causes the writer to consider what the writer has done and not done, what the writer has achieved and what the writer needs to attempt. The writer whose writing improves must not only produce a text but reflect upon it, must not only practice a craft but reflect upon that as well. The listening editor causes this essential reflection during which writers teach themselves how to improve their craft. And there is a bonus for the editor. As the editor performs the unnatural act of listening, the editor learns how effective writing is made.

THIRTEEN
READ THE READING BEFORE THE TEXT

In the craft of teaching—and writing—you have to learn how to do less and less, how to get out of the way of the learning student—and the discovering text. I found it hard to be irresponsible and lazy, difficult to give my students room in which to learn, to give my texts room in which to develop.

When I have stepped back, however, I've learned from the experiment. Of course I can intervene, but it is amazing how rarely I've had to do that. I am convinced that too well-prepared conferences—or sometimes classes—prohibit us from learning or even seeing what needs to be learned. I have found, by trial and error, that I need to know how my students were reading their drafts if I was to help them produce more effective drafts. And by observing their reading, I learned how to read my own drafts more effectively.

It took me years to learn how to read student papers; and years to learn how *not* to read them.

I realized, slowly, as I became expert at the correcting of student papers, that I was learning a great deal during the virtuous—even smug—fumigation of error. My students, however, were only learning what they already believed: they were not writers.

They did, however, expect me to correct their papers as would a secretary or someone from public relations. If they didn't have one of those after graduation, they would buy a computer program that would not only run a spell-check but a rhetoric-check, even a think-check.

Still, I worked hard at doing a better job of correcting their papers, sometimes on the blackboard, sometimes on an overhead projector, often on handouts. I thought my correcting was, well, skillful, even clever. It certainly was responsible. And I confess to acute ego: my students had a chance to see a pro practicing the moves he learned during decades of revision.

The better I did my job the less my students learned.

The focus was all wrong. It was entirely on what *I* thought of their drafts, what *I* knew of their subjects, what opinions or feelings *I* had about those subjects, what thinking *I* would have done faced with their writing tasks, what voice *I* would use and how.

This could have been of interest to my students, but it wasn't, and it took me a while—months? years?—to realize they were right. It really was irrelevant. It did not connect in any effective way with what they went through to create or improve a draft.

It isn't easy, however, to get students to teach themselves. It took me years to learn how not to teach, how to keep from interfering with their education, to follow instead of lead.

The first problem is the teacher. We are all tempted by authority. Power over other human beings—as rapists, clergy persons, corporation executives, therapists know—is a powerful addictive drug, and few jobs offer as much power as teacher.

I fought that power and have retired, in part, because of it. I don't mind a little power and confess I even enjoyed serving as a military policeman for a while. There are places where power is appropriate, but I am suspicious of power in the writing classroom.

Of course I needed that power at first. I was scared in front of the class. I would have loved a lion tamer's chair and whip. Instead I lectured in a positive male posture with a loud, deep voice, depending on absolute answers, overpreparation, an avalanche of handouts, and, sometimes, sarcasm.

I feared the students would rise en masse and toss me out the window; worse, they might expose my ignorance to my colleagues. I mistreated my students and earned a reputation as a good teacher. I behaved as teachers were supposed to behave, and that made me a good one.

When I finally taught myself to relax and learn *with* the class, to deal in questions rather than answers, listening instead of talking, I confused many of my students.

They expected to be taught, and I expected them to learn. They considered me the authority on writing, but I expected them to be the authority on their own drafts.

I wanted them to tell me their subject, to establish their

authorship (child of authority), to look at the subject from their own point of view, to choose their readers and the genre appropriate to subject and reader, to write in their own voice, to read and rewrite and edit, to define and examine and adapt their own writing methods.

I wanted them to learn to write. I wanted them to find and focus on writing topics, to research them, to organize what they found, to create an informing text, to use appropriate structures and languages, to read and revise and clarify.

They wanted instruction: rules and patterns with blanks hungry for their filling. They wanted right and wrong, correct and incorrect, go and no go, and I offered them constructive confusion, productive doubt, possible possibility.

As I unlearned to teach, they began to unlearn what they had been taught in other composition classes and began to make use of the room I gave them. I learned how to allow them to learn—and they did.

In other classes they had learned how stupid they were: they'd never heard of rule five; or were told they could never, ever, *ever* use a sentence fragment (although the models of good writing they were studying were full of them); that effective writing was the product of precise rules that had few exceptions.

Following previous instruction, my students were terrified, lost in a swamp without a map. They had a collection of half-remembered, inappropriately placed, or misremembered instructions that had no apparent reason behind them. They just were. Right you were bright; wrong you were dumb.

Now my students discovered that writing was a matter of common sense. Thinking was allowed. They could describe what they had done while producing a draft, the reasons they had done it, examine the result, see another way to do it, try it, read it, and *think* about it. They discovered how much they knew about how they had written a draft and how they might write the next one.

They were able to do this because I had stopped teaching what they knew or didn't need to know, waiting until they really needed my wisdom. The humbling lesson for me was that they rarely needed me. Their writing improved by their own effort when I learned how *not* to teach but how to create an environment in which they could teach themselves. Each year I taught less and my students learned more.

My pilgrimage toward unteaching began in the weekly writing conference, where I gave my students individual attention—at first, more than they wanted or could handle. I had read their papers, corrected them, and then I told them what I had done and what they should do. Some of my advice was harmless, some was completely wrong, and most of it did not fit the writing situation that my students were in when they created their drafts.

A switch in file cabinets made all the difference. For some incredibly stupid reason, I arranged my office so I had to get up and walk six feet to get my corrected copy of each student's paper. While I was walking I would make some sort of a social sound—"How yuh doin'?" "Mornin'," "Uunnhh"—and many students started telling me what was wrong with their papers, why, and what they intended to do about it. The conference was over before I settled myself into an appropriate professorial position.

I learned slowly, but I learned. I rearranged my office, but then I started writing conferences by inviting my students to speak first, and listening to what they had to say. No, they didn't tell me about their weekend minimarriages, their hangover cures, their problems with their parents; they started talking about their papers.

When they didn't think they had anything to say, I learned to ask questions that invited comment—"What surprised you in writing the draft?" "What did you do differently in this draft than you've done before?" "What did you learn from writing the draft?" "What would you do differently if you had another chance at it?" "How was this written differently than it would have been at the beginning of the course?" "What came easily?" "What are you going to do next?"

Most of the time they had a better insight into their writing procedures than I did. There should be no surprise in that, but most composition teachers seem to feel that they know what their students do and don't do better than the students. Of course, there were times when I would intervene with suggestions, but I tried to answer questions with questions, to make several suggestions so the students still faced choices, to present myself as an interested, supportive reader who is eager to be taught by the next draft.

It is embarrassing to report that the learning I covered in a few paragraphs above took more than a dozen years and thousands of conferences. It is even more embarrassing to report that it took almost an equal amount of time for me to apply what I was learning in my own unlearning to the writing workshop, that had always been taught when I was a student as a test of virility. Yes, that's right, virility. It was a sexist, macho operation, prejudiced against women—and men and beginners and those who were shy, insecure, uncertain of their talent, and anxious to write well. In other words, the best writing students.

Slowly I learned to make the small group and whole class workshop another place where students were able to demonstrate how much they knew. The writer, who is not allowed to speak in the traditional writing workshop, became the person who set the agenda for the workshop, often by answering those two crucial questions: "What works?" and "What needs work?" The student was able to ask the reader for help where the student needed help at a time when the student was ready to make use of help.

Semester after semester I kept trying to learn how to teach—or, rather, how *not* to teach—and how to encourage my students to learn. I experimented with written as well as oral responses by the students to their writing. I had them write comments, such as what works and what needs work, on a three-by-five-inch card attached to their papers. I read those cards before reading the papers. I also experimented with a questionnaire that I stole and adapted from Janet Emig. After the students had finished writing they filled out a questionnaire saying why they had done what they had done.

These activities, and others, combined with my listening in conference and workshop, helped me see how much my students knew. Again and again I was confronted with papers that were rhetorical and linguistic catastrophes. I not only had nothing constructive to say, I had nothing destructive to say. I couldn't understand the drafts well enough to attack them. But when I gave the students a chance to explain what they had intended and what they did, and why, I always found that there was a theory or a misunderstood instruction or an inappropriate rule that caused the disaster. They knew what they were doing and why, and once they knew, they knew that they could suggest better ways of working in the future.

I also learned about writing from my best writing students. They taught me important tricks of my trade, revealed the attitudes that encourage good writing, inspired me by their process and their product.

Finally, years after it should have, this approach allowed me to unteach enough so that I could invite my students to write commentaries each week on what—and how—they had written and on the problems they had to face and solve.

These commentaries were a major breakthrough for me, and they revolutionized the last years of my teaching. My students and I wrote texts, but we found our commentaries on the making of those texts even more important then the texts themselves. I wrote and shared what I was learning with my students, who wrote and shared what they were learning with each other and with me. These relaxed writer-to-writer texts created a real writing community. They blended the best of what happened in conference and workshop, and they, incidentally, gave me a new insight on grading. A writing experiment that did not work but that was accompanied by an intelligent and insightful commentary on the reasons for the experiment, for the failure, and intelligent analysis that might be applied to the next task could, I found, be a more legitimate A than a dumbly created piece of good writing that the student might never repeat.

The quality of their writing improved, largely, I believe, because the students were learning how to read their own papers. They could read to see what went wrong and what went right; they could read for accomplishment and for potential.

I began to think of myself more as a reading teacher than a writing teacher—but a special kind of reading teacher, a coach or colleague who was a good listener, an experienced writer who was helping the student writer read a draft in such a way that the next draft would be better. I was monitoring my students' reading more than their writing.

It became clear that effective writers are expert readers of their own draft and that this is a special kind of reading, a reading with possibility, a dynamic, ever-changing reading in which there are at least three parallel texts: what might have been written, what is written, what might be written.

This might seem an impossible task for many of our students, but I have found it is not. They know what they have done and why, but they do not know they know. When I gave my students the confidence and the opportunity to discover how much they knew by writing about their reading of their drafts, they started to learn to write better. They found out how to take advantage of the failures, the insights, the accidents, the solutions that occurred on the page.

And as I read their reading of their texts, I knew where they were and I knew when not to interfere, when to question, nudge, hint, suggest, support. I had finally learned how *not* to read my students' papers; I had learned to read their reading of their papers. I had taken a step back and given them the room to make their own steps forward toward more effective writing.

FOURTEEN

WRITING ABOUT WRITING —COMMENTARIES IN THE CLASSROOM

I've probably written as much about writing as I've written, and, like the author of the sex manual, I've felt guilty. I should be doing it rather than talking about doing it. Yet this is the way I've taught myself—and possibly others—to write. It took me years to discover that my students should not only do it, but write about it.

In recent years I've asked most students to pass in commentaries with their drafts, telling themselves, their classmates, their instructor what worked and what needs work. They also compared their intentions to their accomplishments, explained their working procedures, defined problems and proposed solutions, suggested what they would do next, reported what they had learned and needed to learn, responded to their classmates' and their instructor's commentaries.

Learning increased. As I learned by commenting on my own craft, so did they. We taught each other what we needed to learn while we were faced with the immediacy of our drafts. Meaning demanded to be made, and we learned how to make it.

I've experimented with different ways of using commentaries and these are the ground rules that work best for me:

- *Write the commentaries quickly and informally. Be honest and direct.*
- *Spend 90 percent of your time on your writing, 10 percent or less on the commentary.*
- *Bring a copy for each member of the class. (I've found that most college students have access to copy machines. When that is not the case, copying expenses may be built into a book budget, or copies may be placed in a notebook, made available to students during writing periods, or posted.) When the commentaries were written just for me, they were ten times less effective.*

The benefits were enormous:

- *Students became more thoughtful writers, constructively self-critical.*
- *Students found they could teach themselves to write.*
- *We learned what we needed to learn, when we recognized the need to learn it.*
- *The destructive power of the teacher was diminished—I became a fellow writer.*
- *The students' voices often became clear in the informal commentaries and later could be used in the drafts themselves.*
- *The students were prepared in conference and workshop to direct their own learning and make use of a reader, telling that reader what they needed to know at that point in the writing process.*
- *The students and the instructor became more perceptive and effective readers of drafts in process.*

When I decided to share some of my commentaries with you, I found I had written hundreds, perhaps a thousand, single-spaced pages of commentary to myself, to my writing friends, to my students. Here are a few samples of my own commentaries:

As you write, moving deeper and deeper into the text, you realize that you are changing the vision of the whole, but that vision remains intact, a sort of tent of meaning that bulges here and there and then organizes itself into new and unexpected shapes.

Will the text tell you how to write it? Don't just think about the text, try it out. Writing, like physics and chemistry, is an experimental art. Try it, step back, observe, think, redefine the problem, redesign the experiment, try again.

There's no one text, no one story to be told, but many—we may hear dozens of the hundreds that lie there waiting to be told. And as many ways to tell them. No right or wrong, no correct or incorrect, not even effective and more effective, just alternatives, possibilities, a never-ending potential.

Really had no idea of what to do in chapter, just wrote my

way in. Two disposable paragraphs I may keep. Must stand back from it. It changes the book but it feels right. It is there, a process of excavation. I just have to scrape away, carefully, the dirt that covers it.

Part of me thinks I can decide what book I want to write, when all I can really do is to listen to the book that is being written and help it make it what it will of itself. I am its teacher, learning from it, encouraging it to learn from itself, to become more of itself with each day.

The best subjects find you. They connect with the reasons we write and, for many of us, they relate to those questions that formed in our early years and cannot be answered but must be continuously explored. Something is read, overheard, observed, remembered, thought, experienced; and it connects with one of those fundamental questions, and we write to imagine an answer.

The ever-changing master plan, if seen at all, must be kept shadowy, vague, erasable, just out of sight. This may be more true of poetry and fiction, but I suspect it is also true of the most explorative nonfiction, that prose from which the writer and then the reader learns.

The experience of collaborating with Chip the past few sessions has gone beyond my expectations. It is true collaboration and must be close to what good jazz players experience during a jam session.

I've gone further in escaping ego than I've been able to alone, even though I think I've made a great deal of progress in this area in recent years. The text is in charge. The voice is not Chip's or Don's but the text's.

I've heard how you can talk *within* the act of writing in a way that is challenging yet supportive. Chip has taught me about this and I hear his voice, not the censor's, while I write other texts.

Collaboration sparks every part of the writing process from concept to editing. Writing does not have to be a lonely, secretive act. Most of my past experiences of being open about my writing and my feelings about writing have not been good. This experience is based on mutual and equal vulnerability, skill, and respect for the shared craft, the shared text, and each other. I was not sure this could be achieved. It has been.

I attempt a kind of seamless writing. My writing flows out of what has been written. My writing is born of my writing, the not-yet-written text flowing out of the just-written text.

The hardest writing, for me, is trying to write before I have that igniting phrase in mind or, at least, that hint of an approach, a feeling, an instinct, or sense of direction. I don't know how to advise others on how to find it, for I don't know how myself. It is the most mysterious part of the process for me. I have to suspend myself half in and half out of life, drift, stare out the window, half reading, half listening to music or TV, half paying attention to those around me, just waiting, knowing that direct seeking will frighten my quarry away.

Writers write, most of all, to hear what they will say. It is traditional to believe that writing reveals your ignorance—and it certainly can—but writing also reveals that you may know more than what you thought you knew.

Subjects are often found by what isn't as much as by what is. What is not being done, said, felt. Be aware of the omissions, the space around and within the potential subject.

Emptiness is terrifying, but it should be accepted, even welcomed, and understood. It is an essential condition of constructing a new meaning. The slate is wiped clean, and we are freed from the failures and the successes of the past, especially from the successes, those attractive prisons of thought.

Silence is an experience so unusual to most of us that we fear it and fill our rooms with noise. Yet silence is where writing begins. Silence will not last; it becomes quiet. Quiet makes it possible for us to hear what we have not heard before.

The writer often hears writing. The clue to the subject comes in a phrase or a line that precedes meaning. The writer learns to pay attention to those words and lines that catch in the ear and are heard and reheard until the writer must write to find out what the words are saying. Often they are quite ordinary words, and it may take a great deal of writing to reveal their significance.

I think of myself as a craftsperson with a small shop on a back street or off in the country where I repair cellos or bind books in leather. In the morning I go to the workbench, putting in my time, doing each job right—at least as right as I can—and then go on to the next project.

But I have a problem. I dream of designing and producing new cellos—perhaps long and thin ones or short, squatty ones; cellos made of copper or human bone—but the world has no interest in new cellos and certainly not in cellos made of impossible materials in ridiculous shapes. But I have to work on the projects at hand, good old familiar cellos. I have no time for the new zucchini cello over in the corner.

I haven't been writing. Simone de Beauvoir says, "A day in which I don't write leaves a taste of ashes." My mouth is full of ashes. To heck with the letters, the planning, the errands, the jobs that must be done before the trip. I grab a piece of writing, or I try to. I suddenly remember the piece I agreed to write for the *Alumnus* magazine. I can't find my notes. I can't find the piece of writing that gave me the idea, a draft of a report I once wrote. I can't find in the computer the draft I began. To hell with it. I just start writing, naturally, talking to myself about the piece. It starts to go. And when I'm into it I race down the page, making notes about what's to come. I have a sense of the proportions. A long chunk about a relatively short period of time. A paragraph about fifteen years, then another long section. I know where I will end, sort of. I have a hint, an idea of what I may end with. I write the piece as fast as I can, letting the typing be sloppy, dictating a section to Minnie Mae that takes off and says what I did not expect it to say. I go back and revise it, line by line. There is so much joy and satisfaction in this for me. It's not that I have written something, it's that I am writing something. It's the fun of the making. The piece is too long, but I'll give it to the editors, see what they think. Probably cut it, maybe from seven pages to four. And again, if I do I will enter into the piece and into the making. People don't believe me when I forget pieces I've published. Why not? Once they leave my desk they are no longer mine, but the reader's. Let them worry about which pieces have my name on them. I'll be busy working on another.

I am never so much myself when I am out of myself, fled into the writing.

I go to hear Nancie Atwell in the worst possible mood and that miracle happens that is rare but wonderful at a good reading or talk. My daybook is open and I become calm, listening. I start making notes as I enter into what she is saying and then the real miracle of inspiration. I continue to follow what she is saying. I could report it. It becomes part of my experience but at the same time, as my awareness is stimulated and heightened, part of my mind peels off and starts making its own meaning, sparked by the demonstration of making meaning being provided by Nancie. This is the test of an extraordinary performance.

There are three strands being woven. I am involved with Nancie's text or, at least, the individual text being created between Nancie and myself. I move from her remark about making reading easy for her students to my own problems with writing and know the answer I will spell out later in this document. For weeks I've been seeking a way of working and now I know I have found it and will make it clear to myself when I write about it. Then there is a simultaneous third thread: the talk and paper I am to give at Merrimack. My drafts have been flatulent, full of rhetoric and speaker's tricks. I have called to say the paper will be late. I need time to develop the germ of meaning that I have discovered: the importance of going beyond standards and conventions to the powerful distortions that are the mark of art. How do we support students so they will do this instinctively or break through the prison of conventions or be able to recover their essential innocence after they are educated? I was weaving those meanings and they lead to a new vision of the writing process that may seem obvious to others but will open my mind. All of that and more is in, around, behind these daybook notes.

In the fog, in the car, I can't stop writing. I make notes as I drive, somewhat ziggy-zaggy notes—and keep driving. I make notes while I stop for breakfast, back in the car, in the parking lot outside the University of Southern Maine's Bailey Hall. I have to make a note to relieve myself of the topic.

Description is the center to which I must return. I have colleagues who think description should not be tolerated in freshman English because it is too simple, a lower order of reasoning, but description may be the whole ball game: to describe what we see, what we feel, what we think. No, to describe in such a way that the reader sees, feels, thinks. There is always surprise in description. I surprise myself by seeing in words what I did not see before words, and my readers are surprised at what they see which, when I am successful in communicating, is *not* what I expected them to see. It would be Nazism to see for my readers. I want to do my own seeing so they may do their own seeing.

At the Henri de Toulouse-Lautrec exhibition in NYC at the Museum of Modern Art: Was his vision his alone, or were there hundreds (thousands?) who saw what he saw but did not have the courage to reveal their vision?

When the writer writes well, the reader doesn't so much learn from what the writer knows as what the writer made the reader realize he or she knows. The writer articulates the reader's unspoken (until then) knowledge. It is my job as a writer to allow or stimulate the reader to know what he or she already knows—but doesn't know he or she knows it.

FIFTEEN

CASE HISTORY: WRITING IN CLASS

This case history was shared with the teachers in a summer seminar held at the time when I actually wrote the column. It is an example of professional writing performed under course conditions. If that isn't possible, then the course must be redesigned.

I'm often surprised to find that writing courses often ask the students to do what the teacher—or even a published writer—could not do. I am even more surprised when I create such a syllabus myself. When I do, I have a class meeting and we write a new syllabus. Sometimes I invite students to write their own syllabus, and when they do, they demand—and deliver—more than I could or would ask of them.

The history of one *Boston Globe* "Over Sixty" column:

- *Motivation.* Deadline. I'm going to Nova Scotia August 15 and Canadian mail service is terrible.
- *Support.* Readers I respect have been very kind about my pieces that have been published.
- *Challenge.* I have a limited genre. A limited audience. A range of subjects to be examined from a limited point of view in a limited voice. It's fun to explore those limits.
- *Occasion.* In-class writing. A series of titles and leads that swoop over the landscape of my childhood. A list of titles for pieces not yet written—or thought of—written fast, during a short in-class writing period, without planning or conscious thinking:
  —Learning how to sit
  —whatcha doin there. A porch
  —Rocking but not rolling

Nothing very special but given the in-class exercise pressure to draft a lead to go with a title, I wrote:

> emptying the pan under the ice box, shoveling coal or the Depression, World War II and Mother's daylong boiled meats, I don't miss but I do miss a front porch. We lost something when our houses got turned around and the authorities made us have patios.
> (Now,) I'm going to build a big front porch with rockers, bamboo sunshades, a canvas hammock. Somedays it'll take me from breakfast to supper to try them all out.
> No TV. Perhaps radio if the Red Sox are winning. They were losing in 1938 and I stopped listening. Mostly what I'm going to do is watch the neighbors.
> That was pretty exciting in Wollaston in 193X. It ought to be real good these days.
> Course, I may change things. One of the reasons I didn't do what I wanted to do when I was a kid was the old folks in the rockers. Watching.
> I thought they were keeping order. Now I know they were hoping for disorder, real sinful stuff. Sin. They lived in hope of sin. And they found it. If they didn't they made it up. They didn't have gossip papers. Their gossip was homegrown.

- *Support.* I shared it with the class when they shared theirs, and they laughed.
- *Doubt.* Since they laughed I worried that there were just one-liners. Dishonesty. Tricks. Glibness.

This morning, about five days later, I sat down and drafted the piece quickly, not paying too much attention to what was in my daybook. It seemed to keep going. I had a strange combination of delight and doubt. I kept being pleased by what popped up, and worried about whether it was too slick, too tricky, not honest. During the drafting and a quick revision I had to rationalize this writing. Of course it was sentimental and not a totally realistic picture of either the past or the present. Neither was it the most serious piece of literature ever attempted. Perhaps it was amusing and had a bit of content too. Maybe that was OK.

I did feel strongly during the draft that I was being led by the piece. By that I mean that the voice, the word play, was moving me forward. There were twists of phrase that were unexpected and words that were unexpected, and I seemed to be going somewhere. But I guess what kept me most interested was the sense of fun in the language. That's both good and dangerous. Read what I have sent to the *Globe* to see if you can read it the way I read it as I wrote it. And then let's discuss the writing of the piece and the implications for our teaching that come from this example of process. The draft follows:

> I don't miss emptying the pan under the ice box, shoveling coal, or eating meat that has been boiled since breakfast, but I do miss the front porch. Something important was lost when we turned our houses around, built patios, and hid in the backyard.
>
> I'm getting ready to retire and I think I'll build a huge wraparound front porch on my phony colonial home. I'll equip it with rolled-up bamboo sunshades, a long line of rockers, and a huge canvas three-sided hammock hung with a chain that squeaks satisfyingly both forward and backward.
>
> No TV. No boom box. No radio. We turned it off when the Red Sox blew a lead in 1938. I'm going to do what we used to do when life became boring: watch the neighbors.
>
> That was pretty exciting back in Wollaston when people —mostly—led quiet lives. Or at least secret ones. Not many people could afford much fooling around in the Thirties. And if the watching was good then, it ought to be really something these days.
>
> After supper—I'll never eat dinner after I retire—we'll sit out on the porch, shove off for a good rock, and fold the paper so we can appear to read as we wait to see what's going on.
>
> I used to think the old people—anyone that was married or over 27—sat on their porches of an evening to protect the world against sin. Now I know why they were rocking madly; they were all tensed up hoping for sin.
>
> They weren't out there to maintain order, they were looking for disorder. Of course they had an advantage. There was sin then, plenty of it to go around.
>
> Sometimes the people in the house across the street didn't pull their window shades exactly halfway. Sometimes they kept some of their shades down all day as if they had something to hide. Sometimes they kept some of their shades up at night as if they had nothing to hide.
>
> They were foreigners and different. They came from Allston.
>
> They ate fish—you could smell it—when it wasn't Friday. The man of the house didn't water the lawn and they had a

daughter who had a wedding ring but lived with her parents.

Not often enough for me, only once or twice a year, the butcher up the street got drunk and chased his wife and their children with a cleaver. Now it seems terrible, but then it was like a living cartoon. I knew he would never catch them, and he didn't, but it was exciting.

I heard talk of Roosevelt and jobs, and I knew there was going to be a war and I would be in it, but there was an entire world close at hand that I found more interesting. One day I was out on the porch reading in the afternoon and I saw Russell's father come home in the middle of the day, walking slowly. I knew it meant he'd been "let go" and I knew what that meant to the family.

I knew what I feared when my father started talking angrily about the bosses, the college men who didn't know the work. I worried that I'd see him coming home in the afternoon.

There were no stories about single mothers in the newspapers but I knew what it meant when the girl diagonally across the street stayed home from school and only went for walks when it was dark and she could move from shadow to shadow.

We all knew. For we were all the watched as well as the watchers. I used to hate those old people on porches. Gossips. But now there is a gossip industry, and we all share the news of Rock Hudson or the rumors about the film star who gave birth to a swan fathered by a famous politician, you know who.

Our family didn't need to buy gossip. We brewed our own. We could be vicious but there could be the knock on the door and the hard voice and the fists ready at the side and the correction of mistruth. When a kid got out of line, he or she didn't just have a parent saying it was time to shape up. There was a chorus of moral instruction from the porches all the way up and down the block.

And there could be neighborliness. A blueberry pie might be delivered when it would do the most good. A tip that they were hiring at Fore River could be mentioned in a casual conversation, as if no one listening needed to know that. A fellow who liked a bit of the sauce himself might drop by the butcher, and the girl in the shadows might find that the spinster who sat on the upstairs porch, watching, had knit sweater and booties.

It wasn't Disneyland, but, mean or helpful, the people

> knew each other, and once I build my porch the people up and down the street may realize that someone's watching them. The only thing for them to do will be to build their own porches, stop eating dinner and gulp supper early so they can get out on the porch to watch me watching them.
>
> After a while we'll start strolling, not getting exercise, just happening to be going by. Perhaps then someone will stop by, standing at first, then sitting on the porch steps, maybe graduating to a rocker after a season or two. Gossiping, talking about the neighbors, becoming aware of who's sick and who's well, who needs supper brought by, who needs to know where you can pick up a flivver cheap, who wants to be left alone and who might just appreciate somebody stopping by.

And that was pretty much the way it was published.

You mean you publish first draft stuff?

If I can, if I can.

Isn't revision necessary? Yes. Often. When the writing doesn't come easily, when the voice doesn't lead and instruct. But the longer I teach myself writing, the better I learn how to write naturally, easily, the first time. I learn how to get ready to write, how to relax and listen to the writing.

Is it possible you are just lowering your standards?

Very possible. I've worked hard to achieve lower standards.

III

EXPLORING FORM

SIXTEEN
TRICKS OF THE NONFICTION TRADE

One of the things I've learned with long experience is how to cultivate ignorance and simplicity. School often makes us hide those essential intellectual qualities, but I have a natural talent for ignorance and simplicity and I have learned to respect—even flaunt—them.

When I receive an assignment or an invitation to write on a subject—sometimes I am self-assigned—I usually work without looking back at what others have written and never *look back at what I have written. I am terrified of consistency.*

Of course I often repeat myself but never intentionally and often in at least a slightly different way. This cultivated ignorance allows me to find the unexpected in the obvious. One newspaper editor said that a good reporter is forever astonished at the ordinary. I hope I am as well. I have found fascination with returning again and again to the basic elements of my craft.

When I first taught, I caught the contagious academic disease of making the simple complex. It is an attractive game and impresses your colleagues, but it leads you away from the truth that in the simple lies the true mystery. I often learn most when I write a piece such as this that retells me what I already knew. And, of course, I didn't always know I knew it, until I wrote it.

Under the apprentice system still practiced in most crafts, a beginner has the opportunity to work beside an experienced worker and pick up small but significant tricks of the trade. Writing, however, is a private business. Few of us ever observe a writer at the workbench, turning a phrase, cutting a line, or reordering a paragraph so that a meaning runs easy and runs clear. Here are a few of the tricks I've picked up from other writers or taught myself during more than forty years of trying to make writing look easy.

ASK THE READER'S QUESTIONS

An effective piece of writing is a dialogue between the writer and the reader with the writer answering the reader's questions just before they are asked. Each piece of writing usually has five or four or six questions that must be answered if the reader is to be satisfied.

I brainstorm and polish the questions first, then put them in the order the reader will ask them:

- What is diabetes?
- How can I tell if I have it?
- What's the latest treatment?
- Do I have to give myself shots?
- Where can I get that treatment?
- How dangerous is diabetes?

1. *Lead*: What's the latest treatment for diabetes?
2. How dangerous is diabetes?
3. What is diabetes?
4. How can I tell if I have it?
5. Do I have to give myself shots? No. New treatment.
6. Where can I get it?

As I write, I may have to reorder the questions if I "hear" the reader ask the question earlier than I expected, but that doesn't happen very often. Most times the reader's questions and the order in which they will be asked can be anticipated. It is also helpful to write these questions down before researching a story, beginning the first draft, or revising a draft—especially a confusing one. Just role-play a reader and put down the questions you would ask, combining them if necessary, and then put them in order. This trick will help you anticipate what readers want to know and when they want to know it. It will help you understand what is significant in an abundance of confusing material, and also help you organize it.

READ FRAGMENTS

Professionals don't wait until they have a completed draft to read what they have written. They learn to pay attention to lists, collections of information, partially drafted sentences and paragraphs, abandoned pages, notes, outlines, phrases, code words that constitute the kind of writing we do on the notebook page and in our heads before the first draft.

Reading those fragments, the writer discovers a revealing or organizing specific around which a story or an article can be built, a pattern of action or argument on which a meaning may be hung, a voice that tells the writer what he or she feels about the subject and that may be used to communicate that feeling to the reader.

SELECT AN EFFECTIVE DISTANCE

Many writers write everything at the same distance from the subject. It becomes an unconscious habit. Academic writers may stand too far back from the subject, so that the reader is detached and really doesn't become involved with the content. Magazine writers usually move in close, many times getting too close, so that we are lost in the details of a particular person and are not able to understand the significance of the story.

The writer should use an imaginary zoom lens before writing the first draft and decide the proper distance for this particular story, the point at which the reader will see the story clearly, understand its context, and care about the subject. The writer may stand back and put the winning play in the context of all Army-Navy football games or move in close and tell the story of the game in terms of the winning play itself, concentrating on the fifty seconds that made the difference.

PLAY WITH LEADS

The first line, the first paragraph, the first ten lines of a piece of writing establishes its direction, dimensions, voice, pace. "What's so hard about the first sentence is that you're stuck with it," says Joan Didion. "Everything else is going to flow out of that sentence. And by the time you've laid down the first *two* sentences, your options are all gone." It's worth taking time to get those sentences right.

The more complicated the subject, the more time you may need to spend on the lead to make sure that you're giving the reader the information needed to become interested right away. You can't start too far back with background, and you can't plunge into the middle of the story so that the reader doesn't know what he or she is reading. You have to start at the right point in the right way, and the more time you spend drafting new leads, and then refining the leads you choose, the faster you will be able to write the whole piece. Most of the major problems in a piece of writing are solved when the right lead is found.

Leads can be drafted in fragments of time: during commercials on television, sitting in a supermarket parking lot, waiting for a meeting to start, suffering a traffic jam. Once the lead is found it can be saved until there is time to draft the piece.

AIM TOWARD AN END

When I worked as writing coach at the *Boston Globe*, I found that the best writers usually knew where they would end. They had a quote, an anecdote, a scene, a specific detail with which they would close. It would sum up the piece by implication. The good writer has a sense of direction, a destination in mind. The best endings are rarely written to solve the problems of a piece that just trails off. The best endings are usually seen by the writer as waiting just ahead for the draft to take the writer and the reader there.

REHEARSE VOICE

Experienced writers rarely begin a first draft until they hear in their heads—or on the page—a voice that may be right for a draft. Voice is usually the key element in effective writing. It is what attracts the reader and communicates to the reader. It is that element that gives the illusion of speech. Voice carries the writer's intensity and glues the information together that the reader needs to know. It is the music in writing that makes meaning clear.

Writers keep rehearsing possible first lines, paragraphs, or endings, key scenes or statements that will reveal how or what is to be said may be said. The voice of a piece of writing is the writer's own voice, adapted with written language to the subject and audience. We all speak differently at a funeral or a party, in church or in the locker room, at home or with strangers. We are experienced with using our personal voices for many purposes. We have to learn to do the same thing in writing, and to hear a voice in our head that may be polished and developed on the page.

WRITE WITH YOUR EAR

The voice is not only rehearsed but practiced. We should hear what we're writing as we write it. I dictate most of my writing and monitor my voice as I'm speaking so that the pace, the rhythm, the tone supports what I'm trying to say. Keep reading aloud as you draft and edit. If you use a word processor, it may be helpful to turn off the screen and write, listening to what you're saying as you're saying it. Later you can read it aloud and make the changes you need to develop a voice on the page that the reader can hear.

WRITE WITHOUT NOTES

Put your notes away before you begin a draft. What you remember is probably what should be remembered; what you forget is probably what should be forgotten. No matter, you'll have a chance to go back to your notes after the draft is completed. What is important is to achieve a draft that allows the writing to flow.

WRITE FAST

Planning allows the writer to write fast without interruptions, putting a space or TK (to come) in the text as we used to at *Time* for the quote or the statistic that has to be looked up later. There are some writers who proceed slowly, but most of us learn the advantage of producing a draft at top speed when the velocity forces unexpected connections and makes language twist and spin and dance in ways we do not expect.

STOP IN THE MIDDLE OF A SENTENCE

When you finish your daily stint or if you are interrupted during the fast writing, stop in the middle of a sentence so you can return to the text and start writing at a point when you know what you have to say. It's always a good idea to stop each day before the well is drained dry, when you know what you'll try to deal with the next day. This is the best way to overcome the inertia we all suffer when returning to a draft. If we know how to finish a sentence, the chances are the next sentence will rise out of that one, and we'll be writing immediately.

WRITE TO FIND OUT WHAT YOU HAVE TO SAY

Planning is important, but it isn't writing. You want to be free enough in writing a draft to say more than you expect to say. Writers do not write what they already know so much as they write to know. Edward Albee echoes many writers when he says, "I write to find out what I'm thinking about." Writing is an act of thinking, and the process of writing adds two and two and comes up with seven.

SAY ONE THING

An effective piece of writing usually has one dominant message. Everything in the piece of writing advances that meaning. The best pieces of writing, of course, have depth and density. There are other meanings that collect themselves around the dominant meaning, but there still is a dominant meaning, and the writer, during the process of revision, needs to make sure that everything in the piece of writing relates to that meaning. As nonfiction writers, we can learn from masters of every genre. Kurt Vonnegut, Jr., tell us, "Don't put anything in a story that does not reveal character or advance the action." We should not have anything in an article or book that does not move the reader forward toward meaning.

DEVELOP WITH INFORMATION

To make a piece of writing longer, the writer should return to specific information, to statistics, anecdotes, evidence, documentation, quotations, material that is represented by language but that is not inflated language, floating free of meaning. Inexperienced writers try to develop their meaning with words. It doesn't work. Experienced writers develop their meaning with information represented with words. They put money in the bank before attempting to write a check.

ACHIEVE BREVITY BY SELECTION

The inexperienced writer cuts a piece of writing by compression, working the way the garbage compactor works, and produces a constipated little package of tight language that can be difficult to understand and is rarely a pleasure to read. The professional writer selects those parts of a text that most efficiently advance the meaning and then develops them fully so that the reader understands the significance of the anecdote, the meaning of the scene, the full strength of the argument.

USE THE 2–3–1 PRINCIPLE

Writing in which the meaning is not clear often occurs because we bury the most important information. One way to make a text clear is to look at the most significant paragraphs and move the information around so that the most important information is at the end of the paragraph, the next most important at the beginning, and the least important in the center of the paragraph.

We need important information at the beginning to attract the reader, but what the reader remembers is usually at the end of the paragraph. This pattern doesn't work for every paragraph, and shouldn't. But it is a way of clarifying a complicated and significant paragraph—and the same rule may be applied to an entire piece of writing.

TO SAVE TIME, REVISE THREE TIMES

Beginning writers plunge into a draft and try to revise and edit at the same time. They attempt to deal with questions of content, structure, and voice simultaneously. Some very skillful writers or editors can do that, but it's a waste of time for most of us. If the first reading reveals that the meaning of a piece of writing isn't clear, or if it has nothing to say, then it's a waste of time to spend energy reorganizing the piece or polishing the language. In fact, there is no way to choose the right word except by looking at content and meaning. If those elements are wanting, then the writer has to go back to reconsider the subject, reresearch it, refocus.

If the writer does have content and meaning, then the writer can deal with questions of organization in a second reading, building a structure that will carry that meaning to the reader. But it is a waste of time to deal with problems of diction, syntax, punctuation, grammar, style, and voice until a working order is established. Again, inexperienced writers will try to solve the questions of language and order at the same time, and because of it they may not solve either.

Finally, if the writer has a content or meaning, and the structure that develops it, then the writer can work line by line during a third reading to develop a text that communicates to the reader. Now close attention to the text is an efficient use of time.

Those are a few of the tricks of the nonfiction trade. Try them out to see if they work for you. Collect others from your writer friends and become aware of those devices that you have used to make your meaning clear, so that you will be able to call on them as you continue your lifelong course in learning how to write.

SEVENTEEN
NEWSWRITING

At first I was not going to include this piece; then I realized I have learned a great deal by crossing the genre boundaries that divide English departments. We separate the forms of writing, approving some, disapproving others, following what is fashionable, what is in, what is out. But effective writing is effective writing in any genre. The basic standards and techniques are more similar than different in poetry, newswriting, script writing, fiction, science writing, business writing.

Economics made me promiscuous, as it has led, so often, to promiscuity in other people. I worked on newspapers when I dropped out of high school, but after World War II I went to college, majored in literature, and became retroactively virginal. I was graduated as a literature major with a single vow to become a great poet. But jobs, in those days, for great poets were limited, and so I went to work on a newspaper as a copy boy. This dates me; there were no copy girls, and therefore no copy persons.

I have written novels, newspaper stories and columns, poems, textbooks; I have ghostwritten for politicians and industrialists. And all this crossover writing has helped me look at writing and the writing process with fresh eyes. Once I was ashamed of my promiscuity, and even published under a pseudonym, but now in old age I am proud of it. I hope that this piece will provide the reader with another view of writing and even stimulate some techniques or lessons that can be applied to whatever genre is being taught to a particular class.

Newswriting puts language to work right away. Newswriters probe, connect, and affect what is happening—while it is happening.

To write under the pressure of the hour, newswriters have developed professional skills we all can use. First of all, we all write to deadline. The term paper, the corporate report, the grant application, the dissertation, the acceptance speech, or the job application letter are usually written at the last moment—and rewritten after the last moment. Newswriters can help us all learn how to perform effectively under pressure.

Newswriters must collect specific, accurate information, then select those pieces of information which are significant and connect into a meaning of importance to the reader. Sounds like all good writing, doesn't it? Our students who go on to law school tell us that newswriting exercises when they have to select and order such specifics is the best training for law school.

Newswriting attempts to make the complicated clear in honest, hardworking language that can be read and understood by many people. Those who can do just that—newswriters—are hired by industry, government, and universities as writing specialists. People who know newswriting themselves have an advantage in the company office and the union office, in the military and in politics, in science and in the academic world. The skills of newswriting can be helpful writing poems, grant applications, stories, press releases, memos, screenplays—and letters home asking for money.

Newswriters are active observers who ask questions, constantly seeking specific, accurate information. They are also continual learners, because it is the newswriter's responsibility to connect the pieces of information, erecting a meaning for the reader from the raw materials of significant detail. And newswriters are participants who, by recording and informing, influence the course of the events they observe.

This is an exciting and important job in a democracy, because the newswriter informs those who are in power and those who put people in power. Our world has grown smaller and become more complicated at the same time. We depend on newswriters to tell us what is happening in our world, to deliver the information we need to know about politics, economics, science, art, education, sports—all of the hundreds of fields about which readers need or want to be informed.

We store and share information through newspapers, magazines, books, radio, television, movies, computer networks. These ways of sending and receiving information may appear different, but they all depend on the basic skill of the newswriter, who can collect concrete information, organize it into a meaningful pattern, and use language—spoken, visual, or written—to make that meaning clear.

All newswriters—young and old; on small papers and huge papers; on radio, TV, and magazines; in sports, business, and politics—start at the same place on every story. They begin with the search for specific, accurate, significant information. Newswriters don't write with pen, typewriter, or word processor, grammar, vocabulary, or spelling; they write with information. They dig for quotes and facts and statistics, check them and connect them with other fragments of information until they are woven into a pattern which carries meaning to a reader.

To learn newswriting, you should pick a subject that has already picked you:

- What did you notice this morning, yesterday, this week that surprised you?
- What's new?
- What's missing?
- What makes you mad?
- What ought to be changed?
- What ought to be kept the way it is?
- What worries you?
- What are people talking about?
- What's the most important thing going on where you live?
- What problems need solving?
- What solutions should more people know about?
- Who—or what—would you like to know more about?

Look into yourself, what you know and don't know and need to know, what you feel and wish you didn't feel or wish you felt. Look at all the people around you. What do they know and not know and need to know? What do they feel, what should they feel? What's new, what's old, what's happening, and who's making it happen?

The newswriter begins with this kind of nosiness—the kind of curiosity we all have—and then does something about it. You can learn how the newswriter works by writing one story from start to finish. It will help you understand how the news you read, hear, and see is made, but, more than that, it will introduce you to a craft you may be able to use all your life.

You will learn best if you stick to one story and follow the steps set aside in italics through the text. To be aware of what's coming up, read all of the suggested writing assignments throughout the chapter before going on.

Ask yourself the questions above until you get an itch to know more that has to be scratched, something you find yourself thinking about in your spare time. Don't be afraid to pick an important subject, even one that involves life and death. If you have a subject that is important to you, it will probably be important to your readers. It should provide them with information they want or need. If it doesn't interest your readers, then it is your challenge to show them why it should interest them. The new toilet seat factory may bring hundreds of new jobs to town, but it also may bring families that have to have houses, houses that need water and sewers and roads, children who need schools. It may, in fact, cost the town more than it gives the town. It's not the job of the newswriter to tell the voters what to do. It is the job of the newswriter to tell the reader the facts and their implications.

To help you experience the making of a news story we have to break down the process into a series of steps. In real life these categories and steps overlap, may appear in a different order, may even be skipped, but in learning any skill you have to see the overall goal—to kick a field goal or to produce a news story—and then figure out the steps that will make it possible to achieve that goal.

REPORTING

A continual, obsessive awareness is the reporter's basic skill. The good reporter never gets too old to keep asking, "Why?" A famous editor once said a good reporter is "forever astonished at the obvious." I am rarely bored, for I can sit in a meeting, on a bench at the mall, or in my car in a parking lot and see a hundred stories. One of the satisfactions of journalism is the opportunity to learn all the time. The newswriter is paid to learn how city hall works, how plays develop in rehearsal, what goes on in the hospital operating room, how fires are put out, how factories mass-produce new products, how a single mother survives on welfare. The writer has a backstage pass to just about everything that goes on in the newswriter's world. The reporter notices what is there and what isn't, what is said and what isn't said, what is new and what is old hat.

FINDING SOURCES OF INFORMATION

In school we all learn to use the written sources of information stored in libraries, and the library continues to be an invaluable resource all the journalist's life. When I was freelancing I paid special out-of-town fees to have cards in four libraries.

Besides what libraries have on their own shelves, librarians can help you get books from other libraries, tell you of books and periodicals on your subject which you can look for elsewhere, and lead you to other sources of information, such as the organizations of people and institutions or companies in the territory of your story.

If you are writing about pickles, local, state, or federal government agencies may have reports on pickle growing, packing, selling, marketing, or eating. There may be government pickle regulations and standards. Pickle growers and packers will have their own organizations. University laboratories may have studies of the advantages or the hazards of eating pickles. Medical schools may have case histories of pickle allergies.

Professional organizations may send you enormous amounts of information. This information can be extremely helpful as long as you recognize the prejudice of the organization. Pickle packers will tell you that pickles are good for body, mind, and spirit. That's what they are paid to do. Accept what such organizations say with a generous dose of pickling salt.

The most valuable source of information for the newswriter, however, is the live source—the person who can be interviewed in person or on the telephone. And the best people to interview are the ones most involved in the story. Try to go to the top—the person who knows the most about the story—then interview others who are involved.

Most stories have two opposing forces—and many have more. Make sure that you are fair and talk to all sides. You may start by interviewing the hospital administration about a nurses' strike. Make sure you also interview the union. And if the union comes first, make sure you interview the administration. Don't forget that other people may be affected by what is happening. Interview doctors, patients, medical technicians, secretaries, nurses' aides, medical insurance executives, families of patients, fire and police services that respond to emergencies.

Make a list of the sources of information for your story. Put them in order and go after them.

INTERVIEWING

The interview is the single most important journalistic research tool. The interview provides the information and the quotations from which most stories are built. Beginning reporters are usually nervous about interviewing. That's natural and, in fact, the right amount of nervousness can get you psyched up the way a football player is psyched up for the kickoff.

The best antidote for nervousness is to realize that 99 percent of the people you interview will want to give information to you. The interview is an ego trip for the interviewee. The fact that you go to the subject implies that you think that person is the greatest living authority on, for example, the difference between a full sour and half sour pickle.

You should explain to someone who doesn't want to be interviewed that it may be in that person's best interest to speak. The shopping center developer may not want to answer tough questions about the disadvantages of putting stores where there used to be farms, but he won't get zoning laws changed unless he tells voters about the economic benefits he believes a shopping center will bring to the area.

You should do some homework before each interview: find out who the person is that you're going to interview, what that person's job is, what power the person has, what position he or she holds on the issue you'll be asking about. If you're prepared, you'll know how to get the source to talk and you'll be able to understand what the source says.

I like to prepare the five or so key questions that have to be answered if I'm to have a story. Perhaps my story is on the increase in car stereo thefts. If I'm going to be able to write that story, I'd have to have the answers to these questions:

- Have car stereo thefts increased?
- How much?
- How come?
- What can be done about it?

Sometimes there are four questions, sometimes six, but there are always a few questions that will have to be answered. I put the questions down as they occur to me, put them in order, then ask them of everyone I interview despite how many other questions I ask in response to what I hear.

I also try to ask questions that can't be answered yes or no. The shopping mall security police probably won't want to admit that thefts have increased. If I ask that first question they may say no or answer just a terse "yep." I'll probably get a better response if I ask, "Why have car stereo thefts increased?" or "What can car owners do to prevent the increase in car stereo thefts?"

When making an appointment with a subject to be interviewed, identify yourself with both your name and the publication you are working for. Show up on time, dressed in a manner appropriate for the story you are writing. Use a spiral notebook so you won't lose your notes and have your questions ready (I like to write them on the inside cover of the notebook). Most of all, let people talk; don't rush to ask questions, and listen to what is being said, not what you expect to hear. The mall security chief may say it doesn't make any difference how many car stereos are stolen; what she's worried about is the epidemic of rapes in the parking lot. The dumb reporter will go on talking about woofers and tweeters.

It is important to develop a consistent, natural way of taking notes. You may want to use a tape recorder, but you should still take notes in case the tape recorder doesn't work and to record all those visual details that won't be on the tape recorder: how the security chief keeps eyeing the potential shoplifters and rapists who walk by the mall, how the radio on her belt monitors local police calls, how quickly and efficiently she responded when a salesclerk rushed up and said a man had collapsed in her store. Make quick notes of the specific details you may want to use in your story later.

Your notebook should be filled with details. The name of the mall. The name, age, title, and experience of the security chief. The brand of car stereos most often stolen. How they are sold on the black market. Who steals them. The smell of the stale air in the mall. The colors of the lights, the sounds. What tips the chief off to a shoplifter. Who collapsed? How serious was it? What ambulance service responded? Where was the victim taken? A newswriter can't have too many details, for those facts are the raw material the writer will use to build a story.

Although you have prepared for an interview, you are not expected to be an expert on the subject's specialty. Don't be afraid to admit your ignorance when something comes up you cannot understand. You can't bluff the news source who would rather have a reporter responsible enough to admit ignorance than a know-it-all—who doesn't.

Establish an objective stance toward the news source. You are not a participant in the story and you should keep your distance. You are a reporter, a learner, whose responsibility is to the reader. You should be skeptical—questioning—but not cynical—disbelieving. Your job is to keep asking questions and checking the anwers until you believe you have come as close to the truth as possible.

Every story you cover may uncover dozens of other stories if you maintain curiosity. Notice how many stories might have come from that one visit with the mall's security chief. Here are some others:

- How did a woman become security chief, a job that used to belong to a man?
- What advantages does a woman have? Disadvantages?
- Has shoplifting increased? Decreased? Why?
- Who shoplifts?
- Why?
- How do you catch them?
- What does shoplifting cost?
- What should you do if someone collapses in the mall?
- What's CPR?
- How many heart victims have been saved by CPR in this area?
- Who can learn it? Who should? Where? When?

Those are just a few of the possible stories growing out of one simple interview. Be aware, be nosy, be caring, and you will find that each day brings dozens of stories that may be pursued.

Choose the subjects you have to interview to get the information you need for your story. Prepare your questions, make appointments, and then interview, paying close attention to what the person says, to how it is said, and the environment in which it is said. Try to get a phone number or an address before you leave so you'll be able to check back if you need to confirm your notes or ask for additional information.

When you have an inventory of specific, accurate information, then you are ready to write. As you write you may discover other information and you may find that you have holes in your story—you don't know what happened to the man who was taken to the hospital, you need to know how much was stolen by shoplifters at the mall last year—so that you need to go back and fill them in by doing some more reporting. In fact, the more experienced you become, the more likely that you will begin to write early, for the act of writing will help you discover the questions that need to be asked, the reporting that still needs to be done. But this first time through you should decide when you have enough information to allow you to shift from reporting to writing.

WRITING

News is written in a style that is the logical result of the journalist's job:

- News stories are written while events are taking place.

Readers need stories that put the information into context, connecting it with what has happened and what may happen.

- News stories are read in a hurry by people who are distracted. The most important information must get to the reader right away. The reader may only read the headline, the lead, or the first paragraph.
- News readers—and listeners—want specific, accurate information. New stories deliver concrete, factual information.
- News readers are *not* experts in most areas in which they are being informed. News stories are written as simply as possible without oversimplifying the story.
- The reader doesn't have the time or the patience to dig for information. Information is displayed clearly. Sentences are short, and paragraphs deliver one chunk of information. Some paragraphs are a sentence long; rarely are paragraphs more than three sentences long. Newswriters know that a line they write will become two lines in the newspaper. A five-line paragraph becomes ten lines of type, a huge gray mass that's hard to read in a hurry.
- Readers have only minutes, sometimes only seconds, to absorb the information from the story. News stories are written with active verbs, specific nouns, direct sentences. "Considering the energy shortage, the decision was made by the school committee to close schools all winter" becomes "School will be closed all winter. The school committee took that action because of the energy shortage."
- Readers want to see and hear the story, not the reporter. Newswriters follow George Orwell's advice, "Good prose is like a window pane." They try to get out of the way and reveal the story to the reader. "There was an exciting play during the last minutes of the basketball game when the crowd went wild and I lost my glasses as Elmer Monk made a spectacular shot to win" becomes "Elmer Monk blocked an East High shot with only ten seconds left in the tie game. He faked left, dribbled right, and shot from midcourt as the buzzer sounded. It hit the rim, rolled around once, and fell in. West High won 63 to 61."

News style appears simple—the flight of the seagull—but it is a lot harder to write than to read. My colleague, Andy Merton, has an exercise that can turn a wordy writer into a newswriter in a hurry. Follow two simple rules:

- Write one sentence to a paragraph. This forces the writer to say one thing in a paragraph and to get right to it.

- Use only one comma to a page, except in names and addresses. This eliminates all clauses but one on a page. It forces the writer to produce the direct, subject-verb-object sentences that are the strength of journalistic writing—and the foundation of a good English prose style in any genre.

Most reporters hate the result when they finish, but a day later they realize that their writing has become crisper, tighter, more efficient.

BEFORE MERTON

Settling a bitter zoning dispute, the Board of Selectmen, last night, by a vote of 3–2, taken on a secret ballot, agreed that Morison Construction, who will appeal the decision, will not be granted a variance, an exception from normal zoning, and be allowed to build a shopping center on top of Colonial Cemetery, the oldest burying ground in the state.

AFTER MERTON

Morison Construction will not be allowed to build a shopping center on Colonial Cemetery.

The Board of Selectmen voted 3–2 to refuse the company an exception from normal zoning laws.

The vote was by secret ballot.

Colonial Cemetery is the oldest burying ground in the state.

Morison Construction will appeal the decision.

Decide for yourself which style makes the information and its meaning clear to the reader. Of course, news style is not always as rigid as the Merton exercise, but it is a disciplined form of clear writing that builds on the foundation of that exercise.

Take a page from a textbook and use the Merton exercise to turn the text into news style so that you get the feel of newswriting.

PLANNING

The experienced newswriter, even when writing against a close deadline, takes time to plan. But one of the most exciting things about writing is that the plans don't always work out. The writing comes alive under your fingers and teaches you what to say. You discover new meanings and new ways of sharing those meanings with the reader. That will not happen unless there is a plan—the explorer makes plans to climb Everest, probe space, or map the Antarctic. Plans do not prohibit adventure, they make discovery and adventure possible.

Several planning techniques help the newswriter produce stories under professional pressures of time and space. They overlap, of course, and they do not always come in the same order. Sometimes they will take a long time to work out; other times, with an experienced reporter, the planning will occur so fast that you may have the illusion there was no planning at all. These elements are:

Focusing. A news story—and probably every other form of writing—should have one dominant meaning. In a complex story there may be many pieces of information and meanings. But the reporter and the reader should be able to answer the question: "What's the single, most important element in the story?"

Take a piece of scrap paper and put down—in just a word or two or three—what the main points may be in your story. For example, shoplifting, woman security chief, rape in the parking lot, stolen car stereos, man in ambulance. Pick the one point on your list that will be the main point of your story. Rape would be the most important element in the mall story. Put a star next to it. That will be the north star that will guide you through the story. Everything in the story must connect with and relate to that point.

Rehearsing. Experienced reporters listen to write. They rehearse what they're going to say by saying it in their heads, out loud, or on paper, to hear how it sounds, and keep saying it over again in different ways until it sounds right.

We all rehearse when we want to ask someone for a date, a raise, a loan; when we write a note or make a phone call to congratulate or offer sympathy; when we hope to make a good impression at a party or make a sale. We say, over and over in our heads, what we hope we'll be able to say later. We listen to how it sounds, trying—by practice—to sound natural, trying out different words, in various orders, changing paces and rhythms.

Rehearsal is a vital part of planning for most newswriters. They won't proceed until they hear language that seems appropriate to the meaning, illuminates it, makes the meaning clear, and emphasizes it. Each reporter has his or her own voice, a personal way of using language, that has to be adapted to a voice that is appropriate to what is being written. You speak with your own voice at the family reunion, at a formal meeting, in the locker room, at a wake or viewing, at a wedding. Your voice is yours but you tune it so it is effective in each situation. Voice is style, and more; it is intensity, caring, and above all illumination.

The experienced reporter learns how to hear a fragment of language, a paragraph, a sentence, a phrase, and know that the voice is right. You can only do this with experience, but the ability comes early. For a mood piece on a mall, a newswriter might write:

> "The mall is crowded with shoppers looking for bargains, trying to find out what's in and what's out, hoping to see friends or make new friends, trying to decide to buy a pistachio walnut chocolate chip mint cone or a slice of pizza. It is the Medieval carnival re-created seven nights a week."
>
> or
>
> "The mall is where the lonely go. They hope the artificial lighting, the electronic music, the plastic bargains, the imitation new styles, the crowds of other lonely people will make up for the lack of friends or family but, of course, it doesn't, but they return, night after night. Where shall I go tonight? Where else? The mall."
>
> or
>
> "All malls are the same. Visit Texas, Florida, New Jersey, Illinois, California, Portland, Maine, or Portland, Oregon, and the same stores are in the same places. They have the same garish lights and fountains; the same stale air; the same bargains already out of fashion; and the same people searching for what they will not find."
>
> or
>
> "The malls have turned the developers' lonely housing tracks into villages. Here people can meet and shop and gossip and even share the new folk arts that people have used to escape the plastic society."

The voice in each paragraph is different and each would lead the writer—and the reader—into a different story.

Sketch half a dozen sentences or short paragraphs that allow you to hear the different voices in which your story might be written. Read these fragments aloud to hear the voice. If you don't hear a voice, read them aloud to see what you would have to add or change to make the voice distinctive and appropriate to the subject.

Writing Leads. The lead, the first ten lines or less, in a news story must capture the reader in three seconds. It must attract the reader, competing with all the other stories that are fighting for the reader's attention. The lead delivers the most important information in a news story—the news—to the reader as fast as possible.

The lead combines focus with voice. It aims the story, and by doing that, makes it possible for the newswriter to produce clean, well-directed copy, in a hurry.

Some of the common forms of leads are:

- *Statement.* Shopping malls are the loneliest places in our society according to sociologist Horatio Graves, who has been studying loneliness in America for ten years.
- *Quotation.* "There is no place as lonely as a crowded shopping mall," says sociologist Horatio Graves, who has been studying loneliness in America for the past ten years.
- *Fact.* Eighty percent of the Americans surveyed said they felt most lonely in a crowded shopping mall.
- *Description.* The people in the shopping mall shuffle back and forth, back and forth, until the electronic voice says the mall is closing. They always look up surprised as if they had nowhere else to go.
- *Anecdote.* Mary M got up early, made sandwiches for her husband and the twins, cooked breakfast, drove her husband to the bus and the twins to school and then went to the mall where she spent the day—every day.

  Now President of Mallers Anonymous, Mary says, "Housewives, the unemployed, the retired, teenagers, people from every part of society are attracted to the shopping mall if they are lonely. We are trying to show people there is life outside the mall."

There are many other ways to lead into a news story. Read newspapers, magazine articles, and books to find leads that make you continue reading and try their techniques on your stories.

Newswriters know the time they spend on the lead is well spent because almost all important decisions that have to be made during the writing of the story can be decided in the lead. Writing the lead, you know where to start, where to go, and how to get there.

Draft ten leads for your story. You may use one of them to start the story or start it with an entirely new one. Remember that the time you spend finding the lead will save you time in writing the story.

Ending. In traditional news stories there is no formal ending. The stories just trail off. Such stories are called inverted pyramid stories with the information important to the reader up front, the next most important information next, and so forth.

Nowadays news style is changing and endings are more important. Writing ends helps the writer because they increase the writer's sense of direction. Inexperienced writers, however, must learn that news endings are not conclusions or summaries. News stories conclude with specific pieces of information that summarize by implication. Do not, for example, end a story on loneliness by saying it's a lonely place. Instead, use a quotation from a lonely person or a description of someone at a mall being lonely.

Sketch five different endings you may come to by writing the article.

Designing. Although experienced newswriters have combined focus and voice in a lead, they will usually delay writing until they see the design—or pattern or shape or structure—of the whole piece. Writers use different language to describe this. They may say outline, but most do not, for the outlines they were taught in school are too formal, too structured, and too limiting. Formal outlines imprison the newswriter and prohibit the important discoveries that must take place during writing. Writers usually talk about a thread that runs through the story, or a spine to which everything in the story is connected.

The reporter who has a lead—a starting place—and an end—a destination—can go back and mark down the three or four or five landmarks that have to be followed to get there. These are the main points that have to be made in the story—in the order the reader needs them. Sometimes it is helpful to think of the landmarks as the reader's questions. These questions do not appear on the page. The skillful reporter anticipates the questions and provides the answers at the moment the reader would ask the question.

Write down the four or five questions the reader has to have answered to get from the lead to the end. Then put them in the order the reader will ask them. If you're not sure what questions the reader would ask or the order, ask a potential reader to help you.

DRAFTING

Writing is rewriting for most writers—but not for newswriters. They have to produce first drafts that can be edited, published, and read in hours. They write directly on typewriters or word processors, and once they have committed themselves there's little time for looking back. That's why experienced newswriters learn to plan so well, focusing, rehearsing a voice, trying out leads, playing with endings, anticipating the reader's questions, seeing a pattern all in their heads so that they can write a clear, accurate, interesting story in an hour.

And after newswriters learn to write fast, they discover speed has so many benefits they continue to write first drafts in a hurry, even if they have the time to write slowly. The pressure of speed increases the intensity, the flow, the natural connections within the writing that can't be planned but occur when writing is working at high speed.

Writing a draft, newswriters keep their notes simple, or put them aside, start with the rehearsed lead, and move as quickly as they can to the end. They know that what they remember is usually what should be remembered, and what they forget is usually what should be forgotten.

Newswriters know they will go over the piece after the draft is done, so they don't let anything interrupt the flow of logic and voice that is vital to produce a coherent piece of prose. When they come to a fact or a quote or a statistic they can't remember, they leave a blank or put the letters TK (for *to come*) into the text. TK will flag their attention when they revise the piece. At that point they can take the time to get the detail right. When there is a fact or a quote that has to be checked, they usually stick CK after it as a reminder to make a phone call or in some other way confirm the point.

When interrupted, reporters will try to wave off the interruption and keep pouring the words down on paper or video tube as fast as possible. If the interruption can't be waved off, experienced reporters try to stop in the middle of a sentence so the thread of the sentence can be picked up when the reporter returns to the draft.

In drafting a story there are some important things to keep in mind. They are important, but it's more important to keep the draft flowing.

Remember:

- Keep the paragraphs short. Vary the length according to what you have to say, but five lines is a signal that your paragraph is getting long.
- Be specific. Readers have a hunger for concrete, precise, accurate information. Use full names with middle initials, addresses, ages, titles, where appropriate. Say how many people attended the meeting, where the meeting was held, exactly how long it lasted, precisely what was accomplished. Give the exact vote, the correct name for the action taken. But, of course, use only significant specifics, details that

move the story forward and increase the reader's understanding.

- Attribute information so the reader knows who is the source for each piece of significant information that's not directly observed by the reporter. And even when the reporter has observed the event, the reader will appreciate information from someone in authority, the fire chief or the judge, rather than the reporter. Reporters must accept the idea they are not the authorities for the story and the reader needs to know the information in the story and who is responsible for it.
- Use direct quotes—the exact words of the speaker—for the most important points, if possible. The direct quote is precisely what the person said. Put quotation marks at the beginning and end of direct quotes. Identify the speaker of each direct quotation before, after, or right in the middle of the quotation: "I'm worried about the rapes we've had in the parking lot," said Anne Hannah, mall security chief. "They're far more serious than the car stereo thefts." Always remember to put the quotation in context. The person may have said, "I'd like to kill him," and mean that she would really like to murder him, or that she's delighted he's given her an expensive gift she really wanted.
- Use paraphrase—putting information you have received in your own words when the direct quote is too long, unclear, or less important. For example, "The mall security chief said that other crimes at the mall included shoplifting, passing bad checks, stealing cars, and using stolen credit cards."
- Do not write transitions. The information should come to the reader when the reader needs it. If the information is in the wrong place, move it to the right place. Do not try to solve it by writing, "Meanwhile, back at City Hospital . . ."
- Reveal the story to your reader. Show rather than tell when possible. It is not your job to tell the reader about the story. Your challenge is to get out of the way and let the reader see and hear the story directly. Put the reader in the hearing room or on the sidelines.
- To write short but effective copy, do not try to pack everything into the story, the way you use a garbage compactor. Instead, select the information your reader needs to know and develop it fully.

The reporter producing a first draft is a mad weaver, combining information, structure, voice into a tightly woven and effective whole. It is a task that takes concentration and usually can be done only in relatively short spurts.

PROOFREADING

When the story is finished, the writer has the responsibility to read the story line by line. The writer should be the enemy to the writer's own prose, challenging each fact, each word, each detail, so that the story will be accurate, easy to read, and easy to understand.

It may help you to follow

The Proofreader's Checklist

- Is each fact correct?
- Is each fact fair?
- Is each fact in the right context?
- Is every quote accurate?
- Does the reader know who is speaking?
- Does the reader know who is responsible for the information in the article?
- Is the information as specific as possible?
- Does the lead give the reader important information right away?
- Does the story fulfill the promise of the lead?
- Are the reader's questions answered when they are asked?
- Is there adequate evidence to support each point?
- Does the story flow gracefully from point to point?
- Can it be read aloud?
- Does each paragraph say one thing?
- Does every sentence advance the meaning of the story?
- Is every sentence a sentence?
- Is each word the best word?
- Does the punctuation work to make the meaning clear?
- Are the nouns concrete whenever possible?
- Are the verbs as active as possible?
- Is there anything that can be made more simple without oversimplifying?
- Is there anything that can be cut?
- Is each word spelled correctly?
- Is the story accurate and fair?

One story doesn't make a newswriter. But once you have passed through the process and produced one story, you know how to write another—and another. You can begin the life of learning that is the challenge and the satisfaction of every newswriter.

Take what you have learned seriously. To write clearly, you

have had to think clearly. The newswriter gathers accurate facts and uses language to connect those random fragments so they make meaning. It is hard, disciplined work, but satisfying and important work. What all of us know—whether we like the press or not—depends to a great deal on what newswriters tell us. They do it to deadline and they make it look easy. It isn't easy but, as you now know, it is the kind of hard work that can be fun.

EIGHTEEN
UNLEARNING TO WRITE

And again we look at our writing craft from the perspective of another genre. In this case I also gave myself the opportunity to discuss an important issue in teaching writing: how to instruct unlearning.

One of my last teaching assignments was a freshman English honors section. It was a tough assignment because they had so very much to unlearn. They could spell better than I could. They could organize. They could follow—rigidly—the rules of usage and mechanics. They could say nothing, absolutely nothing, with enormous skill and correctness.

Their detachment from their writing was terrifying. They had become honors students by playing it safe. They knew how to write without voice or meaning just the way they had stamped out burgers at fast-food restaurants. And so I had to unlearn 'em. They were terrified and so was I but we made it just in time for the end of the course.

When students sign up for a fiction course they are usually experienced writers—too experienced. They have done well at introductory writing courses and literature courses. Many are skillful writers of nonfiction, some have published nonfiction or earn their living writing. All have enough interest and confidence to dare to study fiction. They want to be fiction writers or, for a few hours a week, to imagine themselves short story writers or novelists.

The problem is not motivation, the problem is that the students have learned to write. They bring with them knowledge that may be true for some of the writing they have done but which makes the writing of fiction difficult. The better educated the student, the harder it is to return to the natural, magical art of narrative—the mother of all forms of significant discourse.

> But what do beginners know? Too much. It is what they think they know that makes them beginners.
>
> *William Gass*

A process of unlearning has to take place. This is painful and frightening for students and for an antique nonfiction writer tutoring himself through a period of unlearning when he returns to fiction.

Old rules become comforting to us all. Skills—and the attitudes behind them—become beliefs raised to the power of Truth. I am used to unlearning, but most of my students have come to learn new truths, not to have old ones stripped away; they have come to construct a system of higher skills on the foundation of old ones, not have the cathedral of their learning razed so that the wondrous and essential mists of unknowing can take their place.

> You write—and find you have something to say.
>
> *Wright Morris*

> I write out of ignorance. I write about the things I don't have any resolutions for, and when I'm finished, I think I know a little bit more about it. I don't write out of what I know. It's what I don't know that stimulates me.
>
> *Toni Morrison*

Producing constructive unlearning is a challenge for the teacher. To replace rules with rules, an old theology with a new one, inappropriate formulas with appropriate-appearing formulas, is easy compared to replacing knowing with doubting, answers with questions, dependency with independency.

Yet this is what has to be done if students are to learn to seek, respect, and make use of doubt, questions, wonder, surprise, failure, accident, discovery to explore the uncomfortable, exciting territory of the fiction writer.

Most students arrive in the fiction class with a dangerous assumption: they believe in the precedence of theme. They have the misconception that idea always precedes story. They see fiction as propaganda, the illustration of a preconceived concept.

> One is not free to write this or that. One does not choose

> one's subject. That is what the public and the critics do not understand.
>
> *Gustave Flaubert*

Oddly enough, the ideas that seem vague and useless—"love is complicated," "people need love," "outsiders (parents) don't know how love feels"—are often the ideas that *may* develop into a piece of fiction. It is easy for teachers to dismiss such ideas as banal, but the "idea" of a Shakespearean play or a novel by Tolstoy can also be reduced to such a statement. Often they are banal, but they also may be code words for the deep-running experiences, fears, concerns, and needs of the student writer. "I worry about an unhappy married woman" can become pure flapdoodle or *Madame Bovary*.

> The beginning of every short story is ridiculous at first. There seems no hope that this newborn thing, still incomplete and tender in every joint, will be able to keep alive in the complicated organization of the world, which, like every completed organization, strives to close itself off. However, one should not forget that the story, if it has any justification to exist, bears its complete organization within itself even before it has been fully formed; for this reason despair over the beginning of a story is unwarranted; in a like case parents should have to despair of their suckling infant, for they had no intention of bringing this pathetic and ridiculous being into the world.
>
> *Franz Kafka*

The idea for fiction is a question to be answered, a feeling or a place to be explored, a what if to be observed. It is private, an obsession that has an importance for the writer which cannot be seen by others until it is written (when it will be seen far differently by the writer). The idea is just that—a hint, a clue, something overheard from the next book, a reflection in a store window caught in the corner of an eye.

> All I have to go on is something I caught a glimpse of out of the corner of my eye.
>
> *John Updike*

> I start my work by asking a question and then try . . . to answer it.
>
> *Mary Lee Settle*

> What if? What if? My mind raced, and my emotions kept

> pace at the sidelines, the way it always happens when a story idea arrives, like a small explosion of thought and feeling. What if? What if an incident like that in the park had been crucial to the relationship between father and daughter? What would make it crucial? Well, what if the father, say, was divorced from the child's mother and the incident happened during one of his visiting days? And what if . . . ?
>
> *Robert Cormier*

But students have been taught to write thesis statements, sentences that contain the conclusion that will be reached after the writing is done. Writers write to explore, to discover, to know. The writer has to keep the idea open so there is room for the story to happen.

> I write because I don't know what I think until I read what I have to say . . . The more you write, the more you will realize that the form is organic, that it is something that grows out of the material, that the form of each story is unique . . . a story is good when you can continue to see more and more in it, and when it continues to escape you. In fiction two and two is always more than four.
>
> *Flannery O'Connor*

> Let the story arise of itself. Let it speak for itself. Let it reveal itself as it goes along.
>
> *Eudora Welty*

The greatest joy in writing fiction is surprise, but students have been taught that they should know what they want to say before they say it. If I did that, I would have no need to write. I would seek a craft in which I could not predict the product before it was begun.

> That's not what writing is—writing what you know. You write in order to find things out.
>
> *Garrison Keillor*

> We write about what we don't know about what we know.
>
> *Grace Paley*

Students who seek literary fame have often been taught literature in such a way that they do not understand that the writer was conducting an experiment in meaning; the writer usually finds the theme after reading with surprise what has been written. The fiction writer doesn't intend, but observes and records. Yet the literary writer thinks the story rather than writing it, choosing subject matter, actions, the author's voice, the theme, the background from literary history, the way the student shops for the back-to-school wardrobe, selecting what is in, rejecting what is out. Their work is clever, imitative, and as pointless as wearing a fake Reebok—or even a real one, as I am at this moment.

And, as I am carried away with these beliefs of mine, I have to remember to temper what I am telling my students with contradictory information: that Steinbeck often wrote a sentence or two on a three-by-five-inch card saying what the book was about, and kept it in front of him as he wrote the book, and I may do that too; that many writers know the end before they begin; that planning is part of preparing to write. The secret is balance, and the balance may be different for the experienced and inexperienced writer, may change with the writing task, may vary according to the personality and thinking style of the writer.

> I don't know how far away the end is—only *what* it is. I know the last sentence, but I am very much in the dark concerning how to get to it.
>
> *John Irving*

> If I didn't know the ending of a story, I wouldn't begin. I always write my last line, my last paragraphs, my last page first.
>
> *Katherine Anne Porter*

Writers who scorn "literary" writing and seek an immediate cash return on their talent revere plot above all else. They design their stories the way you design a supermarket. The book is constructed to appeal to each reader: sex, violence, laughter, a behind-the-scenes background that reveals the world of toilet bowl manufacturing or summer waitressing, characters who can be ordered off the TV shelf—one urbane, one crude, one pretty, one plain, one a user, one used.

> I have no regular system for writing . . . I sit down at the typewriter when I feel like it. Something—an image or phrase—from five years earlier may suddenly come out as I type. I try to follow it. I never think to myself, "Boy, would such-and-such make a good story." I don't have any

> preconceived ideas of plot. When I start writing it is a process of discovery.
>
> *Ann Beattie*

> Plot might seem to be a matter of choice. It is not. The particular plot for this particular novel is something the novelist is driven to. . . . It is what is left after the whittling-away of alternatives.
>
> *Elizabeth Bowen*

> When I start a book I have no idea of how it's going to end. I really don't know what's going to happen more than a chapter or two ahead. The characters audition in their opening scene—I listen to them, see how they sound. The plots develop on their own. If I'm curious enough to turn the pages, I figure it will have the same effect on readers.
>
> *Elmore Leonard*

Some students want both literary fame and the large cash advance; they want the in's reputation and the out's best-seller status. And they suffer writer's whiplash as they try to be all things to all readers.

It is hard for any of these students who have been asked "What did the writer mean when . . . ?"—and been given a precise answer—to be patient with a teacher who says that the writer was probably dumb before such questions, that the writer may not have known where the story was headed until it got there.

> Creation must take place between the pen and the paper, not before in a thought or afterwards in a recasting.
>
> *Gertrude Stein*

> Any man who knows in advance what he's going to write about would be so bored that he'll bore his readers, or he won't finish it.
>
> *Paul Theroux*

My teacherly task is to make my students uncomfortable, to lead them into unknowing, but not to abandon them there—to be an effective Maine guide, paddling them toward the salmon but allowing them to make their own catch.

I encourage my students to start with a character or, if they have an idea, to populate it with a character, an individual who is seen and heard and felt, who can hurt and be hurt, who can act when it would be wiser not to and not act when it is important to act. They should start with a person who is complicated, probably drawn from those we know, but not too consciously, and not drawn in a sketch but in dramatic action.

Character meets character. There is action and reaction, push and pull, cause and effect. The scene in which characters act and react is the engine of the story; the energy of this dramatic interaction between characters drives the narrative forward. Not meaning, idea, theme, or thesis; not literary style or voice; not background or setting; but character against character. All else comes from that—the language, the place, the meaning are revealed by the scene and the sequence of scenes.

> I begin to get preconscious intimations of what the work is going to be like, even before I awaken. I see faces and scenes, floors, walls, landscapes. I hear lines of dialogue.
>
> *Saul Bellow*

Dialogue, as Elizabeth Bowen taught me in her fine "Notes on Writing a Novel," is action. Dialogue isn't talk. It is what people do to each other. It is what they say and do not say. It is how they speak and how they are silent, turning away or moving close.

> Dialogue has to show not only something about the speaker that is its own revelation, but also maybe something about the speaker that he doesn't know but the other character does know. You've got to show a two-way revelation between speaker and listener, which is the fascination of writing dialogue. Dialogue is action.
>
> *Eudora Welty*

Dialogue, as much as anything else, reveals the character to the writer and, ultimately, to the reader.

> I don't have a very clear idea of who the characters are until they start talking.
>
> *Joan Didion*

My students and I share our drafts and our *written* commentaries about how we have written that day or that week, how we have felt, failed, attempted; what problems we have defined and solved or failed to solve, what questions we have answered—or not answered.

Our breakthroughs to fiction come as we have the central experience of writing fiction: the characters begin to act on their own and the story is not told but observed and recorded. The writer doesn't make up the story but receives it.

> If you're silent for a long time, people just arrive in your mind.
>
> *Alice Walker*

> The bad novelist constructs his characters; he directs them and makes them speak. The true novelist listens to them and watches them act; he hears their voices even before he knows them.
>
> *Andre Gide*

> It's the characters who direct me. That is, I see a character, he's there, and I recognize someone I knew, or occasionally two who are a bit mixed together, but then that stops. Afterwards, the character acts on his own account. He says things . . . I never know *what* any of them are going to say when I'm writing dialogue . . . I'm very visual when I write. I see it all, I see everything.
>
> *Julio Cortazar*

> It begins with a character, usually, and once he stands up on his feet and begins to move, all I do is trot along behind him with a paper and pencil trying to keep up long enough to put down what he says and does.
>
> *William Faulkner*

> When I construct a scene, I don't describe the hundredth part of what I see; I see the characters scratching their noses, walking about, tilting back in their chairs—even after I've finished writing—so much so that after a while I feel a weariness which does not derive all that much from my effort of imagination but is more like a visual fatigue: my eyes are tired from watching my characters.
>
> *Graham Greene*

> My characters really dictate themselves to me. I am not free of them, really, and I can't force them into situations they haven't themselves willed. They have the autonomy of characters in a dream. . . . It's a mysterious process. The character on the page determines the prose—its music, its rhythms, the range and limit of its vocabulary—yet, at the onset at least, I determine the characters. It usually happens

> that the fictitious character, once released, requires a life and will of his or her own.
>
> *Joyce Carol Oates*

Of course there are writers such as Nabakov who say this is nonsense, and it may well be for him. But the evidence is overwhelming that most fiction writers are in a constant state of tension with their characters, that these writers battle with their characters for control of the story. And most writers learn how to accept defeat gracefully, to give the characters room, to allow them to break free and tell the story.

This is difficult for students, and especially for many literature teachers, to accept. (I am battling it this week as the father in my novel is behaving in such a way that he's taking the story where I do not want it to go. The battle is not over, but he will win.)

This process doesn't feel like thinking; it is irrational, disorderly, at best a dumb kind of thinking. My students, as if they did not have natural cognitive styles, have all been taught to think in a different way, a more logical, more controlled and directed way. Now they find themselves not knowing what they are going to say before they say it. Writing to them is not a matter of discovery but a matter of presenting thoughts that have already been thunk.

> I'm working on something, I don't know exactly what.
>
> *Eudora Welty*

> Writing and rewriting are a constant search for what one is saying.
>
> *John Updike*

> Every short story, at least for me, is a little act of discovery. A cluster of details presents itself to my scrutiny, like a mystery that I will understand in the course of writing or sometimes not fully until afterward. . . . A story that you do not learn something from while you are writing it, that does not illuminate something for you, is dead, finished before you started it.
>
> *Mary McCarthy*

To unlearn most of us have to write fast. We have to push ourselves to describe what is taking place before our mind's eye, because the velocity of the writing seems to cause the actions we record. The energy of the writing causes the energy of the vision.

> There are some kinds of writing that you have to do very fast, like riding a bicycle on a tightrope.
>
> *William Faulkner*

There are other good reasons for speed in drafting. Acceleration of prose causes those accidental connections between what is known and what is suddenly remembered; it causes the interaction of information we would have thought inappropriate but which brings a crucial insight when it occurs on the page. Speed puts a spin on language, causing those phrases and tiny surprises which mark an interesting style.

> Follow the accident, fear the fixed plan—that is the rule.
>
> *John Fowles*

> It tells you. You don't tell it.
>
> *Joan Didion*

> Inch by inch, the words surprised me.
>
> *William Kennedy*

And perhaps most important, speed allows us to outrun the rational mind and its busy chorus of censors—parents, teachers, editors, associates—who tell us what can be done, what we can't do, what is certain to fail. If we write fast enough we enter into the text and are so busy getting down what we are seeing and hearing and observing and, yes, experiencing that we may forget—unlearn—what we know.

> All my life I've been frightened at the moment I sit down to write.
>
> *Gabriel Garcia Marquez*

We may, by writing fast, achieve the gift of concentration. We may be able, for the moment, to lose ourselves in our text, so that the world on the paper and behind it is more real than the world in which we sit writing.

> If it is winter in the book, spring surprises me when I look up.
>
> *Bernard Malamud*

But, of course, we will return to read and revise, read and rewrite, read and edit. The writing act has its intellectual and rational elements. But once we have a text, we can learn from the text. We have been taught that the answers are in the handbook or writing text (perhaps even one by Don Murray), but if we listen to our emerging text, it will teach us to write. It will tell us what the text needs and what it cannot take. The text will establish its directions, its voice, its own meaning.

> The writer himself studies intensely how to do it while he is in the thick of doing it; then when the particular novel or story is done, he is likely to forget how; he does well to. Each work is new. Mercifully, the question of *how* abides less in the abstract, and less in the past, than in the specific, in the work at hand.
>
> *Eudora Welty*

Students who have come to class full of external rules and laws and theories and standards and skills that they have been taught to apply to a text will begin to see that the writer's craft comes from within a text that the writer has learned how to receive. It is a matter of acceptance and cultivation and harvesting what is not what was hoped for; it is not a matter of making but accepting.

> An artist observes, selects, guesses, and combines.
>
> *Anton Chekhov*

> [Writing] is sort of like when you've got no electricity and you've gotten up in the middle of the night to find the bathroom, feeling your way along in the dark. I can't hardly tell you what I do because I really don't know.
>
> *Carolyn Chute*

> The material itself dictates how it should be written.
>
> *William Faulkner*

In the academy, we separate the writing of fiction and poetry from the serious writing of the essay, the thesis, the term paper. We seem to fear the creative and want to fence it off as if it would contaminate other forms of writing. But the students who experience characters taking over their story often discover they have learned a new and powerful way of thinking that will help them in scholarly research and vocational pursuits. They have found how to use written language not just as a method of recording thought but as a way of thinking.

How do I know what I think until I see what I say?

E. M. Forster

I write both fiction and nonfiction, "creative" (a term fiction writers hate), and, I suppose, "noncreative" work, and I find that my articles on composition theory and pedagogy, my textbooks, my newspaper columns all work best when the ideas take off like characters and surprise me during the act of writing. In fact, I, like most writers in all genres, find out what I have to say as I say it. Writing is an act of discovery; and it may be just as important in the freshman English class, in the advanced composition class, in the courses in non-fiction writing that we help our students unlearn to write and encourage the experience of allowing characters—or ideas—to take off, with the writer racing after them, at top speed, to discover what the text is thinking.

NINETEEN

CASE HISTORY: DEALING WITH THE PERSONAL

The following case history was written for presentation at a session for journalists at the Poynter Institute for Media Studies in St. Petersburg, Florida. I simply followed the process of writing an essay, documenting what I was doing as I did it.

Later, I revised the piece, and it was one of the three I submitted to the Boston Globe in suggesting my "Over Sixty" column. It was the third column they published, and I've included the final version at the end.

In writing the piece, I faced a problem shared by many of my students through the years: how to write about a very personal and painful subject. I realized I had to write this, that I had to confront this topic, but I knew I would never put it to rest. As a professional I instinctively moved toward narrowing the topic, not writing about the death of children but to the unexpected focus of how a combat soldier used some lessons of war to survive the dying of his daughter. I don't like saying this now. It seems to diminish the piece, but it is important for students to deal with moments, glimpses, fragmentary ideas and explore them in writing.

Is this what we should be doing, encouraging therapy in our classrooms? Well . . . writing is therapy for this writer and for most others I know. We should certainly allow life in the classroom when it walks through the door. Some of our students will find it healing to write about the pain and anger in their lives. And it is, after all, the raw material of art.

As the narrative about my drafts reveals, I was attacked publicly for doing this kind of writing. And I suppose my only defense is the text and the knowledge that each reader will respond individually, out of his or her own need and own pain.

Yesterday I read an article by Julio Cortazar in the *New York Times Book Review* in which he cited Pablo Neruda's "My creatures are born of a long denial." Today Don Fry suggested I write of Lee's death. He had a market—the men's column in the *New York Times Magazine*—and a reason—it would help people. I wanted to run out of the room, but I sat in his office politely turning him off—or trying to. But I knew I had the lead written in my head, the anecdote I wrote to Ed Corbett Saturday on the death of his wife.

Six weeks after we lost Lee, at the age of 20 to Reye's Syndrome, we were invited to go back to the hospital. The invitation was to all who sat through those endless days, waiting, waiting, waiting. So Minnie Mae, our daughters Anne and Hannah, Lee's boy friend, Paul, and I went back.

I didn't want ever to return to this hospital where I had left my father and now my daughter—and where I had recorded, guilty, what I saw and felt with a writer's eye.

And the first thing Dr. Shannon, the doctor in charge, asked in our postmortem session was if I was going to write about my daughter's death. I get tears writing this 11 years later. He plunged a dagger in my heart. He knew I had not only been a father but a writer during those days of her dying.

I heard myself saying no and adding something about a quotation from de Maupassant which had haunted me there and since, the writer "says to himself as he leaves the cemetery where he has left the being he loved most in the world; it is curious what I felt . . ."

But the wise doctor said that I must write about it, and the people who I cared most about agreed.

But not everyone agrees and the guilt surfaces. Curiously, it was most relieved during a summer writing session on another campus. I write when I ask teachers to write and I share my writing. I think it is an ethical obligation. If they are to reveal themselves to me and to their colleagues, I must reveal myself to them. And, of course, Lee returns to my page.

When I shared my piece about her, the head of the program accused me, before the teachers, of exploiting my daughter's death. It was what I feared most, but once it happened, I felt a calm. The worst is rarely as bad as what I imagined. And I knew Lee understood.

But now that Don Fry had sparked this piece I wondered, do I have the need or the courage to write it? What do I tell my students? "Write about it (a death, divorce, illness that's tearing at them) if it feels good, if it's healthy for you. If it doesn't feel good, don't do it." But I don't know how I feel, I haven't done it.

A week and a day after Don Fry mentioned the piece, I find myself almost involuntarily picking up my daybook and making such fragmentary notes, translated here from my scrawl:

Jess lead
    what do I do
    walk under water
    "gte" [Jess']
comfort
not quite true, true enough
xxxxxxxxxxxxx

war—I slept on floor
decision—father
        —mother
        —daughter
reaching out—brain tumor
             students
             xxxxxxxxxx
blind sided
Next aug. it will be nine yrs
        it doesn't get any easier, lee. we don't forget
But I have the lead, I have no choice.

It is the next day, and I am going to dictate a rough draft to my wife. I had asked her if I could. The subject makes it difficult, but she said to go ahead, and so we'll try it. Dictating is something we have done since the birth of Lee. We started it just after Minnie Mae came home from the hospital, because we had a huge book insert to complete in a ghostwritten business book that would pay for Lee's birth. Perhaps it's particularly fitting that we dictate this, if I can keep my voice from choking up. The great advantages of dictation are, first of all, speed—I'm a poor typist—and flow. It is easier for most of us to be fluent speaking than writing. The process is strange. It is not conversation; it is intensely disciplined. But I'm usually saying words that are just beyond what I know I will say. At least that is true if it goes well. And dictating marvelously helps me to take advantage of voice and the music that not only underscores the meaning, but often produces the meaning. I know the topic as I start to write, but only have hints at how it will be developed. I know the audience and the market I intend to aim it toward: the column, "About Men" in the *New York Times Magazine*, as Don suggested, and the length, about three pages, or a bit more of my double-spaced pages. I can't forget Don's quiet anecdote about the pain of a family he knew who lost a child, and how it might help if I wrote the piece. Lee's death taught me how much it helps to reach out, and so I will attempt to write it.

I wake the morning after I had given the family decision to the doctor that Lee, our daughter and sister, should be allowed to die.

I am aware before waking that the world will never be the same, and I have to ask myself what I do in the morning. I swing my feet toward the floor and push my body up. I push away from the bed and stand up, walk slowly to the bathroom, return, and dress, making decisions about what had once been instinctive habits. And then I stop. What do I do now? I go to the store to buy the morning papers—the *Boston Globe* and the *New York Times*.

At the store Jess, who has lost a son, sees me and says, "It won't get any better, Don."

I knew instantly that there would be strange comfort in those words. I was exploring landscapes of pain and loss I had never understood when others had a child die before them, but I knew that this was a condition of my life, and I did not want to evade it or lose it.

It would not get any better. We would learn how to live with it, but we would not get beyond it and recover. We would not forget Lee.

At the beginning of that August week our sunny middle daughter, 20 years old, healthy, in love with Paul, was preparing to transfer to the New England Conservatory, after two years of college, to study the oboe. At the end of the week she had survived Reye's Syndrome, but lay terribly still, healthy, beautiful but with flat brain waves.

It will be nine years this August, and it doesn't get any better, at least not that much better. I can, sometimes, hear an oboe solo she played without rushing to turn the radio off. I still see her on the street, or standing smiling, just outside of the corner of my eye in our house. She is the unspoken inhabitant of our lives.

We did learn some important things. We rediscovered the importance of family and the fragility of life. We are not obsessive about death, but we are careful, we know it can happen to us, and our daughters and ourselves call without prompting to report the successful end of a trip.

We learned to be less critical of ourselves and of others in how we live our lives. We did what we could do, and we understand others who grieve and survive in their own way.

We are still humbled and grateful to our friends, who took care of us after we came home from the hospital. I will never forget Phyllis, the Jewish mother, kneeling on the floor beside me, literally forcing food into me. We learned to accept, and our friends fed us and cared for us, even organizing themselves so that we were never alone, but never overwhelmed by kindness.

During the days at the hospital we all drew on what wells of strength we had. I was surprised to find how much I drew on the lessons of manliness that had been drilled into a frightened, resistant, spoiled and lonely only child. The simplicities and cruelties of the street, the YMCA camp, and the football field had all given me a masculine code that I thought superficial and rather silly. And yet I found that I turned to those lessons of behavior to be the man, the father.

I did not think I had been the Veteran, but surviving those days which were worse than combat, I turned back to what I had been able to do in the paratroops, in combat, in World War II. I remember in the tiny waiting room apologizing to the family, and lying down on the hard floor to nap, turning my mind off from insanity, the way I had learned to do it under shellfire. I am still blessed and guilty that I can at night turn off the thoughts that will prohibit sleep, a skill my wife has never learned, a skill that was born in terror under fire. It is a strange and terrible manly gift of acceptance and detachment.

And so, Lee, we have learned to reach out to others as they reached out to us, and to survive by whatever toughness we can draw on. My survival is that strange, lonely, masculine gift of war. What you seem to understand when I had to make the decision as the only child to let my Father go, and later my Mother, neither of us knowing, although we talked of it, that we would have to make this decision for you. Your mother and your sisters, and Paul, have all survived in their way, and my way has been what I least expected, by trying to be a man, an unpopular stance

> today. It's one I usually attack, for it is so full of such dangerous silliness, and I have been educated to see all of that by my feminist friends. And yet it is what I turned to, alone, when trying to survive Jess' truth, "It won't get any better, Don."

During the writing of this draft I only looked at the notes once. It went along pretty naturally. Every time I began to think critically or to wonder, for example, when or how I could get to the military business I sensed was looming up ahead, I suppressed all that critical stuff. I knew I would go back and revise and edit the piece, as you can see that I have. Toward the end of the piece I felt the writing breaking down, and my first instinct was that of despair. And then I reminded myself, as I always have to, that when the writing is getting out of control, when the syntax is breaking down, that's usually the place where the most significant breakthroughs are taking place. Don't worry about it, plunge on with language. It will be a matter of craft, or carpentry, to make clear what I have to say, if I have said anything worth making clear. I will let it sit, and when I cannot keep from touching it I will start working over, trying to discover what I have said and what I want to say.

My memory of the piece was that it went off in three directions, talking about the lessons of war, the truth of Jess' counsel, and perhaps something about how people helped us. My reading of the piece the next morning was quite detached and confirmed the problem, which Minnie Mae had identified when we finished. She didn't know what it said. In other words, there wasn't one clear message.

The problem may be the lead. The lead is so powerful it controls the piece. And if I use that lead then I must go with it. Perhaps I will. That's probably what I'd use if I were on deadline, but the military idea is one that fits the purpose of the column better. It may be that the market Don suggested is yanking me off my natural course. I'm discomforted by the military angle. I've been educated by feminists over the years, and I'm a strong opponent of the phony macho attitude which pervades most city rooms. I think it hurts the full development of many men I know, and I think it affects, in the worse possible way, both the development of writers and the stories we are publishing and how they are written. I'm uncomfortable with anything that seems to praise a macho attitude of manliness. And yet. And yet. Truman Capote said, "If there is no mystery, for the artist, to solve inside of his art, then there's no point in it." My very discomfort indicates mystery, irony, complication, and so I probably better go with the military one. That will mean ditching the lead and the end. The end's no great loss, but the lead I like.

This is the kind of talking to yourself that the writer has to do. I had thought that I would put my pen, or my cursor, to the copy line by line. But I'm not ready for that yet. I've got to let the piece simmer, and perhaps go back to fiddling around with titles or leads in my head, in my notebook. It won't worry me, since I have no deadline for this piece, if it doesn't surface again for weeks, months, or years. I'll try to bring it up this week for the purposes of the seminar, but I'm not going to force it.

I didn't intend to work on it last night, but I was aware of it as I did my other preparation and reading. I had given a copy to Chip late yesterday afternoon. We all need test readers we can trust but I was skittish about this piece. Outside of Minnie Mae, I wouldn't have shown this to anyone and I sort of flung it at Chip. He called, said he was honored to be allowed to read it, which was nice. He didn't need to treat it as a successful piece, it isn't. He mentioned a few things he liked and talked about the three year writing of his column about his father which he had shared with me in its early, as well as late, forms. This is the kind of companion writer we need, who supports and instructs by sharing. I had no intention of working on the piece when I got off the phone. In fact, Chip had encouraged me not to push it. He'd allowed me to get off my own hook and not feel I had to finish it for the workshop. Within half an hour I had picked it up.

I have a mystical feeling that a text will tell me what to do if I listen to it. To hear the text I have to enter into the text pen—or cursor—in hand. I was at the apartment and so I worked by hand. This was by no means an attempt at a final draft. I was just fiddling with it as you can see.

I wake the morning after I, as the father, had ~~given~~ met with the doctor and gave him, ~~both of us weeping~~ the family decision to ~~the doctor~~ that Lee, our daughter and sister, ~~shoul~~d be allowed to die.

I am aware before waking that the world will never be the same, and I have to ask myself what I do in the morning. I swing my feet toward the floor and push my body up. I push away from the bed and stand up, walk slowly to the bathroom, return, and dress, making decisions about what had once been instinctive habits. And then I stop. What do I do now? I go to the store to buy the morning papers - the Boston Globe and the New York Times.

At the store Jess, who has lost a son, sees me and says, "It won't get any better, Don."

¶ It seemed particularly masculine advice, delivered man to man, eyes staring into eyes. Of course women suffer as much as men, in their way. I only know the way I had been ~~told~~ taught to act: as a man. And I found ~~I knew instantly that there would be~~ strange comfort in ~~loss~~ this other father's harsh ~~those~~ words. ~~I was exploring landscapes of pain and loss I had never understood when others had a child die before them, but I knew that this was a condition of my life, and I did not want to evade it or lose it.~~

It would not get any better. We would learn how to live with it, but we would not get beyond it and recover. We would not forget Lee.

At the beginning of that August week our sunny middle daughter, 20-years-old, healthy, in love with Paul, was preparing to transfer to the New England Conservatory~~, after two years of college,~~ to study ~~the~~ oboe. At the end of the week she had survived Reye's Syndrome, but lay terribly still, healthy, beautiful but with flat brain waves.

It will be nine years this August, and it doesn't get any better, at least not that much better. I can, sometimes, hear an oboe solo she played without rushing to turn the radio off. I still see her on the street, or standing smiling, just outside of the corner of my eye in our house. She is the unspoken inhabitant of our lives.

We did learn some important things. We rediscovered the importance of family and the fragility of life. We are not obsessive about death, but we are careful, we know it can happen to us, and our daughters and ourselves call without prompting to report the successful end of a trip.

We learned to be less critical of ourselves and of others in how we live our lives. We did what we could do, and we understand others who grieve and survive in their own way..

hard to that code I had been questioning and doubting as a teacher and a writer in a world of changing (sex role) consciousness. But

We are still humbled and grateful to our friends, who took care of us after we came home from the hospital. I will never forget Phyllis, the Jewish mother, kneeling on the floor beside me, literally forcing food into me. We learned to accept, and our friends fed us and cared for us, even organizing themselves so that we were never alone, but never overwhelmed by kindness.

During the days at the hospital we all drew on what wells of strength we had.' I was surprised to find how much I drew on the lessons of manliness that had been drilled into a frightened, resistant, spoiled and lonely only child. The simplicities and cruelties of the street, the YMCA camp, and the football field had all given me a masculine code that I thought superficial and rather silly. And yet I found that I turned to those lessons of behavior to be the man, the father.

I did not think I had been the Veteran, but surviving those days which were worse than combat, I turned back to what I had been able to withstand in the paratroops, in combat, in World War II. I remember in the tiny waiting room apologizing to the family, and lying down on the hard floor to nap, turning my mind off from insanity, the way I had learned to do it under shellfire. I am still blessed and guilty

Father + Mother ?

Expand? Examples?

Expand? Examples?

that I can at night turn off the thoughts that will prohibit sleep, a skill my wife has never learned, a skill that was born in terror under fire. It is a strange and terrible manly gift of acceptance and detachment.

And so, Lee, we have learned ~~to reach out to others as they reached out to us, and~~ to survive by whatever toughness we can draw on. My survival, in part, ~~is that strange, lo~~nely, masculine gift of war. What

---

you seem to understand when I had to make the decision as the only child to let my Father go, and later my Mother, neither of us knowing, although we talked of it, that we would have to make this decision for you. Your mother and your sisters, and Paul, have all survived in their way, and my way has been what I least expected, by trying to be a man, an unpopular stance today. It's one I usually attack, for it is so full of such dangerous silliness, and I have been educated to see all of that by my feminist friends. And yet it is what I turned to, alone, when trying to survive Jess' truth, "It won't get any better, Don."

Now it is early the next morning and I am going to run the piece through the word processor, paying some attention to my editing, as much or more to the evolving text.

> I wake the morning after I, as the father, had the lonely task of delivering the family decision to the doctor that Lee, our daughter and sister, should be allowed to die.
>
> I am aware before waking this next morning that the world will never be the same, and I have to ask myself what I do in the morning. I swing my feet toward the floor and push my body up. I push away from the bed and stand up, walk slowly to the bathroom, return, and dress, making decisions about what had once been instinctive habits. And then I stop. What do I do now? I go to the store to buy the morning papers—the *Boston Globe* and the *New York Times.*
>
> At the store Jess, who has lost a son, sees me and says, "It won't get any better, Don."
>
> It seems particularly masculine advice, delivered man to man. As soon as I feel that, I suffer guilt, as if I am saying that men suffer in a special way. Perhaps they do. So do women and my wife and my surviving daughters are

suffering as much, or more, than I am, but each of us suffers alone. And my way of handling it is, in part, a man's way, taught and learned. I found strange comfort in this other father's harsh counsel.

It would not get any better. We would learn how to live with it, but we would not get beyond it and recover. We would not forget Lee.

At the beginning of that August week our sunny middle daughter, 20 years old, healthy, in love with Paul, was preparing to transfer to the New England Conservatory to study the oboe. At the end of the week she had survived Reye's Syndrome, but lay terribly still, healthy, beautiful but with flat brain waves.

It will be nine years this August, and it doesn't get any better, at least not that much better. I can, sometimes, hear an oboe solo she played without rushing to turn the radio off. I still see her on the street, or standing smiling, just outside of the corner of my eye in our house. She is the unspoken inhabitant of our lives.

Through it all I had been consciously trying to be a man, to hold hard to that male code I had found dangerously silly in an academic world of changing consciousness. I had even called myself a feminist, but during the days at the hospital we all drew on what wells of strength we had. I was surprised to find how much I drew on the lessons of manliness that had been drilled into a frightened, lonely only child.

[expand and document?]

> The simplicities and cruelties of the street, the YMCA camp, and the football field had all given me a masculine code that I thought superficial and rather silly. And yet I found that I turned to those lessons of behavior to be the man, the father.

I had not been the professional Veteran, did not join the Reserve or the Legion, never tried to get back into uniform (fat chance) and march in a Memorial Day parade, but when I had to remove "extraordinary means" from my father, had to convince the nurses two years later to let my mother go, and now had to attend to a daughter's dying, I turned back to what I had been able to do in the paratroops, in combat, in World War II.

In the tiny waiting room, I apologized to the family, and lay down on the hard floor to nap as I had under shellfire.

> Several times I, a Protestant, had been given the last rites in combat. I took them with gratitude, but I had only been asleep. Sleep was my retreat.
>
> [Bit more documentation?]
>
> I am still blessed and guilty that I can at night turn off the thoughts that will prohibit sleep, a skill my wife has never learned, a skill that was born in terror under fire. It is a strange and terrible manly gift of acceptance and detachment.
>
> And so, Lee, we have learned to reach out to others as they reached out to us, and to survive by whatever toughness we can draw on. My survival is that strange, lonely, masculine gift of war. You would have seen the irony in that. And as much as you always wanted us to be happy, I think you would understand the hard comfort of the fact that it doesn't get any better, and never will.

Maybe. Maybe, a piece. I don't know. I've been lost in it for the past half hour or so. Lost in the experience and lost in craft, trying not to feel guilty that the craft is there. Telling myself that Lee, the oboe player, would understand that.

I'll let it rest and try not to worry if I'm forcing the masculine angle. I do know the market. I am a pro, and yet I seem to be telling the truth I knew before I wrote this, but didn't know I knew it because I hadn't articulated it. Let it rest for now.

The next morning I come back to it. Now I am distant from it. I just want to work on it as a matter of craft. I made a couple of quick notes during one of the sessions yesterday. I open the daybook to where they are, put it on the stand and move on to the text itself, reading it line by line as a reader might—quickly.

> I wake the morning after I, the father, had the lonely task of delivering the family decision to the doctor that Lee, our 20-year-old daughter, should be allowed to die.
>
> Before waking I am aware that my world will never be the same, and I have to ask myself what I do in the morning. I swing my feet toward the floor and push my body up. I push away from the bed and stand up, walk slowly to the bathroom, return, and dress, making decisions about what had once been instinctive habits. And then I stop. What do I do now? I go to the store to buy the morning papers—the *Boston Globe* and the *New York Times*.
>
> At the store Jess, who has lost a son, sees me and says, "It won't get any better, Don."

It seems particularly masculine advice, delivered man to man. As soon as I feel that, I suffer guilt, as if I were saying that men suffer in a special way. But perhaps we do. Women—certainly my wife and my surviving daughters—suffer as much, or more, than men, but each of us suffers alone. And my way of handling it is a man's way, taught and learned. And I found strange comfort in this other father's abrupt advice.

It would not get any better. We would learn how to live with it, but we would not get beyond it and recover. We would not forget Lee.

At the beginning of that August week our sunny middle daughter, healthy, in love with Paul, was preparing to transfer to the New England Conservatory to study the oboe. At the end of the week she had survived Reye's Syndrome, but lay terribly still—healthy, beautiful but with flat brain waves.

It will be nine years this August, and it doesn't get any better, at least not that much better. I can, sometimes, hear an oboe solo she played without rushing to turn the radio off. I still meet her on the street or crossing campus; evenings or mornings, she often stands smiling, at the edge of the living room door. She is the unspoken inhabitant of my life.

Through her dying and afterwards, I realize I have been consciously trying to be a man, to hold hard to that male code I had found dangerously silly in an academic world of changing consciousness. I call myself a feminist, but during the days at the hospital we all drew on what wells of strength we had. I was surprised how much I drew on the lessons of manliness that had been drilled into a frightened, lonely only child.

I had almost drowned as a child, and it took three summers of cruel Christian ridicule to learn to swim at a YMCA camp. The fourth summer I had the responsibility, mine alone, to lead to safety a young camper frozen on a narrow trail across a cliff in the White Mountains. A Depression boy, I had to go out in the alley to fight a young father for my paper route—after bribing the man in charge. I won a prizefight after being knocked down 13 times. Being Scotch stubborn and Scotch stupid could pay off. A right tackle on scholarship, I played 60 minutes in 1942 on a knee that still hurts. Pain was a condition of that life. I don't approve of it, but I took strength from having survived it.

In the Army I went on forced marches where I got my second wind—and my third. I found I had reserves I didn't know I had. I could crawl under live fire; I could jump out of a perfectly good airplane. Once, when my chute did not open, I opened my reserve, got it tangled with another jumper, took the knife off my leg, cut myself free, jiggled my own chute half open and landed OK. In training I was told that machine guns rose during a burst of fire. That's the time to crawl forward, an unnatural act. In combat, I practiced it. I survived and returned home, surprised to be alive.

But I did not like the Army and hated war in the way a person can who has found, firsthand, what he and other human beings can do to each other. I had not been the professional Veteran, did not join the Reserve or the Legion, never tried to get back into uniform (fat chance) and march in a Memorial Day parade, but when I had to remove "extraordinary means" from my father, had to convince the nurses two years later to let my mother go, and now had to attend to a daughter's dying, I turned back to the manly attitudes and tricks of survival I had tested under fire.

I was not afraid that week—and afterwards—to weep, and I did. But I also knew that a man, a father, was supposed to be strong, so I played the role of the father as I had played the role of the paratrooper. I fooled myself and was strong.

When things got too much, I apologized to my family in the tiny waiting room, lay down on the hard floor and napped as I had under shellfire. Several times I, a Protestant, had been given the last rites in combat. I took them with gratitude, but I had only been asleep. Snoring was my retreat.

I am still blessed and guilty that I can at night turn off the thoughts that will prohibit sleep, a skill my wife has never learned, a skill that was born in terror under fire. It is a strange and terrible manly gift of acceptance and detachment.

And so, Lee, we have all learned to survive by whatever toughness we can draw on. My survival has, to a large degree, been a strange, lonely, masculine gift of war. You would have seen the irony in that. And as much as you always wanted us to be happy, I think you would understand the hard comfort of the fact that it doesn't get any better, and never will. We won't forget.

This was hard and fast editing, many line by line touches, a few fast written inserts. I felt the pride, the satisfaction, even, despite the subject, the joy of craft, a pleasure an oboe player would understand. Does it work? I don't know, let Minnie Mae, my daughters, my readers (especially Chip Scanlan and Don Graves), you, perhaps an editor, tell me.

Minnie Mae has doubts about the piece. It may be the writing (she is a good judge) but it also may be the subject and the military feelings so different from hers. She doesn't know. Again, another lonely choice of the writer. You must pay attention to your reader or editor—but not too much attention. Let me know what works and doesn't work for you. I'll pay attention—but not too much attention.

When I submitted three potential columns to the *Boston Globe*, I sent this one and it was published August 1, 1986, nine years to the month of Lee's death. And the reaction to this column assures me that at least a few readers found comfort in it.

> I wake the morning after I fulfilled the lonely task of delivering the family decision to the doctor that Lee, our 20-year-old daughter, should be allowed to die.
>
> Before waking I am aware that my world will never be the same, and I have to ask myself what I do in the morning. I swing my feet toward the floor and push my body up. I push away from the bed and stand up, walk slowly to the bathroom, return, and dress, making decisions about what had once been instinctive habits. And then I stop. What do I do now? I go to the store to buy the morning papers—the *Boston Globe* and the *New York Times*.
>
> At the store Jess, who has lost a son, sees me and says, "It won't get any better, Don."
>
> It seems particularly masculine advice, delivered man to man. As soon as I feel that, I suffer guilt, as if I were saying that men suffer in a special way. But perhaps we do. Women—certainly my wife and my surviving daughters—suffer as much, or more, than men, but each of us suffers alone. And my way of handling it is a veteran's way, taught and learned. And I found strange comfort in this other father's abrupt advice.
>
> It would not get any better. We would learn how to live with it, but we would not get beyond it and recover. We would not forget Lee.

At the beginning of that August week our sunny middle daughter, healthy, in love with Paul, was preparing to transfer to the New England Conservatory to study the oboe. At the end of the week she had survived Reye's Syndrome, but lay terribly still—healthy, beautiful but with flat brain waves.

It will be nine years this August, and it doesn't get any better, at least not that much better. I can, sometimes, hear an oboe solo she played without rushing to turn the radio off but I still meet her on the street or crossing campus; evenings or mornings, she stands smiling, at the edge of the living room door. She is the unspoken inhabitant of my life.

Through her dying and afterwards, I realized I had been consciously trying to be a man and holding hard to what I learned in the infantry and tested in combat. That male code I had often found dangerously silly in an academic world of changing consciousness. I call myself a feminist, but during the days at the hospital we all drew on what wells of strength we had. I was surprised how much I drew on the lessons of war.

In Basic Training I went on forced marches where I got my second wind—and my third. I found I had reserves I didn't know I had. I could crawl under live fire; I could jump out of a perfectly good airplane. Once, when my chute did not open, I opened my reserve, got it tangled with another jumper, took the knife off my leg, cut myself free, jiggled my own chute half open and landed OK. In training I was told that machine guns rose during a burst of fire. That's the time to crawl forward, an unnatural act. In combat, I practiced it. I survived and returned home, surprised to be alive.

But I did not like the Army and hated war in the way a person can who has found, firsthand, what he and other human beings can do to each other. I had not been the professional Veteran, did not join the Reserve or the Legion, never tried to get back into uniform (fat chance, pun intended) and march in a Memorial Day parade, but when I had to remove "extraordinary means" from my father, had to convince the nurses two years later to let my mother go, and now had to attend to a daughter's dying, I turned back to the manly attitudes and tricks of survival I had tested under fire.

I was not afraid that week—and afterwards—to weep, and I did. But I also knew that a man, a father, was supposed to be strong, so I played the role of the father as I had played the role of the paratrooper. I fooled myself and was strong.

When things got too much, I apologized to my family in the tiny waiting room, lay down on the hard floor and napped as I had under shellfire. I am still blessed and guilty that I can at night turn off the thoughts that will prohibit sleep, a skill my wife has never learned, a skill that was born in terror under fire. It is a veteran's trick of acceptance and detachment.

And so, Lee, we have all learned to survive by whatever toughness we can draw on. My survival has, to a large degree, been a strange gift of war. You would have seen the irony in that. And as much as you always wanted us to be happy, I think you would understand the hard comfort of the fact that it doesn't get any better, and never will. We won't forget.

IV

SITTING TO WRITE

TWENTY

GETTING UNDER THE LIGHTNING

Writing is primarily not a matter of talent, of dedication, of vision, of vocabulary, of style, but simply a matter of sitting. The writer is the person who writes. The best writing is self-commanded, and most writers have the problems of life: eating, paying the mortgage, getting the kids off to school, responding to those to whom they have commitments. The world intrudes.

Only a handful of writers can attend to their own work full-time. Most writers in the United States hold staff writing jobs, teach, doctor, lawyer, sell, buy, serve society in a way which society will reward with salary—and health benefits.

At times I found it hard to accept this double life, getting up early to write or staying up late when my peers in other professions could lawyer or doctor or insure from eight to five. But then I would remind myself that writing isn't a profession, it is a calling—and the only one calling is yourself. I had no choice; I had to write.

Recently Annie Dillard put all this talk of discipline and work habits in perspective:

> *Let me close with a word about process. There's a common notion that self-discipline is a freakish peculiarity of writers—that writers differ from other people by possessing enormous and equal portions of talent and willpower. They grit their powerful teeth and go into their little rooms. I think that's a bad misunderstanding of what impels the writer. What impels the writer is a deep love for and respect for language, for literary forms, for books. It's a privilege to muck about in sentences all morning. It's a challenge to bring off a powerful effect, or to tell the truth about something. You don't do it from willpower; you do it from an abiding passion for the field. I'm sure it's the same in every other field.*

> *Writing a book is like rearing children—willpower has very little to do with it. If you have a little baby crying in the middle of the night, and if you depend only on willpower to get you out of bed to feed the baby, that baby will starve. You do it out of love. Willpower is a weak idea; love is strong. You don't have to scourge yourself with a cat-o'-nine-tails to go to the baby. You go to the baby out of love for that particular baby. That's the same way you go to your desk. There's nothing freakish about it. Caring passionately about something isn't against nature, and it isn't against human nature. It's what we're here to do.*

Whether we are motivated by love, hunger for fame, or just plain hunger, the fact is that most of us find it hard to get our rump in the writer's chair and keep it there. I wish more could. I don't need the competition, but most of my students and the teachers with whom I have worked could be writers. But whether they are writers or not, writing is an act of therapy and an act of power. Armed with the craft of writing, each individual can decide to use that craft or not.

Our students have important messages to deliver and their own language in which to deliver them. We need to hear their voices and they need to hear their own voices. I hope the following selections will help make more of those voices heard.

And I hope that by taking the teacher into the writer's studio, the teacher will see the possibility of the powerful interaction I have experienced between practicing my craft and sharing that craft with my students. Each activity has stimulated the other.

Writing is easy; it's *not* writing that's hard. The writing comes in a bolt; one moment there is nothing and the next there are a thousand words or more, an always unexpected burst of language that is frightening in the power and complexity of its connections, in the sudden clarity where there was confusion a moment before. It's easy to receive the bolt of lightning when it strikes; what's hard is to create conditions that cause lightning to strike—morning after morning—and then wait for the bolt to hit.

Every six weeks or less I get drawn away from the writing—too many interruptions, too much traveling, too much talking about writing, too many meetings, too much nonwriting writing (letters, memos, handouts)—and I have to reteach myself the conditions that allow me to receive writing. These include:

SITTING

WAITING

Lightning hits twice, thrice, a thousand times in the same spot. Flannery O'Connor teaches and comforts me: "Every morning between 9 and 12 I go to my room and sit before a piece of paper. Many times I just sit for three hours with no ideas coming to me. But I know one thing: If an idea does come between 9 and 12, I am there ready for it." She was a magnificent sitter; I wish I could sit as well as Flannery O'Connor.

But sitting has its price. Watch writers waddle across campus and you'll notice they grow broad in the beam, their spines shaped like a question mark, their necks crane forward as they peer at you. Writers are sedentary hunters. They wait for the lightning and keep making New Year's resolutions to sit better a dozen times a year—each resolution is aimed at getting the rump in *the* chair on a regular basis. My present resolutions:

- *Only* write before lunch.
- *Never* write after lunch.

If I write in the afternoon and the evening—when I don't write very well anyway—I put off all those things that interfere with writing but have to be done. Soon they build up and steal my mornings. Then I don't write and become mean.

IMMERSION

I am involved with the subjects I write about long before I know I am going to write about them. And I am involved to a degree I cannot demand of my students. I am on duty twenty-four hours a day, reading, observing, absorbing, connecting, thinking, rehearsing. The subjects I write about are never far from me: the death of my daughter, the questions about my family and myself I am still trying to answer, the war in which I learned I could kill, the way I see others and myself behaving toward each other, the process of learning to write.

Of course, I suffer all the guilts that my students admit and my colleagues usually try to hide. I do not read enough; I do not read effectively enough; I do not read what I should read. I'm not up on the latest work—or I do not understand it. And yet I realize that never a day goes by that I am not grabbing hold of new information about the subjects on which I write. I am a continual student, and that is the resource from which all my writing is drawn.

NEED

Writing for me is more than a vocation; it is a need; it is the way in which I make meaning of my world, the way I collect and relate, explore and comprehend, speculate and test in a dialogue with myself that never ends. If you don't have to write, don't.

I don't (and didn't) write to win tenure, to get promoted, to make money (with this energy and commitment I could have made eleven killings in real estate). I don't write for fame, since I had a teaspoon of fame early and found it was both irrelevant—the process of doing the writing was long gone and I was doing new work—and unsatisfying—win one award and you want a dozen more.

I write because I have to write. Meet writers and they look ordinary because they are ordinary. It's important for students to become familiar with that ordinariness. We have many writers in our department and our students learn from their ordinariness. "Gee, I look more like a writer than Murray, perhaps I . . ."

But you'll never know writers as well in person—even lovers, wives, children?—as you'll know them from their writing. And you won't know them from their writing either. The more open and revealing writers are, the more they may be hidden, the more successful at camouflaging their necessary loneliness.

Writers are here and there at the same time, living while observing their living. Talking to you we are also often talking to ourselves in an interior dialogue which discusses—silently, secretly—what is being done while it is being done. Writing, for the writer, is an essential kind of talking to yourself. You may like what you hear, be amused, stirred, stimulated, angered, encouraged, startled, comforted, but what you are hearing is only part of the conversation by which the writer lives. If you don't have to talk to yourself, if you have no need to teach yourself by writing, then writing may not be essential to you. Talk, play the flute, paint, build a bridge, do business, bake, hammer, and do not worry that you're not writing. Society has never said it needed writers. We are all self-appointed and rise to speak without being called upon.

I have no choice. I must write to answer questions I am asking myself, to solve problems that I find interesting, to bring an order into an area where the confusion terrifies me. Donald Barthelme said, "Write about what you're most afraid of," and I nod, smiling. I write to hang on.

READERS

I also write from an external need, to share what I am thinking with that tiny audience of intimates whose respect I need and with whom I am learning. I need to share my writing with my wife, my daughters, Don Graves, Chip Scanlan, Tom Newkirk, Jane Hansen, Carol Berkenkotter (who makes science of pauses, hesitations, and what is left out), and a changing audience of readers, always small, mostly writers themselves, who may respond or not. If hundreds or thousands of other readers tune in later, that's nice, but I really can't see that vague, distant audience who will not see the work until I am two or three projects down the road anyway. Publication is nice, but it is not significant enough to motivate me to place my rear end in the writing chair each morning. I write mostly for myself—and a handful of patient friends.

CRITICS

I must confess those friendly readers on whom I depend are appreciators mostly. I am too immature to enjoy criticism; more sadist than masochist. I hunger for appreciation, and my writing takes its largest steps forward after praise, not criticism, no matter how much the constructive—or even destructive—comments are deserved. As a teacher I try to remember that.

I find little criticism relevant to the work in progress. Critics usually have their own idea of what I should say—based on their own beliefs—and how I should say it—based on their own ideas of good writing. Even the praise of nonwriting critics has little relationship to the writing in progress, and it can even be destructive—if that's what they think I am saying, I'm really in trouble.

INVITATIONS

When I receive an invitation to write a chapter such as this, to produce a journal article, to give a talk, I try to combine an internal need—how *do* I write—with an external need—maybe students *do* need to know what their teachers practice—and I have a condition for receptivity. The lightning may strike again.

INNOCENCE

I have the advantage in being undereducated for my trade. I'd like to be well educated but I am surrounded by people who are too well educated, who know too well what has been done and what can't be done. If you have the disadvantage of a fine and complete education, move out from that center of comfort to where you don't know everything, where there are dark forests, looming mountains, shadows that move, strange noises in the night.

I write out of what I don't know, not what I know, and that exploration of my ignorance makes each draft, the failed ones even more than the successful ones, fascinating, a challenge for another morning. Of course I keep discovering what others already know—but I have the challenge and the joy of exploration.

ACTING

FRAGMENTS

I need something to say—an idea, a subject, a theory, a thesis—but what the lightning bolt leaves is usually just a fragment, a puzzling piece of information, a question without an answer, an answer without a question, a detail, an incomplete observation, a partial pattern, an image, a phrase (a fragment of voice), a problem not yet defined, a feeling of anxiety that may be relieved by writing. Writers have learned to pay attention to fragments that others do not even see lying at their feet.

CONCENTRATION

Well, yes. Perhaps stubbornness is what I mean, a dumb determination to finish what is started. But that isn't all of it—a good deal of it—but not all of it. With all the necessary distraction and all the unnecessary interruptions, I need to be able, at the time of prewriting and writing, to concentrate on one task over all the others—at least for an hour, an hour and a half, two hours, half an hour, fifteen minutes, ten, less, but still a moment when I fall out of the world, forgetting time, place, duty, and listen to the writing flowing through me to the page.

DEADLINES

I have to have deadlines that are self-imposed or imposed by others, and I confess that the deadlines of others are more powerful than my own. I have to be patient, to wait, to listen, not to force the writing, but the day-by-day, hour-by-hour, and louder and louder and louder goose-step march of an approaching deadline is one of the most powerful lightning rods on my study roof.

PLANNING

I spend most of my time planning what I may write, making lists, making notes, making more lists, talking to myself in my head and in my daybook. I try not to be too formal about how I plan—planning should be, above all, play—and I try not to write too early but wait. I will not force the writing—forced writing sounds like forced writing—but hold back until I have to write. The draft must demand to be written. I want to write when I can*not* not write. When the writing will come easily, without effort.

DRAFTING

I write fast. I rush forward, writing so fast my handwriting becomes incomprehensible even to me, typing beyond my ability so that the letters and words pile up on the word processor like a train wreck, or dictating so fast I can produce 500 words or 1,000 in an hour; 1,500, 2,000, 2,500, 3,000 in a morning.

The speed itself is important. The best accidents of phrase or meaning—or meaning illuminated by phrase—occur when I am writing too fast.

REWRITING

I'm doing it less and less. Rewriting means the creation of a new draft with major changes in subject, focus, order, voice. These days I plan more and rewrite less. But when I rewrite, I start back at the beginning, seeing the subject anew, not through the vision of the past draft. Rewriting is mostly replanning.

REVISING

Of course these first drafts—or third or fourth drafts—will have to be fussed with, cut, added, reordered, shaped, and polished so they appear on the page with the effort hidden, all the spontaneous touches neatly in place. That's fun, once you have a draft in hand.

VOICE

Most important of all, voice. I do not begin to write until I hear the voice of the writing, and when that voice fades during the drafting, rewriting/replanning, or revising, I stop, make myself quiet, and listen until I hear it again. The music of the writing, more than anything else, teaches me what I am learning about the subject, what I am feeling about the subject, how I must write the subject to make those thoughts and feelings clear.

And when the writing doesn't go well, the most effective tactic is to listen, quietly, carefully to the writing. If I listen closely enough the writing will tell me what to say and how to say it. As Jayne Anne Phillips says, "It's like being led by a whisper."

BELIEVING

ACCEPTANCE

Of what I am, not what I wish I were. Acceptance of the writing I am receiving, remembering that intention is the enemy and surprise the friend. William Stafford reminds me:

> I can imagine a person beginning to feel that he's not able to write up to that standard he imagines the world has set for him. But to me that's surrealistic. The only standard I can rationally have is the standard I'm meeting right now . . . you should be more willing to forgive yourself. It really doesn't make any difference if you are good or bad today. The *assessment* of the product is something that happens *after* you've done it.

The way I write today is the way I can write today. I must accept what the lightning delivers and make use of it. I can't imagine another text, written by someone other than myself, into being. I must accept myself to write—and accept the fact that writing reveals, not just what I say but who I am. Of course, I am afraid I will be found out—and I will.

SELF-CONSCIOUSNESS

I used to worry that my compulsive study of my craft—"Don't think" we used to tell the goalie, knowing that if he thought, the puck would be in the net before the decision was made—would paralyze my writing or at least cause terminal constipation. Perhaps it hasn't helped, but I had no choice; long before I taught or made a profession of studying the writing process, I was a student of my craft. Aren't most writers?

Writing is luck but writers are repeatedly lucky. They hit the lottery number again and again. To be a writer, you have to be unself-conscious enough to allow the writing to strike, to allow it to surprise you, to accept the gift. But you have to be prepared—calculatingly prepared—to be lucky, and you have to have the cunning to allow what is written to appear spontaneously in the reader's mind. William Shakespeare: "The truest poetry is the most feigning."

ESCAPING CRAFT

Skill is our goal and our prison. We have to learn the tricks of our trade. We apprentice ourselves to our craft to learn to write better—and we do. Our words are surer, stronger; our sentences grow lean; our paragraphs are packed. We learn to turn a phrase, to shape, to polish until our writing becomes professional, polished, slick. Our pieces are so well constructed they say what we have already said—better and better and better until we are hidden within our too well-constructed pages. We are safe. Skilled. Craftpersons. Publishing scholars. Pros.

We have constructed a prison around ourselves with our own carefully crafted words and we can't see out, can't hear out; can't see what needs attending to; can't hear the voice of what we might write on the outside. So we have the obligation to break out, to push beyond our skills, to try and write what we cannot yet write but what needs writing in ways that we have not yet found so that we write with less polish and craft and learn the craft of not finishing the writing too much, to make it rough enough (to leave the roughness in [to remember what Amiri Baraka wrote, "Hunting is not those heads on the wall"]) to let our writing be finished enough so that it helps us do our thinking but not so finished that our readers can only stand and gaze in awe at our clever thinking when we should invite them and allow them to do their own thinking, messing around with our drafts so they will not respect the text too much.

would I stop and mess around with a finished text, unpolish it, unshape it, incomplete it?

you know it

if I can learn how.

know your craft

yeah—that's the complicated thing. Exactly. If I get to know how to do that too well, then I'm crafty again, blinded by my carefully unfinished drafts.

But we *do* want to allow the reader to get into the writing with us, so that the writing doesn't get in the way of the experience of writing/reading reading/writing, so we aren't blinded by the conventions, deafened by the traditions, made dumb by our own hard-earned craft.

unfinishing a text

it is necessary and will be necessary again

as we learn how to get out of the way—how to write rough—when we become crafty enough to allow the writing to appear spontaneous. Even when it is really spontaneous, when we have not got in the way, then what we have done is to learn a new craft, a new skill, a new way of digging in where it is safe and the lightning can never find us. so

INCOMPLETENESS

This is a new draft, but it isn't the last word on how writing is made or even how I make writing. It contradicts some things I've said about how I write, and what I say in the future will produce more contradictions. I just wrote a new version of *A Writer Teaches Writing* without opening the previous edition; I am writing a novel without referring to the last draft. I don't want to be imprisoned by my own ideas and my own words. I don't want to be either consistent or proudly inconsistent. I want, each morning to find out what I have to say that day. Each publication is nothing more or less than an entry in my daybook where I talk to myself about what I don't know and need to know, imagining answers to questions that really can't be answered: How do people stay with us after they die? Why did my family do what it did to itself? Why are we able to make war—and to be proud of it? Why did I survive? How do people take experience and re-create it in the minds of others through some squiggles on paper? How do we learn from writing? How can we help others learn to learn from writing? I don't want any questions that have answers—they aren't any fun.

FAITH

Hardest of all for me. Faith that I can write, that I have something to say, that I can find out what it is, that I can make it clear to me, to a reader, that I can write so that the reader is not aware of the writer but the meaning.

Faith enough not to read what is written until the entire draft is done and then not to compare it to what might have been or what others have done, but to listen to the writing, to see in it its own meaning, its own form, to hear its own voice. Faith enough to stand out there all alone and invite the lightning.

TWENTY-ONE
ONE WRITER'S SECRETS

Arriving as a professional writer in the academic world, I was astonished at the importance of publishing to the careers of young academics and even more astonished by their total lack of training for publication. People would talk more easily—often too easily—about their intimate fears and parental drinking customs than how they wrote.

I proposed to the editor of College Composition and Communication, *Richard Larson, that he devote an issue to the practical questions of scholarly life, possibly tied into a special session at the annual convention. That didn't work out, but this article was invited and published after some very wise editorial suggestions from Larson.*

I was very much aware of my own eccentricity—a bustling duckling among swans. I was far from the normal academic, and I hoped that my confessions would inspire others whose counsel might be more helpful to young scholars and researchers. I haven't seen a flood of such helpful material, but I hope that my article has been helpful to a few graduate students or beginning assistant professors.

And I hope that this look backstage at a writer who has been considered "productive" will strip away the mystery and help more teachers write.

It is good form in English department offices and corridors to grump, grouse, growl, even whine about how the writing is going. Such labor, such a dreary business, how grubby, how ridiculous to expect publication, as if an article could reveal the subtleties of a finely tuned mind. The more you publish, the more tactful it is to moan and groan. The danger is that young colleagues, new to the academy, may believe us. They may think we who publish are performing penance, obediently fulfilling a vow to publish out of fear of perishing, when this academic and others will slyly look around to see who is listening, then confess, "writing is fun."

The focus is on writing. That is where writers discover they know more than they knew they knew, where accidents of diction or syntax reveal meaning, where sentences run ahead to expose a thought. If the writing is done, publication—perhaps not this piece but the next or the one after that—will follow. And publishing promises a lifetime of exploration and learning, active membership in a scholarly community, and the opportunity for composition teachers to practice what we preach.

I will share some of the methods that have helped me publish what some would say—and have said—is an excessive number of articles and books on the composing process. I do not do this to suggest that others should work as I work, but as a way to invite others who publish to reveal their own craft so those who join our profession can become productive members of it—and share the secret pleasure in writing which we feel but rarely admit.

ATTITUDES THAT ALLOW WRITING

Our attitudes usually predict and limit our accomplishments. I find that I have to encourage, model, and continually relearn certain attitudes if I want my students to write—and if I want myself to write.

- No publication is the final theological word on a subject. Too many academics believe they have to write *the* article or book on their topic. That is impossible. Each publication is merely a contribution to a continuous professional conversation. I was paralyzed by the idea I had to deliver the Truth—Moses-like; I began to write when I realized all I had to do was speculate, question, argue, create a model, take a position, define a problem, make an observation, propose a solution, illuminate a possibility to participate in a written conversation with my peers. There is an increasing emphasis on research, but still it is not necessary to wait to report on the ultimate, all-inclusive research project.
- There is no need to be consistent. Learning does not stop with publication. I continue to learn from my students, my colleagues, my reading, my observations, my researches,

my teaching, and my writing. I learn from each draft. Change is essential to learning. Of course, I will contradict myself from time to time.

- Ask your own questions and find your own answers. Few people talked about the writing process when I started publishing in this field. No matter, it was what interested me. I didn't think my articles would get published, but I sent them off, and most of them were.
- Use the mail. My articles, poems, and short stories that don't get into the mail never get published. Submit. Maybe you'll find an editor who is suffering empty journal terror. We like to believe that all acceptances are rational and all rejections irrational. I've learned from participating on both sides of the process that acceptances are often as irrational as rejections.
- Start at the top. Maybe the best journals will not publish my stuff, but at least they've had their chance.
- Remember what Al Pacino said: "Forget the career and do the work." The doing is far more satisfying than the done. The discoveries made during the writing—the thinking process—are far more exciting than receiving half a dozen copies of a journal with your article in it a year or two later.
- If it isn't fun, don't do it. The lack of fun will show. Since both acceptance and rejection are irrational, you might as well have the satisfaction of doing what you want to do. We are lucky to have a vocation of scholarship, a calling. But who is calling? Ourselves. We are all self-appointed authorities. If our work is not our play, then we should quit, take a job, and make some real money.

SOME TRICKS OF THE ACADEMIC TRADE

As you develop the attitudes that will allow you to publish, then you may be able to develop techniques and strategies that help get the work done. Some tricks of my trade are:

- Keep a planning notebook with you to play in at the office, at home, in the car, on the airplane, at faculty meetings (especially at faculty meetings), while you're watching television, sitting in a parking lot, or eating a lonely lunch. Such play has allowed me to write on the advantages of writer's block, to catch a glimpse of ideas about planning and vision, which have become talks, articles, and sections of my books. I pay most attention to the questions that keep reoccurring, the connections that surprise me, the patterns that give the familiar an interesting unfamiliarity.

The notebook, which I call a daybook, will make it possible for you to use fragments of time, and fragments of time are all that most of us really have. Fifteen minutes, ten, five, two, one, less. In this book you can make lists, notes, diagrams, collect the quotes and citations, paste in key articles and references, sketch outlines, draft titles, leads, endings, key paragraphs that will make it possible for you to be ready to write when you have an hour, or two, or three clear.

- Write daily. I try to follow the counsel of Horace, Pliny, Trollope, Updike: *nulla dies sine linea*—never a day without a line—but a line for me does not mean a polished sentence of finished prose. It means the daily habit of talking to myself in writing, playing with ideas, letting a piece of writing grow and ripen until it is ready to be written. It is intellectual play, self-indulgent, introspective, and immensely satisfying. Each time I play with an idea I purposely do not look back at my previous notes. Then, after I finish the daily entry, I look back to see what I'd said on the same subject before and add ideas that seem worth adding. In this way I keep turning over the compost of my thoughts and discover what I didn't know I knew.

The academic schedule encourages the illusion that you can get your writing done on the day free from teaching, during the semester with a lower teaching load, between semesters, next summer, or on sabbatical. Nonsense. When those times come you can't suddenly take up an alien craft. The productive scholar is in the habit of writing, at least notes, at least lists, at least fragmentary drafts, at least something that keeps the topic alive and growing so that writing will come that is ready to be written.

If I have a good title; a well-honed first sentence, paragraph, or page; a hint of the ending; a list of three to five points that will lead me toward that end, I can put a draft on hold, for weeks, if necessary, and not lose the freshness of the first draft that will follow.

- Pick the best time for your writing and try to protect that time. Be selfish. Writing is the best preparation for teaching. I schedule my teaching in the afternoon, which is my normal slump period. In the afternoon I respond to the stimulus of the class, the conference, or the meeting. But only in the morning do I respond to the stimulus of the blank page.

My most difficult problem is to keep the moat around my writing time filled with alligators and absolutely terrifying snakes. I do not spring out of bed ready and eager to write. I need time I can waste in which my subconscious can prepare itself for the period at the writing desk. And I need time on the other end of the writing period. If I start to write too close to when I have to be at school, the demands of teaching invade my mind and I cannot concentrate on the writing task. Bernard Malamud described this too rare concentration best when he said, "If it is winter in the book, spring surprises me when I look up." Concentration is not only important for the work but to the mental health of the worker. My agent did not want me to accept a teaching job. I think she said it would be like "being bitten to death by ducks." I didn't know how wise she was. It was far easier to achieve concentration in the confusion of the city room on deadline than in the distracting, fragmented academic world. Wasn't it Mencken who said, "Campus politics are so vicious because the stakes are so low"? The hardest thing I do is to find time, to sit, to wait, to listen for writing.

- Read widely as well as deeply; read writing as well as writing about writing. Our training teaches us to read critically and narrowly, and it is vital to probe deeply into a specialty or a text. The best ideas, however, come from connecting information from different disciplines. We should also be bottom-feeders, gobbling up everything that comes our way—reading a book on science, a line of poetry, a newspaper story, a picture in a museum, a question by a student, a move by a hockey player, a pattern of music, a comment overheard in an elevator, the look on a face seen from a bus window, reading our world in such a way that our scholarly work is fed by connections from the world, so that the work we do is in context. If it is fed by the world, it may, if we are effective, return to feed the world.
- Keep a list of questions to which you want to seek answers, answers for which you wish to form questions, territories of fascinating ignorance you wish to explore. How do writers choose and use test readers? How does thinking style affect writing process? How does a writing task change process? Does MTV have a positive influence on the writing or reading process? How do good student writers read their evolving drafts? Keep moving around, and don't be trapped in your own specialty. Some people took my work on

revision more seriously than I took it myself, and I consciously moved toward studying prewriting. Use your list to turn class presentations, invitations to give talks and workshops, opportunities to publish articles or chapters or books to your own advantage. Set your own agenda, so that each year you sniff along two or three new trails of thought.

- Put yourself on the spot. Accept teaching, speaking, and writing assignments that are just beyond reach—but within reach. Join local, regional, and national organizations within our discipline and participate so that you become a working member of the profession. In this way you will learn what others are doing and you will have a balance wheel to counter the niggling problems within your own department that can so easily get out of proportion.
- Respect your own judgment. Of course, you should be aware of the scholarship that has preceded you, but pay close attention to what you see with your own eyes, hear with your own ears, think with your own mind. Ours is not only a profession of confirmation but also of exploration. I have published personal answers to my own questions about how writers read and write, not so much to provide answers as to provoke research, since I have found few people dealing with questions in our discipline which I believe are obvious—and fundamental. If I publish my guesses, others may respond with their truths.
- Write for yourself. Don't try to figure out what other people want but try to figure out what you have to say and how it can be best said. The standards for academic writing are contradictory and confused. In many cases what is considered to be the standard forces bad writing. Most editors want good writing. Decide how best to say what you have to say. You may have to compromise your voice to be published in some journals that require educationese or excessive formality, but certainly do not compromise in advance and write in a parody of academic writing. Submit writing that is as clear and graceful as you can make it.
- Write early. Remember that you are not writing the ultimate article that will cause all other scholars to pack up their tents and go home. Write early to find out what you know and what you need to know. Publish early to participate in the game of academic exploration. You will learn by committing yourself and by developing colleagues in other schools who are interested in the same topics.

- Yet be patient. This is hard for me under any circumstances, for I was born twitching to get on with it, whatever it was. It is often difficult for a young faculty member under the threat of tenure. To be patient, it is important to develop a pace appropriate to the work you are doing. It takes time for ideas to be planted and cultivated. There has to be a habit of work that allows this to happen. Those of us who publish extensively are harvesting what has been put down years before.

  Most of my articles have a five-year history. It takes about a year for my reading and thinking and conversing and note making to work their way toward a topic which is more interesting than I had expected. Once I recognize the topic's potential significance I play around with it for at least a year, taking advantage of opportunities to talk on the subject or to teach it. I receive reactions from my colleagues and my students, and then in the third year I may accept a chance to give a paper or to attempt an article. Now I begin to plan in earnest. My play becomes more intense, and eventually there is a paper or a draft. My colleagues, often my students, and my editors or audiences react. In the fourth year it is usually rewritten and edited. And in the fifth year it is published. And to those who do not work continually, it appears as if I had suddenly produced another piece of work, when it is really the product of a rather plodding habit of thinking through writing.
- Write to discover what you have to say. You do not have to know what you want to say to be able to say it. Just the opposite. You have to write to find out what you have to say. This is the never-ending attraction of writing. We write more than we intend to write, reaching beyond our goals, finding within ourselves how much more we know than we thought we knew. We need to write drafts with such speed and intensity that they propel us toward unexpected possibility. Then we can learn from those drafts as we revise and clarify. We are, first of all, students to our own writing.
- Write without notes. Much academic writing is poor because it is note-bound. Write out of what is in your head; write what you remember from your notes. What you forget is probably what should be forgotten, but you will have time after the draft is completed to go back and check your notes. If you absolutely have to have key references in front of you, use as few as possible in producing the first

draft in which speed and flow produce both grace and the unexpected connections which are the mark of good thinking and good writing.

- Lower your standards. I carry two paragraphs of counsel from poet and teacher William Stafford with me at all times and turn to them morning after morning:

> I believe that the so-called "writing block" is a product of some kind of disproportion between your standards and your performance. . . . One should lower his standards until there is no felt threshold to go over in writing. It's *easy* to write. You just shouldn't have standards that inhibit you from writing.
>
> I can imagine a person beginning to feel that he's not able to write up to that standard he imagines the world has set for him. But to me that's surrealistic. The only standard I can rationally have is the standard I'm meeting right now. . . . You should be more willing to forgive yourself. It really doesn't make any difference if you are good or bad today. The *assessment* of the product is something that happens *after* you've done it.

- Write easily. If it doesn't come, don't force it. Forced writing reads like forced writing. Putter. Fiddle around. Stare out the window. Keep coming back until your head is ready to produce the writing almost without effort. Hard writing usually means that you're not ready to write. You have to start the writing process early enough ahead of deadline to allow the essential backing up—the planning and rehearsal that will eventually allow the draft to flow. As Virginia Woolf said, "I am going to hold myself from writing it till I have it impending in me: grown heavy in my mind like a ripe pear; pendant, gravid, asking to be cut or it will fall."
- Write with your ear. Writers feel that the voice may be the most important element in writing, and few writers will proceed until they hear the voice of the text. Voice is the magic ingredient in writing. It carries all the meanings that are not within the world. It allows the individual writer to speak to the individual reader. It is style and grace and tone, and it reveals the character of the writer as well as the content of the text.

  Listen for a voice in fragments of writing in your notebook, in lines rehearsed in your head, in early drafts. Your voice will help you understand what you have to say and how you have to say it, and a strong voice will be the element that will make significant content available to your colleagues. It will bring you publication, and publication will bring you the opportunity for further exploration.

- Write writing. Try a poem, a familiar essay that can be published on the editorial page of a newspaper, a novel, a TV or movie script, a magazine article, a short story, a news story, a play. The experience of writing writing, not just writing about writing, will help the soul, the scholarship, and the craft. The poem may not be anthologized, but it may reveal a leap of language, a turn of a line that will free your prose and allow the poet's skills of grace and clarification that are so often missing from academic writing.
- Reach out to colleagues. This will be your most difficult—and the most valuable—professional activity. The academic world can be a closed place, a landscape of monasteries and convents, moated castles and isolated villages. Even when I am intimidated by the walls and parapets erected by colleagues I try to remember how lonely they must be, imprisoned within their knowledge and high standards.

  Invite colleagues to lunch, suggest a cup of coffee, ask a colleague to visit your class, set up brown bag lunches of colleagues to share common interests, arrange team teaching, travel together to conventions. Most of all, reach out by sharing your own drafts. I have received insult, scorn, ridicule, jocular remarks that burn like acid, and, worst of all, silence. And for many good reasons. Most of us do not know how to respond, and we are all busy. But through this reaching out in my own department, across my campus, to colleagues I meet at meetings, to students and former students, to friends in other fields, I begin to develop a small group of helpful colleagues in each of the areas in which I work. I share work with them; they share work with me. They know how to give me criticism. But even more important, they know how to give me strength and support. They know because they are writing, are exposed and vulnerable in the same way I am. If we can discover the attitudes and the techniques that allow us to write we will experience the joy of writing. First will come the lonely surprises that occur on the page. A life of writing is a life of learning. There are the tiny discoveries that may not shake the universe but that may bring a grin or sometimes even a laugh of victory from the academic at the desk. Writing is more likely than teaching to produce an active intellectual life and to be a defense against boredom, burnout, and age. The writer can always ask new questions and draft new answers, can always explore new territories and experience new genres.

Writing is also an extension of teaching and a stimulation to teaching. Our students, wave after wave, may change their lingo and their dress, but they remain at the same intellectual level when they come to us. We need to be practitioners of our discipline if we are to stay alive and if we are to bring new ideas to our teaching. Publishing allows us to belong to a large community of scholars. We can contribute to that community, and the more we put in, the more we will take away that is of value to both ourselves and our students. Publication obviously has its rewards—promotion, tenure, occasional recognition in an elevator at a convention, and even royalties, although most books I have produced have never made their advance. But the more you experience those rewards, the more you realize that the real satisfaction comes during the process of the writing itself. The true rewards are internal—the satisfaction of asking your own questions and finding your own answers.

TWENTY-TWO
FOUR NEWSPAPER COLUMNS ON WRITING

In 1986 as I moved drafts around the office, I realized there were three pieces I had written in workshop sessions with teachers, students, or journalists that had a similar perspective: they were written after my sixtieth birthday and I was looking far back and briefly forward from that position.

In a sudden burst of oh-what-the-hellness, I polished the three pieces up—one on an angina patient's experiences in a strange hospital, another on dieting, the other on the death of a daughter and how the lessons of combat helped me survive—and sent them off to the editor of the Boston Globe, *suggesting a column "Over Sixty."*

I heard nothing for weeks and imagined Globe *editors sitting around giggling at the evidence that another writing teacher can't practice his preaching. Then I got a phone call. The monthly column would begin the first of next month and the first three columns were fine. When I retired from the university sixteen months later, the column began to be published every other week.*

It has been nothing but a delight to write these columns. It allows me to make use of my living and that making, of course, makes me more aware of the world in which I am reporting of the experience of growing old. They are what my high-school teacher would call personal essays.

The topics appear, unbidden, in my daybook, inspired by a reaction to what I am feeling, observing, thinking, doing. What is interesting is that they arrive as a line, something we should teach our students and something I document through much of this book. I don't write down a summary topic or thesis statement. I scrawl something that is less than a sentence but more than a phrase. It is a line written in a private language, but it is a line that has enough tension within it to release a sequence of thought in the play we call writing.

Here are some lines from my daybooks that have produced columns. Yes, I think the lines produced the columns. I followed the line to see where it would take me.

- *I've picked up a few trades/crafts in my day [The third column published here.]*
- *programmed by our parents—y chromo, heart—behavior [Not written yet but I can hear the voice expressing the joke our parents play on us, that we play on our children.]*
- *playground [That one word reminds me of the territory I hated most as a child. The tension is within the word.]*
- *touch—old—NYT—hands in middle of the night—football—parents' marriage bed [Very private language but a piece was published from this sequence of notes.]*
- *i'm not going to write a column about Hannah's wedding. [Of course I did and that was the lead.]*
- *sleeping late—guilt [All I needed for a column.]*
- *i didn't know it would be a full-time job to do nothing [Another column.]*
- *Boston—drive to market—durgin park 1.25—narrow guage—summer street—singing—alleys—casino burlesque [Not yet a column but it will be. I find a potential lead in my notes I'd forgotten: "Each of us has a secret place where we went as a teenager, our own private world, different from our parents." I wonder if that lead will take me to Boston as I expected or not.]*
- *when you're old, you ought to have a young doctor [Overheard and stolen.]*
- *report from the front. Over sixty you keep an eye cocked for the big surprise. You have to take care it won't come ahead of its time and live as if it couldn't. [This was the scrawled beginning of a column written after a heart attack and an angiogram on the eve of bypass surgery.]*

I think we should encourage our students to play with language so that they will find their own lines and then follow them, writing so fast and uncritically that they will discover where the line leads.

For a year or more, my columns were written in the following manner:

- *A line, and possibly a few notes, in my daybook.*
- *A lead and about ten to fifteen lines written on a morning. This took about fifteen minutes.*
- *A complete draft, written as fast as possible, in forty-five minutes to an hour. A draft is four to five double-spaced pages.*
- *A careful revision and editing, cutting, developing, pacing, tuning the voice, correcting.*

I still seem to write the line the same way, but to do the entire column in one sitting, it takes about two hours in all.

The following column was inspired by the experience described. A hand surgeon told me he was going to be a writer when he retired. I wrote him the following unsolicited advice. I sent him the column, but he never responded.

---

so you want to be a writer

"I'm going to write when I retire," said the hand surgeon. "When I get tired of 80-hour weeks, I'm going to sit by a pool in Hawaii and be a writer."

The ex-Marine would have received a right cross from the former paratrooper, whose writing hadn't gone at all well that morning, except that the doctor was wiggling a long needle around in my writing fist. Everybody's going to write a book after they retire, lawyers, doctors, taxicab drivers, college presidents, waitresses, airline pilots, call girls, priests, dentists, even my financial adviser.

And they may. There are certainly worse things to do in retirement, such as play golf, bail out a boat, kill a fish on a dock or paint seascapes. Why not write a book? A little research on the bestseller list will convince you that you don't have to know a great deal about our language; what you have to have is a working combination of arrogance and stubbornness. Most successful people, especially surgeons, have that.

Before selling the practice and investing in a pool in Hawaii, I have some counsel based on my experiences as I've arrogantly and stubbornly completed more than a dozen books.

- *Take a typing course, or marry a secretary.* (The secretary adds, "a willing secretary.") I couldn't pass the typing course, so I married a woman who is now sitting with her back to the view in a Nova Scotia vacation cottage accepting dictation. In these days of liberation it may be easier to pay for a pool in Hawaii than to find a woman who would sit by the pool being dictated to by a male.

- *Find something to say—worth saying.* It's easy to ramble, but not easy to find editors and readers who will pay you to ramble. Writing has to have a focus, a purpose, a point of view. Ninety-eight percent of the unsolicited manuscripts I read (readers please note: what I'm doing in retirement is *not* reading unsolicited manuscripts) simply do not have a point. Ask yourself the question an agent used to ask me: "So what?" Having a point looks easy, just like knowing the place to stick that needle in my paw looks easy.
- *Put in.* Most amateur writing is undeveloped. You think the reader knows what you know, or you imagine that since you're writing for general readers that your writing should be general, vague, a sort of blank check for the reader to fill in. Writing that is read is built from revealing details that are specific, insightful, and interesting. Finding just the right specifics can keep you out of the pool for weeks.
- *Take out.* Now writing gets interesting. Once you've considered and reconsidered and reconsidered what to put in, you have to reconsider and reconsider and consider what to take out. The trick is to take out those things that are still, after they are taken out, in the piece. It's easier to swim in an empty pool than to understand how you can stimulate the reader's mind so that there is more in the reading than there is on the page.
- *Move it around.* After you've put it in and taken it out, you're ready to move around what's left. It often takes all morning to jiggle some sentences or paragraphs so that they create a meaningful meaning. And it can take all the next morning to untangle the mess. All you have to do, really, is to figure out the questions the readers will ask when they read your piece, and answer them in the order the readers will ask them. Sometimes it takes weeks to mess around until you find the natural order of information, the one that is obvious after you've found it. Then you can spend a few more days to put in the touches that make it all sound spontaneous.
- *Read as a reader.* If you want to publish your own books with the profits from selling your practice, then you can just sit back and read what you've written, smiling with pride. If you want to get paid for it, you have to stand back and read what is on the page, not what you hoped was on the page. I find it helpful to role-play a specific reader, someone who is intelligent, but basically uninterested in

my subject. I read aloud and hear what I have to say with my reader's ears. After doing this you'll cancel the plans to go deep-sea fishing with the other retirees and start rewriting. Rewriting. Rewriting.

- *Find an editor.* An editor is someone, like a doctor, whom you don't want to know but have to. The editor will ask all of the questions you have avoided asking yourself. You will rewrite. Rewrite. Rewrite.
- *Use the mail.* Don't worry about all those other retirees who tell you they are writing books. Most of them are talking about writing, not writing. Those who do not write have Depostalize Syndrome. They are incapable of putting their manuscripts in the mail. Publishers—look at what they are stuck with publishing—are looking for better stuff. Give them a chance to discover you, and you may find that, in your retirement years, you have become an author.

If you become a writer you slowly discover that the writing itself, painful as it may have been, is the best part of the writing process. No one knows you're an author, even after publication. If you tell them they look at you with suspicion. You don't look any different from anyone else. How can you be an author? Fame is no problem. Neither is money. Most books pay the author, when you figure back, about 3 cents an hour, and in my case two-thirds of that goes to my advising-editing-typing partner.

But you can work on one thing. You can polish a rejoinder and be ready when your lawyer, your minister, your auto mechanic, your insurance salesman, your doctor says they are going to retire and become writers. In the future my response will be, "I'm going to become a brain surgeon when I retire and make people happy."

The next column has a curious history. While writing the second edition of A Writer Teaches Writing, *I wrote the draft of an essay, "The Weight of Sunlight on a Maple Leaf." I then shared the draft with a seminar I was teaching, along with my own comments, "The Writer Reads." I eventually decided against including the essay in my book but held onto it anyway, thinking that perhaps, just perhaps, I could do something with it later.*

Years later, having forgotten in my conscious mind about the original essay, I wrote and published "Reflections from a Sick Bed" for my "Over Sixty" column. Until I began dredging up pieces for this collection of essays, did I remember the column's origins.

The column documents how the writer keeps returning to the fundamental experiences which will be a known—or unknown—guiding mystery all the individual's life. Some writers believe that we have all our subjects by the time we are fourteen or fifteen. I certainly believe that is largely true for me, and if it is a truth, then we should encourage our students to look back, explore, reflect, and learn from those experiences which are significant to them.

"THE WEIGHT OF SUNLIGHT ON A MAPLE LEAF"

Every winter when I was a boy, I would come down with the flu or bronchitis, or pneumonia, or whooping cough, or measles—both flavors—or the mumps, or chicken pox. One spring I had my tonsils out; another my appendix. Every ailment had the same treatment: bed rest. I fussed to be allowed to go out and play, because I was supposed to act like a boy, but I think I knew even then that those days when the worst was over and I drifted between sickness and health would be among the most valuable days of my life.

When I got the fever or the spots or the cough or the aches Dr. Bartlett would be called, and he would shamble into the bedroom and sit down on the bed, and I would let him "have a look." He smelled of tobacco, an alien smell in our house, and medicine—ether if he had come from the operating room—and I took great comfort in those manly odors. He was from Maine, had black hair combed over his bald spot, a long deeply lined face, like a bloodhound's, that was made for bad news (I kept thinking he would say, "heart murmur," and I wouldn't be allowed to play games, but he never did), but his jet black eyes seemed to sparkle, and he knew how to kid a boy as if he were a man. His skin was the color of his leather doctor's bag, and with his dark hair and eyes I liked to believe he had Indian blood. I was a secret Indian. I favored moccasins and spent years trying to walk with my feet straight ahead as I had been told Indians walked.

I believe I remember waking when I was very sick to find him sitting on the edge of the bed. There wasn't much doctors could do then—though I didn't know it—but to wait for the crisis to pass. It was enormous comfort to have Dr. Bartlett visit during the waiting. He didn't say much, or do much; he was not much for words or false hope, but he was a good waiter. Several times the crisis almost didn't pass for me, and years later I was to lose a daughter in a great medical center when she suffered an old-fashioned disease in which there was a crisis. I remember wishing for old Dr. Bartlett with his solemn bloodhound face and his magnificent calm.

Most of the time, of course, he just came, thumped me, stuck a stick down my throat, prescribed medicines that were so bitter they had to do some good, and recommended the old familiar: bed rest. His face nodded seriously at my complaints about staying in bed, but I think his eyes knew that I really wasn't too upset at his command. Today miracle drugs give the illusion of health and prop us up so we can return to busyness almost instantly. But before World War II the body—and mind and spirit—were allowed a time of recovery from illness. It was called convalescence, and I remember it as a special time indeed. It was a time of orange juice and beef tea, a time of more than ordinary maternal concern, of uncles dropping by, and a time when Father, coming back late from a trip, might drop a New York magazine or even a book about business on my bed.

When I arrived at junior, and later senior, high school, far beyond childhood, I thought, I continued to have childhood diseases, and there would be mornings when the guys on their way to school would yell, "Hey, Murray, ya goin' to school?"

My bedroom then was a sleeping porch just above the sidewalk, and I would shove open a window, lean out, and shout, "Naw, I gotta stay in the rest of the week. The doctor says."

I tried to sound angry and put upon so they would believe I wanted to walk to school with them, nudging each other, laughing, talking about girls, playing our way to school by tossing a football two telephone poles down, cut to the left, and laughing at the curses of drivers when the ball bounced out into Hancock Street. And part of me did want to return to the world of streets.

But only part of me, for I can still feel the teenage agony of not belonging—and I can admit it now. I was cowardly, scared, sickly, and felt I was always an outcast—an evangelical Christian in neighborhoods of Irish Catholics or Orthodox Jews, the son of parents with middle-class pretensions in working-class neighborhoods. I didn't know then that everyone else was lonely and scared—and didn't realize then how well I hid myself in my street costume and my street walk, how successful I had become at being someone else.

When I was ordered to bed I had relief from being "outgoing" and healthy and could attend to that part of my life that required privacy and looking inward. In those days family and neighbors worried about a child who had a talent for solitude, who liked to stay indoors, who enjoyed reading and sitting. It can, indeed, be disconcerting to share rooms with someone whose hobby is staring at a world others cannot see.

Although I was a reader I didn't like school, for I found it boring. It was far slower moving than life on the street, yet too busy for proper staring, drifting, dreaming. I did have a good teacher in the sixth grade, a teacher who would surprise me by expecting as much as I, secretly, expected of myself. I was to have another teacher in junior college before my war and still another in college after the war. Later I would learn that one might be enough, that the three I had from first grade into graduate school were over quota. But I didn't know that then, and the school seemed a terrible interruption to my education on the streets and in the sickroom.

And so I felt no regret as the gang swaggered off to school, walking tough, lying to each other, yelling at clumps of other young males, making comments about the clumps of females, while I returned to a bed piled with books and magazines and pads of paper. First I turned on my own bedside radio, a contraption more astonishing than people can imagine today, and listened through the day to a strange sequence of breakfast clubs, soap operas, comedy shows, Fred Hoey broadcasting the Boston Bruins, and, late at night, the great swing bands brought to me "on the radio airwaves" from some ballroom a world away from my Baptist home.

While the radio played, I read. I had no mentor for my reading. Lorna Doone was the highlight of my English classes, and I had long since read beyond any teacher I discovered in the public school. I read haphazardly—not unlike the way I read today—through the library, mixing good authors and bad, reading history and biography—especially of writers and foreign correspondents—reading politics, poetry, religion, and novels, most of all adventure novels that put me with pirates or soldiers or Indians. I also read magazines, all the women's magazines that my mother got, and that new magazine, *Time*, never imagining that I would work there someday. If I had imagined it, I would have imagined it glamorous, not the dreary game of conformity that was like high school, only worse. I read newspapers, three in the morning then, and three at night, reading the funnies and the sports, and page one without any pattern at all.

Today I have little memory of the convalescent mornings and evenings when the world, and presumably I, was busy, when people came and went, and there were things to do. What I remember most were the timeless afternoons. The pillows were marvelously lumpy, the blankets entangled in a glorious mess of sheets, and the bed piled with books and magazines and pads of paper. I might have written or tried to sketch something, and I certainly would have designed some football plays or an Indian fort or a medieval castle. Moving between them all, I would pass into a state that was as far away from the rush of my healthy life as could be imagined.

I started working when I was twelve, learning the addictive dependence on busyness I've been trying to cure ever since. I learned to wait on people, to deliver, to pile and stack and chop and mow and shovel, to drive a truck, to chauffeur, to do office work after school and weekends. I took stairs two or three at a time, ate at meals, before meals, and after meals, and never walked when I could run.

It was a relief to have those long afternoons. I could drift from book to dream to story to daydream, I could wake, sleep, half-wake, half-sleep until I could suspend myself between the conscious and the unconscious, between the reality of a dreary life in a double-decker behind a filling station and a future life that would certainly take me to war, and I knew not where beyond that.

I had a ceiling to which I had thumbtacked *National Geographic* maps, and I would climb Mt. Everest, spend a winter in the Antarctic with Admiral Byrd, sale the Atlantic alone, explore the Amazon. I would read in this book and that, keeping half a dozen going at the same time, and I would travel into the future with Buck Rogers, into the past with Kenneth Roberts or Rafael Sabatini, and into the world of the Red Sox, where I would hear the crack of the bat, turn and run without looking, and at the last moment reach up and find the ball ever so gently arriving in my glove. It was always the last of the ninth, and I always saved the game.

I had an inkling even then, pun intended, that I might become a writer and make my living telling others the stories that I told myself. During those slow afternoons I explored an interior world that I value more the longer I live. When I grew beyond reading of imaginary battles and found myself in my own real battles I think I survived, in part, because of those afternoons when I was able to begin to map my own interior geography.

I also had an opportunity to visit the castled world etched in frost on my window, to understand the texture of a handwoven blanket from Scotland, to comprehend the architecture of a straight-backed chair. One spring when I was convalescing from an appendix operation I noticed the way a maple leaf outside my window turned toward the sun, and I believed I could tell when the weight of sunlight pressed it softly down.

I still lead a life of busyness, but there are times when the burden of what I ought to do becomes far heavier than the weight of sunlight on a maple leaf. Then I pick up books, magazines, notebooks, and go upstairs to the bedroom where I turn on the radio, pile my stuff around me, and journey back to the timeless afternoons of convalescence.

Below are the comments I made in sharing the draft with a seminar.

THE WRITER READS

The essay, or whatever it is, called "The Weight of Sunlight on a Maple Leaf," was written for a book. The editor's reaction to the piece included some complimentary phrases I had not remembered until I looked her letter up now ("works fine for me in its final draft," "the final draft *does* hold together for me"), but she did find the piece inferior to another piece of mine, and she had some questions: "I wanted to know *more* about that inward journey. For instance, you commented in the piece that you covered your ceiling with maps of Antartica, the Himalayas, and other faraway places; that intrigued me, and I wanted to know more about your imaginary travels. I wanted to know more about your other daydreams; you commented that you suffered from teenage insecurities the way everyone else did, but I wanted to know how you arrived at that comment."

I realized that in part she was reading her own experience into the piece and inadvertently telling me the piece she wanted me to write. She is a good editor and I respect her, but I can't write a piece (won't) unless I have the illusion, at least, that it's mine. One reason I did so badly in school. And yes, I overreact to criticism. Of course I do. All writers do. Their lives are on the line. I'd suspected that I would dump the ceiling of maps, perhaps just because I'd used it before, but she was headed off to a trek in the Himalayas. I was, in other words, suspicious of her reading, but she had questioned the piece, and once questioned it wobbled.

A writer friend who I admire and trust read the piece and talked to me about it on the phone. He made a similar comparison to the one she made and said, "This one is not as fully realized," and asked me if I should "plumb deeper?"

I decided to cut the piece out of the book; it would have to be made a lot better. In the end, I cut the piece for reasons that had nothing to do with the quality of it. It didn't work in the book, but when I cut at least 200 pages from the manuscript I decided to save this essay.

I had read a first draft to Don Graves and Virginia Stuart when they were on extensions of the same phone line at the university. I had a lot of doubts about the draft but they felt that there was something there. I needed that reassurance, but I was suspicious of it. I was, after all, reading it, and I think we are less critical when we hear a piece than when we see it.

Now Don called me and said he wanted to use it at the IRA convention in a workshop. I was flattered, but worried. I went back and read the piece, and then drove out to see him. At best I felt that the piece was a draft, perhaps not even that. I certainly didn't want people to think it was a final draft. Perhaps he could use it if it was marked DRAFT, and if I could present my reading of the piece. He told me his reading of it. I was flattered again. He saw far more in the piece and a far better piece than I saw. It was his piece, and that seemed interesting for a convention of readers. I was glad that the piece meant something to him, but I was astonished, the way you are when a teacher tells you that a thoroughly messy child of yours is noted for her neat work in school.

Here is my reading of the piece:

I want to see something in it that's worth keeping. No, not really that; I want to find something—a voice, a message, a pattern—that's worth making something of. That's makeable. That's workable. I want to find potential in it, and I want to be fair to myself. At the moment I think it should be burned, but then I've got to remember that I was burning everything I wrote when I married Minnie Mae. Much of what would have gone into the fireplace has gone into print. Blame her.

I'm trying not to read this with my stomach. My stomach is sinking. Cramping. My stomach is a good editor. The editor only gave it faint praise. My friend only gave it faint criticism. I don't know what there is here. OK, push on with the reading.

The title seems a bit precious. Cute. I thought it was great when I wrote it. Now it seems a trick.

The lead seems badly written now; the first phrase is awkward, "Every winter when I was a boy." It seems silly somehow, and the lead has to be reworked. I think I could get into the paragraph a little more directly. No, I won't give it a line-by-line reading. Not yet. It may be a waste of time. The piece hasn't earned that attention yet.

I like Dr. Bartlett, but it seems to me that the piece gets

badly out of proportion right away. There are almost three full paragraphs about him. It's probably too much about him for the length of the piece. It's certainly not enough to do him justice. I'd have to cut him down to a paragraph or cut him out and do a separate piece about him.

I think the business about convalescence at the end of the fourth paragraph needs to be a separate paragraph and be set up just a little better, be a bit richer, have a little more weight or density—more specific information.

The next paragraphs about the guys coming by on their way to school seem clumsy, badly crafted. And I wonder if I'm really being honest. Am I trying to jam too much in here. I think the second half of the second page tries to do too much, and because of it what should be done isn't developed appropriately. It isn't specific enough; it doesn't really put the reader there.

The first two paragraphs on the third page go off on two different tangents, and I think the piece jumps around a lot through the rest of the page. I'm all over the lot, and the piece is marred by too many clever phrases, a certain glibness—for example, the last clause of the essay. Also, some of the stuff about busyness.

I think the piece doesn't work. I do think there's an idea in it, and I had thought, until Don called and I reread it, that I could dust it off, touch it up, and peddle it to a newspaper or magazine. Not now. I'm worried, for example, about the dishonesty. Did I really seek sickness? I doubt that. But I learned, or now learn retrospectively, about its value. Or perhaps I've learned how it shaped me, how it made me the private public person, or the public private person I am today. The piece is too glib, too superficial, not focused and probing enough. It's full of writerly tricks, a rather disgusting slickness. I'm embarrased by it now.

Will I go back and write a piece on this subject? Perhaps, if I can get free of this draft. Not free of the reading of it, for I probably wouldn't reread it to write a new piece, but free of the memory of it.

Is Don's reading the right one? It is for him. He created his text out of his life and his needs when he read it. I like his piece but it isn't mine.

Years later, never looking back at the draft I didn't know I had, I wrote and published the following column. Someone once said that the criminal keeps returning to the scene of the crime. And we do, reconsidering and remaking those experiences which haunt our lives.

---

reflections from a sick bed

At 62, I don't take miracle drugs for granted. At 62, I don't take 63 for granted, but I know I've gotten this far because of pills that are still magic to me and drugs that still make me wonder.

I can still remember the red quarantine cards of the houses with scarlet fever inside. I still dream of the hearse that so carefully, so slowly backed down a neighboring driveway, turned in the street, taking away Butler Mitchell who had polio. We had an abundance of justified fears, blood poisoning and food poisoning, rheumatic fever, diphtheria, typhoid, the flu that had touched every family I knew, consumption, whooping cough, measles (German and native), mumps, chicken pox, small pox, pneumonia—I had double lobar.

Things were scary all right and they were treated with medicines that tasted like medicine: no cherry syrup then. Children today would take parents to court who poured acidy things into their throats that tasted as if they were made of mashed tree roots, squashed beetles, shaved toad—and probably were. I can still hear the rip of a mustard plaster being removed, and sometimes, in a strange social situation when people turn away and I am left alone with a glass of tomato juice in my hand, I imagine the guests have smelled the odor of ointments that were massaged into my flesh when I was young.

In a time when I have rarely heard the word *poultice* and medicine tastes so good that the great worry is that children will steal it and make themselves sick on a cure, I grow nostalgic for my sickly childhood, in which God punished me for my sins with sickness and my parents punished me with their treatments. The good part came afterward during a period described by that wonderful, long, musical word so rarely heard today: convalescence.

Now I am not romanticizing the experience of children today or yesterday who battle fatal disease, but I do remember—with a surprising nostalgia—the prescription that followed the crisis of those old-fashioned diseases: bed rest.

As a boy, I often heard Dr. Bartlett rumble, "Now, Donald, you'll have to stay in bed for a week or two."

"A week?" I'd yell as my mother said, "Shush."

"At least a week. I'll come by and we'll see about that second one."

He smiled as he said that and I suspect that he knew, more than I did then, how much I looked forward to long days in bed with no school—and no after-school.

The gang would come by the house in the morning shouting, "Murray, Murray," on their way to school, and I'd appear at the window and wave them on. They'd grin and yell and cavort—they knew I was faking it to get out of school, and I mimed a response that played to such an idea. In the afternoon, I'd hear, "Murray, Murray," again and I'd signal how much I wished I could go out to play.

I was lying. They would leave, and I would return to the warm tangle of quilts, blankets, and pillows in which I would spend those long, lonely days without time. Sometimes I feel that I have lived my life on the resources I developed when I was my only companion.

In that bed I was free of all the pressures to conform and belong. On the street, I was a coward playing the role of a tough kid, and never quite making it. Alone I didn't have to worry about what others thought of me, how I was dressed, how I spoke, how I walked. Turning inward I could travel further than I could biking the streets of North Quincy.

I read without plan or counsel. My teachers assigned books, such as *Lorna Doone*. I had always been a more adventuresome reader than school, in those days, would allow. I read sports stories and reread tales of adventure and exploration, such as Admiral Byrd's *Alone*. As a teenager I joined and paid for the packages that came from the Book-of-the-Month. Membership, in my neighborhood, had to be kept a secret. It was open season on intellectuals. Eyeglasses could get you beaten up. Glasses and books took a form of manliness I had not yet achieved.

In bed I read Baptist sermons, sometimes the Bible, even mother's magazines, the *Woman's Home Companion* and *McCall's*, *Ladies Home Journal*, and I believe something called the *Delineator*.

I was doing badly in school but I was a reader, an insatiable, promiscuous reader of stories about love and home-making, hockey and history; I read the *Boston Globe* and the *Boston Herald*, the *Record*, the *Post*, *Quincy Patriot Ledger*. When I found an author, such as Sabatini or Horatio Alger or Kenneth

Roberts, I would search for all the books by that author, gorging myself the way I did when I found a new ice cream flavor such as black raspberry.

I took advantage of every accident to expand my secret curriculum. My father, for some reason, was given a book I found in his desk drawer. I asked to read it and he blushed. He told me he had not read it. It had been a gift from a college man he worked with. It was a dirty book and a Commie book. Ceremonially we walked to another neighborhood to put the book in a stranger's trashcan.

The book was *Anna Karenina* by Tolstoy. The next day I went to the Wollaston Public Library and introduced myself to the world of Russian fiction.

These books were all, like the *National Geographic* maps on my ceiling, invitations to escape. I didn't read these books, I went into them. I joined the march to Quebec; I was in the Russian railroad station, my nostrils filled with coal smoke. I even entered into the alien worlds of my mother's fiction reading. I moved back and forth in time, crossed oceans, became lonely housewives, sad old men, and more than once a young lover.

I would also travel into my radio, becoming Jimmy Foxx or Tiny Thompson in the net for the Bruins. I played in the big bands with Dorsey and Miller and Goodman. Walter Damrosch introduced me to Tchaikovsky, Sibelius, and Debussy. I followed the convoluted plots of the soapies, surely good training for an intellectual, and got goosebumps hearing the convention hall boom "We want Willkie."

What I read, what I heard on the radio, what I dreamed in my daydreams and my night dreams, what I thought and what I imagined, all ran together. It was all part of a rich tapestry of memory and imagination, experience lived and relived. And the best part of it often was when the radio was off and the books and the magazines and the newspapers slid from the bed to the floor. And I was just there, in my bed, able to follow my mind wherever it went.

Those imaginings of mine were so vivid that sometimes, when I was in a real war, I was disappointed that it was, well, boring, and my life has to some degree always been like that, a wonderful blurring between what was, what might be, what might have been, with make believe often more real than real believe. I learned in those lonely days of a sickly childhood something that many Americans have never seemed to learn, that there are worse things than being in a room by yourself.

I can remember one afternoon looking out the window on Chester Street, where I watched the leaves on the maple tree slowly turn, palms out toward the sun. That was a better lesson than most I learned in school.

I want no sickly second childhood to provide matching bookends to my life, but sometimes, in retirement, when the present is too present, I will take to bed and practice the art of convalescence, tracing a map on the ceiling with my imagination, reading a mystery and putting it aside to continue the story, watching the leaves outside the window to see if I can catch them turning toward the sun.

Several years ago the editor of an academic journal tracked me down on vacation and invited me to write the lead article in a special research issue. I expressed great doubt, saying I was not a researcher, but she answered that was why they wanted me. They wanted a personal "Murray" piece to point out the importance of writing. I was flattered—it is easy to flatter me—but I said no. There were more calls and the editor persisted, flattered again and flattered some more. She won.

Eventually there was another phone call. They loved the piece but could I take out the personal stuff. I said I was sorry, I'd reread the piece, but without the personal stuff, it would probably say nothing at all.

Apparently the editors felt I didn't know how to cut the personal stuff, and so I received a marked-up copy showing me how to remove the offending personal matter. I still declined. The piece went to the firm publishing the journal. They said no personal material; no first person. They wanted the piece but I would have to change it. I refused and some time later cut out the academic, impersonal stuff and published it as the following column.

---

a healthy obsession

I've decided there are four things to take into retirement: a well-ripened pension check, a patient companion who doesn't mind having you home for lunch, a Morris chair worn to the peculiarities of your hind end, and a full-grown, out-of-control obsession.

I suspect the object of the obsession isn't very important if you don't break the law or shock the neighborhood—and shocking my neighbors these days would take some very strange obsession, perhaps playing the bagpipe at dawn without kilt.

I know elders who delight in scraping boat bottoms, spreading chicken dung on flower beds, dangling fake flies over innocent fish. I don't understand their needs, but good luck to them. I can even nod without smiling—not very much anyway—when a neighbor is costumed for tennis. An obsession can make empty days full.

I used to be ashamed of my obsession. My parents, school, and society told me to become well rounded. My body achieved that goal, but not my head. Behind my mask, I have been obsessed with pursuing the active verb.

Writing, for me, has always been a necessary, secret act of selfishness—and survival.

A few years ago I suffered a sudden paralysis and wrote its story in my mind as I was hauled away in the ambulance. Recently, when I was assigned to intensive care, I asked the nurses to attach the IV tubes to my left, nonwriting arm.

I cannot remember when I was not a writer, at least in my own mind. I have never recovered from the magic of crayons, chalk, scratchy steel dipping pens and their rebellious blots, the smell and feel—and taste—of pencils. I remain astonished that you can scratch two lines that cross in the sand and read X.

I did not know then that writing would become the way I experienced life and that I would read my X's—and their companion letters—to discover what I saw and felt and thought.

My daughters who grow toward middle age—and the one who never will—walk in and out of my poems. I am writing a novel to discover what meaning—if any—is hidden in the haunting memories of the hours I spent in foxholes under fire 42 years ago.

I compost my life, piling up phrases which do not yet make sense, lines overheard in a restaurant, scenes caught in the corner of my eyes, pages not yet understood, questions not yet shaped, thoughts half begun, problems unsolved, answers without questions—all the fragments of lives to be lived if I were to write them.

I am not bored, even at dinner parties. Others leave the table to stroll down imaginary fairways: I slip into the skin of the woman with the lavender hair and chat with her first husband, the one I didn't know she had. Others nod, smiling, to their companions, while imagining the grin of a trout or the seductive shape of a jib; I daydream metaphors, violent verbs, taunting sentence fragments.

Some of these fragments give a still-hesitant voice to unspoken feelings, others begin to describe the dark shapes that lurk at the edges of our days. Still more are fantasies— those imaginary lives that run counterpoint to our actual existence. Most arrive as scenes—moving pictures in my skull to which I may fit words.

What is seen is soon heard. The writer sees with the ear as much as the eye. The music of language is not, to the writer, just entertainment. The music of language is thought: our voices tell us the meaning of what we are seeing, thinking, experiencing.

Sometimes the words are specific, their unexpected meaning hidden until it comes clear through writing and rewriting. I creak out of bed, read of a high-school classmate in the obituaries, feel the chill, but then go to my desk as others go to paint the back deck or shop for the ultimate zoom lens. I have no choice: I must follow these elusive, beckoning words.

The words collide with other words, and potential meanings fly off from the collision. Occasionally the phrase grows into a line, rarely to a sentence this early in the hunt, almost never to a paragraph. Sentences and paragraphs are thoughts: they bring with them the clarity of completion. I do not have thoughts; I have language events to be thought about. I am drawn into the events of my language, the way we are drawn to accidents or fire.

William Gass, in his preface to the second edition of *In the Heart of the Heart of the Country*, attempts to tell us how his stories were made:

"They appeared in the world . . . slow brief bit by bit, through gritted teeth and much despairing: and if any person were to suffer such a birth, we'd see the skull come out on Thursday, skin appear by week's end, liver later, jaws arrive just after eating."

Writing, for me, can never be predicted—the jaws *do* arrive after eating. I cannot tame the writing. I am lured by language to edge out on the thin black ice of my own existence.

The writer's explorations fail more often than they succeed.

The ice creaks, bends, breaks. Failure is ungraceful and it may even appear in the *Boston Globe*. Writing is always revealing, because of the terror—to edge out beyond what is known, seeking questions, contradictions, surprise.

And surprise is found. Enough times to keep me returning to the page. The trout rises to the fly: the ball, often enough, gently curves, then drops into the cup.

We are not yet old when we see graceful bowls in shapeless hunks of damp clay, winds that are hungry for sails, flowers in black specks of seed, yellow-bellied sap-sucking tweeters that do not yet fly into our binoculars, words that have not yet found our sentence.

The fourth column was written but never submitted to the Boston Globe *and never published until now. I wrote it unexpectedly as I write most of my columns. I really liked it when I finished but needed a reader. I called Chip Scanlan in Florida and read it to him. He told me how well it was written. He's a writer and knew I needed to know that. And then he paused. I tucked my tummy in, got my chin up, and he told me it was written for a specialized audience. He added that no one in the general public would actually think a writing teacher could be criticized for clarity, brevity, and sincerity in writing.*

As soon as he said it, I knew he was right. But I asked my wife to read it while I was off to lunch where I showed it to Bob Connors, a good writer and good critic. They agreed with Chip—and so did I.

But they all said I should publish it in this book—and so I have.

---

guilty as charged

When you get to the age of sixty or more you often realize that you've picked up many trades along the way.

Every once in a while I pick up a newspaper and my hands will quickly fold it and tuck it together tightly. I might not be able to ride no-hands up and down the familiar streets of Wollaston, but if I could toss that paper on the porch of #133 it would hold.

I haven't tried it recently, but I could probably fieldstrip and reassemble a thirty-calibre machine gun blindfolded. Although, since the statute of limitations must protect me, I can confess that in 1943 I used the latrine to flush away some mystery parts of .45s I'd been assigned to clean.

I know that if the Durham laundry still existed I could pick up and deliver the laundry as I did in college—but I suspect most doors would be locked today. None were then—and there were no surprises when I walked into homes unannounced in the middle of an afternoon. I'm sure *that* has changed.

Some things I might even do more efficiently. Once I was running just ahead of a general when the Germans started shelling us. I hit the ground immediately and expressed surprise that I landed on top of the general, serving as a human flak blanket for the old man who was behind me. He said, "Private, experience counts."

But experience doesn't help when you receive a review of a book that is only 90 percent favorable. One of the strange trades I've picked up along the way to second childhood is the writing of textbooks. In my case, I have written textbooks about writing, and there are times when I wished I'd had a private to wear as a flak blanket.

The other day I opened an academic journal and started to read a review of the second edition of one of my texts. I felt the smile on my face in the beginning and I left it there, frozen, in case anyone was watching. He had several serious criticisms.

Now, I might as well confess that for years I thought that when I matured I would learn to appreciate criticism, make use of it, or, at least, become impervious to it. Not true. I've matured, if ripeness is the measure of maturity, but I hate criticism, know that it is always personal, prejudiced, unfair, and utterly stupid. A wise person once said, "Asking a writer about critics is like asking a hydrant about dogs."

But today, I've decided to report and answer one of the criticisms of my text.

The critic charged, "There is something worrisome about Murray's untroubled endorsement of what Richard Lanham calls the CBS Style: clarity, brevity, sincerity. Aren't there valid alternatives to journalistic economy? Murray also seems unconcerned that many theorists are suspicious of the commonsensical view that underwritten prose is better because it gives readers a lucid window on reality. This unqualified affirmation of the clear style seems almost naive."

Well, now.

Clarity. I confess I'm all for it. I passed through a rather extended period when I thought my own complicated sentences and paragraphs, woven with clauses, comments upon comments, forward with an assertion, backwards with a qualification, were damn profound. I hope I recovered.

Of course many academics confuse clarity with simplicity. They fear simplicity. It's hard to get a dissertation out of simplicity. But I've found that it took me decades to learn to be simple, and even today I work hard to be simple—and clear. I hope I'm guilty of clarity.

Brevity. It takes about a forty to one ratio to boil sap into maple syrup. In my apprentice years it often took more than forty drafts to boil the sap out of my copy. It isn't easy to be brief, but I think it's good. Guilty again, my brevity is premeditated.

Sincerity. That's a more difficult charge. I believe in my truth, stand behind what I write, that sort of thing—I've discovered I'm not bright enough to lie. Of course, you could say I believe my lies. I sure do.

But during the years that have whitened my beard, I have become suspicious of sincerity. Attila the Hun was sincere, the TV evangelists are sincere, all the presidential candidates who have never been TV evangelists are sincere. I even suspect that my reviewer was sincere. And I'm sincere in this objective, scholarly, nondefensive response to my critic. Guilty again.

Naive. I "sincerely" hope so. As I march forward to seventy, hoping to shuffle onward to 100, I realize my most dependable walking stick is my carefully cultivated naivete.

I don't exactly bound out of bed in the morning, but I get up eager to look out at the woods, rush out to get the papers, chat with my neighbors, delighted anew with the reflected light from the snow, the latest impossible political promise to cripple the economy and therefore create jobs, the gossip about you-know-who's third wife's new friend.

I'm naive enough to be amused and educated by the world. I'm still the kid on Vassell Street, heading off to explore the vacant lot. I work hard at being naive. And if you want evidence that will stand up in court, hear this:

> Each morning I go to my desk, face the blank screen as I did this morning, naively believing that I will see myself saying something that I haven't said before—at least in a way that I haven't said it before.

This morning I expected to write first on my novel as is my habit and found myself folding a newspaper, then unexpectedly cleaning a machine gun, and then, not realizing it until now, aiming this imaginary weapon at my reviewer. It was therapy, it was fun, and it was naive to believe that anyone would read these personal ramblings, but if you are reading this you have.

Guilty of clarity, brevity, sincerity, and naivete? I certainly hope so.

TWENTY-THREE

MAIL INTERVIEW WITH STUDENTS AT KENTWOOD HIGH SCHOOL, KENT, WASHINGTON

One of the delights of being interviewed is not the questions that surprise you, because that rarely happens, but your own answers. It is an opportunity to say what you do not expect to say, and so continue with your own learning.

These questions from students at Kentwood High School in Kent, Washington, sparked my curiosity. Though many of the questions were obvious, I hadn't remembered being asked them before—or answering them. I wanted to find out what I would say—and I did.

When did you start writing?

Apparently long before I had the qualifications to become editor of a newspaper in the fourth grade.

What made you start?

I think it was a natural evolution from telling stories to myself which tried to make sense of my world. I was the only child living with a collection of adults who the world thought very proper, and I thought very odd. I was lonely, had imaginary friends, since I wasn't allowed to play with the neighbors' children. They weren't Baptists. What's a kid to do who lives a life like that? He makes up stories of escape. In the stories he becomes a cowboy, a great hunter, a soldier. He scores the winning touchdown and gets the girl. My stories were a lot better than life.

Where you ever forced to write, either by teachers or by circumstances?

I was forced to write a great deal by teachers. I hated it,

because it seemed to me that I had to say what the teachers wanted me to say in a language that was theirs (but I never heard them or anyone else speak it). Later I had to write to feed my family. I didn't like that much either. I found that I had to write what editors wanted, and that isn't very easy, because editors don't know what they want until after they've seen it.

Were there certain books or people that strongly influenced your writing career?

I was lucky. I had a teacher in the sixth grade, another in my freshman year at a junior college, after I'd flunked out of high school, and a third in college after the war, who saw in me more than others saw in me. To put it another way, they saw what I felt occasionally, that I had something to say and my own way of saying it.

I was, and am, a compulsive reader. I read cereal boxes, match covers, any print that passes in front of my eyes. I've been influenced by a great ocean of books, good and bad.

Where and when did you first get published?

My freshman college teacher sent an editorial off to the *Christian Science Monitor* as I was drafted out of school in World War II, telling me that that proved I would be a writer when I came home. It was accepted and published, and I still get choked up thinking about that act of faith on his part.

Where you good in English classes?

I never did learn no grammar, and although I could diagram football plays I could never diagram a sentence. It depended on the teacher. As I said, I was a compulsive reader, but I had one teacher for two years who gave you an F if she found you had read ahead of the assignment. I'd read the whole book the night I got it, and that would get me in trouble. I had good ideas for writing. I have some of my papers, and they are extremely specific. I had a teacher who jumped me in a stairway because I had written in favor of our getting in the war against Hitler. He was Irish and hated Britain. I won the fight, but it didn't have a positive effect on my grades.

As I said, it depended more on my teacher than me, and I didn't realize it until writing the answer to this question. I went to a high school that was considered to be one of the best in the East, and I didn't think it was as bad then as I do now. I didn't expect much of high school then; I wasn't surprised I hated it. I thought that I was dumb, but I knew I could work hard and figured I could hire people who were smart, because they seemed dumb at the things I knew.

Did school help you learn to write?

See above. It didn't stop me, but it tried.

What methods or experiences helped you most in learning to write?

Writing. I learned to write by writing. I discovered what communicated to readers and, most of all, what communicated to myself. I knew what good writing was before I knew I knew it.

What is your general procedure in writing?

There are variations, of course, but when the writing goes well it usually means that I've mulled over the idea and the material for quite a long while. I know that the material is right by playing around with leads. When I have a lead and some sense of the end I may have a glimpse of how I get from one to the other. I write fast, and these days I do very little revising. This is partly the product of a great deal of discipline in the past. I used to write at least three drafts of every magazine article and read each one of them carefully at least ten times. In other words I would have thirty careful readings in which I would make changes. I also used to force the writing. I don't do that any more. If it doesn't come easily, I go on to something else. It means it isn't ready to be written.

How do you generate ideas?

I don't generate ideas; they come to me. Everything I read, see, experience, think about may spark ideas. I can have a lifetime of writing ideas in one day. I never have to strain to think about what to write.

How do you deal with writer's block?

I follow the counsel of a wise poet from the Pacific Northwest—William Stafford—and lower my standards. I only have writer's block when I'm trying to impress someone else, or when I'm trying to write better than I can write. I can only write as well as I can write. I've never had writer's block, incidentally, when ghostwriting. The disease seems to be a malfunction of ego.

How often do you write? Do you have a regular schedule?

I try to follow the counsel credited to Horace and Pliny and followed by such productive writers as Trollope and Updike: *nulla dies sine linea* (never a day without a line). Somedays my lines are pretty fragmentary, and often they do not make sentences or paragraphs; they are words, lines, chunks, phrases, sometimes just diagrams.

Where do you write best?

The ideal writing environment for me would be a busy lunchroom. I like a lot of noise and confusion that doesn't involve me. I can't stand quiet. And if I'm in my office under the porch I play records, tapes, or the radio. I do a lot of writing in the living room, on the porch, and in the car.

What writing utensil do you prefer—pen? typewriter? computer?

This is being written on a Display Writer. I'm anxious to get a lap computer that is battery-operated that I can carry around with me. I write by hand until I can get to the computer, but the computer is a wonderful tool that makes it possible for me to write at greater speed. And I think speed is important, because it causes productive accidents of meaning in language. The computer allows you to revise and edit easily.

Do you belong to a writing group?

No. That hasn't worked well for me. I do, however, have a few—very few—colleagues I count on as readers. The qualities they all have is that they are writers themselves; they are open and honest about their feelings, and they make me want to write when I leave them.

As old and fat and experienced as I am, I can still be paralyzed by a bad reader. That doesn't mean, necessarily, one who attacks me. It more likely means one who wants me to measure up to his or her standards, who cannot seem to understand what I'm trying to do and how I'm trying to do it.

Do you enjoy being critiqued?

Does a hydrant like male dogs?

Who are some of your favorite authors? Do you read the newspaper? Magazines? What kind of writing do you prefer to read? To write?

My favorite authors are the ones I am enjoying that week. I keep a number of books going and, I suppose, read a couple a week in bed, during the Celtics' games on TV, on the john, in traffic jams. I do not like the game of ranking authors. Literature shouldn't be competitive.

I read the *Boston Globe* and the *New York Times* every day. I read *Time,* where I used to work, and *Newsweek* and the *New Yorker* each week and a bunch of other magazines I buy on impulse at the newstand. I also read a number of professional teacher and scholarly journals.

I prefer to read and write poetry and fiction, although I'm having a great time reading a wonderful new biography of Thomas More by Richard Marius right now. I read a great many books on writing, especially collections of interviews with writers.

Do you think your life is exciting?

More exciting than playing right tackle, jumping out of airplanes, getting shot at, being a police reporter. I am never bored. I am constantly writing, standing in line at a supermarket, trapped in a traffic jam, listening to a boring lecture. I'm making up stories about the people around me, trying to capture and understand what I am seeing, hearing, feeling.

I'm as surprised by what appears on the page as I was at sixteen, perhaps more, because I've learned to lower my standards and allow more to happen on the page.

What is the typical or average salary for a writer?

It's OK on a newspaper these days. Not much compared to a lawyer, doctor, real estate developer, or a mortician, but who'd want to be any of those things if you could write. Real writers have to have other jobs so they can afford to write. I teach—it's good inside work. Composers and artists have it much worse than writers so I don't complain. Besides, those who support writers—popes, kings, governments, corporations, foundations, universities—soon begin to think they know what good writing is, what it should say and how it should be said. Better to be free even if it means working two jobs, one for the belly and one for the heart.

How do you get your work published?

By using the postal service. Writers who do not put their work in the mail never get published; writers who put their work in the mail sometimes get published. Editors are looking for good stuff, but they can't publish what they don't see.

Do you involve your family life in your writing?

Most of this has been dictated to my wife. Writing has allowed me to be around my children when they were young. For that I'm enormously grateful. I've never made writing a secret activity.

Have you always enjoyed being an author?

I have to write. That comes from some deep, psychological need of mine. When I think of being anything else it seems great to be a writer. I'm a fortunate man. No one in my family was ever able to afford to do what they wanted to do. They all had jobs. I have a vocation.

What do you like the least about writing and the writing life?

I spend a lot of time grumping and grumbling, but what I'm complaining about are those things that keep me from writing, especially campus politics, campus bureaucracies, the normal institutional manure. I'm looking forward to retiring in three years, or less, so I can spend more time writing. All writers are self-elected. Nobody's asking them to be writers. If they don't like to write, they should do something they like to do.

TWENTY-FOUR
RESEARCHER AND SUBJECT

At an academic meeting I heard Carol Berkenkotter from Michigan Technological University give a very stimulating paper, and I caught up with her to thank her. A group of us stood around, and I found myself criticizing some of the work being done by Linda Flower. I felt that the research was based too much on limited assignments executed in brief periods of time by inexperienced writers. After I had made my case Carol introduced me to one of the people in the group: Linda Flower. She responded graciously and professionally, and we began a friendship of which I am proud. I greatly respect her work and the contributions she and her colleagues have made to our profession.

Carol didn't waste any time in calling my bluff. Would I participate in a long-range study of a professional writer? They all watched for my reaction. I didn't have a chance.

I found the study helpful and instructive for me, but I have two regrets. When the article was published in College Composition and Communication, *it had a serious misprint in the second line of my section 6. A* not *was added, which reversed my meaning. Oscar Wilde said you could recover from anything but a misprint, and he should certainly know.*

I was also disappointed that our study hasn't led to more studies of experienced writers. I have a lot that I need to learn from the study of writers more skillful than I.

decisions and revisions: the planning strategies of a publishing writer

CAROL BERKENKOTTER

The clearest memory I have of Donald M. Murray is watching him writing at a long white wooden table in his study, which looks out on the New Hampshire woods. Beside his desk is a large framed poster of a small boy sitting on a bed staring at a huge dragon leaning over the railing glowering at him. The poster is captioned, "Donald imagined things." And so he did, as he addressed the problems writers face each time they confront a new assignment. During the summer of 1981, as I listened to him daily recording his thoughts aloud as he worked on two articles, a short story, and an editorial, I came to understand in what ways each writer's processes are unique and why it is important that we pay close attention to the setting in which the writer composes, the kind of task the writer confronts, and what the writer can tell us of his own processes. If we are to understand *how* writers revise, we must pay close attention to the context in which revision occurs.

Janet Emig, citing Eliot Mishler, has recently described the tendency of writing research toward "context stripping."[1] When researchers remove writers from their natural settings (the study, the classroom, the office, the dormitory room, the library) to examine their thinking processes in the laboratory, they create "a context of a powerful sort, often deeply affecting what is being observed and assessed."[2] Emig's essay points to the need to examine critically the effects of these practices.

The subject of the present study is not anonymous, as are most subjects, nor will he remain silent. I began the investigation with a critical eye regarding what he has said about revision, he with an equally critical attitude toward methods of research on cognitive processes. To some extent our original positions have been confirmed—yet I think each of us, researcher and writer, has been forced to question our assumptions and examine our dogmas. More important, this project stirs the dust a bit and suggests a new direction for research on composing processes.

I met Mr. Murray at the Conference on College Composition and Communication meeting in Dallas, 1981. He appeared at the speaker's rostrum after my session and introduced himself, and we began to talk about the limitations of taking protocols in an experimental situation. On the spur of the moment I asked him if he would be willing to be the subject of a naturalistic study. He hesitated, took a deep breath, then said he was very interested in understanding his own composing processes, and would like to learn more. Out of that brief exchange a unique collaborative research venture was conceived.

To date there are no reported studies of writers composing in natural (as opposed to laboratory) settings that combine thinking-aloud protocols with the writers' own introspective accounts. Recently, researchers have been observing young children as they write in the classroom. In particular, we have seen the promising research of Donald Graves, Lucy Calkins, and Susan Sowers, who have worked intimately with children and their teachers in the Atkinson Schools Project.[3] By using videotapes and by actively working in the classroom as teachers and interviewers, these researchers were able to track the revising processes of individual children over a two-year period. Studies such as these suggest that there may be other ways of looking at writer's composing processes than in conventional research settings.

There remains, however, the question: To what extent can a writer's subjective testimony be trusted? I have shared the common distrust of such accounts.[4] There is considerable cognitive activity that writers cannot report because they are unable to compose and monitor their processes simultaneously. Researchers have responded to this problem by taking retrospective accounts from writers immediately after they have composed,[5] or have studied writers' cognitive activity through the use of thinking-aloud protocols.[6] These protocols have been examined to locate the thoughts verbalized by the subjects while composing, rather than for the subjects' analysis of what they said. Typically, subjects were instructed to "say everything that comes to mind no matter how random or crazy it seems. Do not analyze your thoughts, just say them aloud." The effect of these procedures, however, has been to separate the dancer from the dance, the subject from the process. Introspective accounts made *in medias res* have not been possible thus far because no one has developed techniques that would allow a subject to write and comment on his or her processes between composing episodes. For this reason I had begun to entertain the idea of asking a professional writer to engage in a lengthy naturalistic study. When Donald Murray introduced himself, I knew I wanted him to be the subject.

METHODOLOGY

The objectives that I began with are modifications of those Sondra Perl identified in her study of five unskilled writers.[7] I wanted to learn more about the planning and revising strategies of a highly skilled and verbal writer, to discover how these strategies could be most usefully analyzed, and to determine how an understanding of this writer's processes would contribute to what we have already discovered about how skilled writers plan and revise.

The project took place in three stages. From June 15 until August 15, 1981 (a period of sixty-two days), Mr. Murray turned on the tape recorder when he entered his study in the morning and left it running during the day wherever he happened to be working: in his car waiting in parking lots, his university office, restaurants, the doctor's office, etc. This kind of thinking-aloud protocol differs from those taken by Linda Flower and John R. Hayes since the subject's composing time is not limited to a single hour; in fact, during the period of time that Mr. Murray was recording his thoughts, I accumulated over 120 hours of tape. The writer also submitted photocopies of all text, including notes and drafts made prior to the study. Thus I was able to study a history of each draft.

In the second stage, during a visit to my university, I gave the writer a task which specified audience, subject, and purpose. I asked him to think aloud on tape as he had previously, but this time for only one hour. Between the second and third stages, Mr. Murray and I maintained a dialogue on audiotapes which we mailed back and forth. On these tapes he compared his thoughts on his composing in his own environment over time to those on giving a one-hour protocol in a laboratory setting.

During the third stage of the study, I visited the writer at his home for two days. At this time I observed him thinking aloud as he performed a writing task which involved revising an article for a professional journal. After two sessions of thinking aloud on tape for two and one-half hours, Mr. Murray answered questions concerning the decisions he had made. Over the two-day period we taped an additional four hours of questions and answers regarding the writer's perceptions of his activities.

Another coder and I independently coded the transcripts of the protocols made in the naturalistic and laboratory settings.

Using the same procedure I employed in my study of how writers considered their audience (i.e., first classifying and then counting all audience-related activities I could find in each protocol), my coder and I tallied all planning, revising, and editing activities, as well as global and local evaluations of text that we agreed upon.[8] I was particularly interested in Murray's editing activities. Having listened to the tapes I was aware that editing (i.e., reading the text aloud and making word- and sentence-level changes) sometimes led to major planning episodes, and I wanted to keep track of that sequence.

The study was not conducted without problems. The greatest of these arose from how the writer's particular work habits affected the gathering of the data and how he responded to making a one-hour protocol. Unlike most writers who hand draft or type, Mr. Murray spends much time making copious notes in a daybook, then dictates his drafts and partial drafts to his wife, who is an accomplished typist and partner in his work. Later, he reads aloud and edits the drafts. If he determines that copy-editing (i.e., making stylistic changes in the text) is insufficient, he returns to the daybook, makes further notes, and prepares for the next dictation. The revision of one of the articles he was working on went through eight drafts before he sent it off. Two days later he sent the editor an insert.

Murray's distinctive work habits meant that all of the cognitive activity occurring during the dictation that might ordinarily be captured in a protocol was lost since he processed information at a high speed. During these periods I could not keep track of the content of his thoughts, and became concerned instead with the problem of why he frequently would find himself unable to continue dictating and end the session. There turned out to be considerable value in following the breakdowns of these dictations. I was able to distinguish between those occasions when Murray's composing was, in Janet Emig's terms, "extensive," and when it was "reflexive,"[9] by comparing the relative ease with which he developed an article from well-rehearsed material presented at workshops with the slow evolution of a conceptual piece he had not rehearsed. According to Emig, "The extensive mode . . . focuses upon the writer's conveying a message or communication to another. . . . The style is assured, impersonal, and often reportorial." In contrast, reflexive composing "focuses on the writer's thoughts and feelings. . . . The style is tentative, personal, and exploratory."[10]

In the latter case the writer is generating, testing, and evaluating new ideas, rather than reformulating old ones. I could observe the differences between the two modes of composing Emig describes, given Murray's response to the task in which he was engaged. When the writer was thoroughly familiar with his subject, he dictated with great fluency and ease. However, when he was breaking new ground conceptually, his pace slowed and his voice became halting; often the drafts broke down, forcing him to return to his daybook before attempting to dictate again.[11]

A more critical problem arose during the giving of the one-hour protocol. At the time he came to my university, the writer had been working on tasks he had selected, talking into a taperecorder for two months in a familiar setting. Now he found himself in a strange room, with a specific writing task to perform in one short hour. This task was not simple; nor was it familiar. He was asked to "explain the concept of death to the ten- to twelve-year-old readers of *Jack and Jill* magazine." Under these circumstances, Murray clutched, producing two lines of text: "*Dear 11 year old. You're going to die. Sorry. Be seeing you. P. Muglump, Local Funeral Director.*" Both the transcript and later retrospective testimony of the writer indicated that he did not have pets as a child and his memories of death were not of the kind that could be described to an audience of ten- to twelve-year-old children. He also had difficulty forming a picture of his audience, since he suspected the actual audience was grandparents in Florida who send their children subscriptions to *Jack and Jill.* Toward the end of the hour, he was able to imagine a reader when he remembered the daughter of a man he had met the previous evening. The protocol, however, is rich with his efforts to create rhetorical context—he plotted repeated scenarios in which he would be asked to write such an article. Nevertheless, it seems reasonable to conclude that Mr. Murray was constrained by what Lester Faigley and Stephen Witte call "situational variables":[12] the knowledge that he had only one hour in which to complete a draft, his lack of familiarity with the format of *Jack and Jill* (he had never seen the magazine), his doubts that an audience actually existed, and finally, the wash of unhappy memories that the task gave rise to. "So important are these variables," Faigley and Witte contend, "that writing skill might be defined as the ability to respond to them."[13]

One final problem is intrinsic to the case-study approach. Although the tapes are rich in data regarding the affective conditions under which the writer composed (he was distracted by university problems, had to contend with numerous interruptions, encountered family difficulties that he had to resolve, not to mention experiencing his own anxiety about his writing), as Murray reported, the further away he was in time from what he had done, the less able he was to reconstruct decisions he had made.

RESULTS

PLANNING AND REVISING

In this study I was primarily concerned with the writer's planning, revising, and editing activities. I had to develop a separate code category for the evaluation of text or content, since the writer frequently stopped to evaluate what he had written. Table 24–1 indicates the percentage of coded activities devoted to planning, revising, and editing for three pieces of discourse.[14] These three pieces were among the projects Murray worked on over the two-month period when he was making the protocols.

The coded data (taken from the transcripts of the tapes he made during this time) showed that up to 45%, 56%, and 35% of the writer's activities were concerned with planning, 28%, 21%, and 18% with either global or local evaluation, 3.0%, 3.0%, and .0% with revising (a finding which surprised me greatly, and to which I shall return), and 24%, 20%, and 47% with editing.

Murray's planning activities were of two kinds: the first were the stating of "process goals"—mentioning procedures, that is, that he developed in order to write (e.g., "I'm going to make a list of titles and see where that gets me," or "I'm going to try a different lead").[15] Frequently, these procedures (or "thinking plans," as they are also called)[16] led the writer to generate a series of subplans for carrying out the larger plan. The following excerpt is from the first draft of an article on revision that Murray was writing for *The Journal of Basic Writing*. He had been reading the manuscript aloud to himself and was nearly ready to dictate a second draft. Suddenly he stopped, took his daybook, and began making copious notes for a list of examples he could use to make the point that the wise editor or teacher should at first ignore sentence level editing problems to deal with more substantive issues of revision (this excerpt as well as those which follow are taken from the transcript of the tape and the photocopied text of the daybook):

> Let me take another piece of paper here. Questions, ah . . . examples, and ah set up . . . situation . . . *frustration of*

Table 24–1 Percentage of Coded Activities Devoted to Planning, Evaluating, Revising, and Editing for Three Pieces of Discourse.

	JOURNAL OF BASIC WRITING	COLLEGE COMPOSITION AND COMMUNICATION	EDITORIAL FOR CONCORD MONITOR
Planning	45%	56%	35%
Evaluating	28%	21%	18%
Revising	3.0%	3.0%	.0%
Editing	24%	20%	47%

> *writer. Cooks a five-course dinner and gets response only to the table setting . . . or to the way the napkins are folded* or to the . . . *order of the forks.* All right. I can see from the material I have how that'll go. I'll weave in. OK. *Distance in focus. Stand back., Read fast. Question writer.* Then *order doubles advocate. Then voice. Close in. Read aloud.* OK, I got a number of different things I can see here that I'm getting to. I'm putting it in different order because that may be, try to emphasize this one. May want to put the techniques of editing and teaching first and the techniques of the writer second. So I got a one and a two to indicate that. [Italics identify words written down.]

In this instance we can see how a writing plan (taking a piece of paper and developing examples) leads to a number of subplans: "I'll weave in," "I'm putting it in different order because that may be, try to emphasize this one," "May want to put the techniques of editing and teaching first and the techniques of the writer second," etc.

A second kind of planning activity was the stating of rhetorial goals, i.e., planning how to reach an audience: "I'm making a note here, job not to explore the complexities of revision, but simply to show the reader how to do revision." "Like many skilled writers, Murray had readers for his longer pieces. These readers were colleagues and friends whose judgment he trusted. Much of his planning activity as he revised his article for *College Composition and Communication* grew out of reading their responses to his initial draft and incorporating his summary of their comments directly onto the text. He then put away the text, and for the next several days made lists of titles, practiced leads, and made many outlines and diagrams in his daybook before dictating a draft. Through subsequent drafts he moved back and forth between the daybook and his edited dictations. He referred back to his readers' comments twice more between the first and last revised drafts, again summarizing their remarks in his notes in the daybook.

To say that Mr. Murray is an extensive planner does not really explain the nature or scope of his revisions. I had initially developed code categories for revising activities; however, my coder and I discovered that we were for the most part double-coding for revising and planning, a sign the two activities were virtually inseparable. When the writer saw that major revision (as opposed to copy-editing) was necessary, he collapsed planning and revising into an activity that is best described as *reconceiving*. To "reconceive" is to scan and rescan one's text from the perspective of an external reader and to continue redrafting until all rhetorical, formal, and stylistic concerns have been resolved, or until the writer decides to let go of the text. This process, which Nancy Sommers has described as the resolution of the dissonance the writer senses between his intention and the developing text, can be seen in the following episode.[17] The writer had been editing what he thought was a final draft when he saw that more substantive changes were in order. The flurry of editing activity was replaced by reading aloud and scanning the text as the writer realized that his language was inadequate for expressing a goal which he began to formulate as he read:

> (reading from previous page)[18] *It was E. B. White who reminded us, "Don't write about Man. Write about a man."* OK, I'm going to cut that paragraph there . . . I've already said it. *The conferences when the teacher listens to the student can be short. When the teacher listens to the student in conference . . . when the teacher listens to the student* . . . the conference is, well, *the conference can be short. The student learns to speak first of what is most important to the student at the point. To mention first what is most important . . . what most concerns . . . the student about the draft or the process that produced it. The teacher listens . . . listens, reads the draft through the student's eyes then reads the draft, read or rereads . . . reads or . . . scans or re-scans the draft to confirm, adjust, or compromise the student's concerns. The range of student response includes the affective and the cognitive. . . . It is the affective that usually controls the cognitive, and the affective responses usually have to be dealt with first . . .* (continues reading down the page) *Once the feelings of inadequacy, overconfidence, despair or elation are dealt with, then the conference teacher will find the other self speaking in more cognitive terms. And usually these comments* . . . OK that would now get the monitor into, into the phrase. All right. Put this crisscross cause clearly that page is going to be

> retyped . . . I'll be dictating so that's just a note. (continues reading on next page) *Listening to students allows the teacher to discover if the student's concerns were appropriate to where the student is in the writing process. The student, for example, is often excessively interested in language at the beginning of the process. Fragmentary language is normal before there is a text.* Make a comment on the text. (writes *intervention*) Now on page ten scanning . . . my God, I don't . . . I don't think I want to make this too much a conference piece. I'm going to echo back to that . . . monitor and also to the things I've said on page two and three. OK. Let's see what I can do . . . The biggest question that I have is how much detail needs to be on conferences. I don't think they're, I don't think I can afford too much. Maybe some stronger sense of the response that ah . . . students make, how the other self speaks. They've got to get a sense of the other self speaking.

The next draft was totally rewritten following the sentence in the draft: "When the teacher listens to the student, the conference can be short." The revision included previously unmentioned anecdotal reports of comments students had made in conferences, a discussion of the relevant implications of the research of Graves, Calkins, and Sowers, and a section on how the writing workshop can draw out the student's "other self" as other students model the idealized reader. This draft was nearly three pages longer than the preceding one. The only passage that remained was the final paragraph.

Granted that Mr. Murray's dictation frees him from the scribal constraints that most writers face, how can we account for such global (i.e., whole text) revision? One answer lies in the simple, yet elegant, principle formulated by Linda Flower and John R. Hayes.[19] In the act of composing, writers move back and forth between planning, translating (putting thoughts into words), and reviewing their work. And as they do, they frequently "discover" major rhetorical goals.[20] In the episode just cited we have seen the writer shifting gears from editing to planning to reconceiving as he recognized something missing from the text and identified a major rhetorical goal—that he had to make the concept of the other self still more concrete for his audience: "They've got to get a sense of the other self speaking." In this same episode we can also see the cognitive basis for alterations in the macrostructure, or "gist," of a text, alterations Faigley and Witte report having found in examining the revised drafts of advanced student and expert adult writers.[21]

PLANNING AND INCUBATION

This discussion of planning would be incomplete without some attention to the role of incubation. Michael Polanyi describes incubation as "that persistence of heuristic tension through . . . periods of time in which problems are not consciously entertained."[22] Graham Wallas and Alex Osborn agree that incubation involves unconscious activity that takes place after periods of intensive preparation.[23]

Given the chance to observe a writer's processes over time, we can see incubation at work. The flashes of discovery that follow periods of incubation (even brief ones) are unexpected, powerful, and catalytic, as the following episode demonstrates. Mr. Murray was revising an article on revision for the *Journal of Basic Writing*. He had begun to review his work by editing copy, moving to more global issues as he evaluated the draft:

> The second paragraph may be . . . Seems to me I've got an awful lot of stuff before I get into it. (Counting paragraphs) One, two, three, four, five, six, seven, eight, nine, ten, ten paragraphs till I really get into the text. Maybe twelve or thirteen. I'm not going to try to hustle it too much. That might be all right.

The writer then reread the first two paragraphs, making small editorial changes and considering stylistic choices. At that point he broke off and noted on the text three questions, *"What is the principle? What are the acts? How can it be taught?"* He reminded himself to keep his audience in mind. "The first audience has got to be the journal, and therefore, teachers." He took a five-minute break and returned to report,

> But, that's when I realized . . . the word hierarchy ah, came to me and that's when I realized that in a sense I was making this too complicated for myself and simply what I have to do is show the reader . . . I'm making a note here . . . *Job not to explore complexities of revision, but simply to show the reader how to do revision.*

From a revision of his goals for his audience, Murray moved quickly into planning activity, noting on his text,

> Hierarchy of problems. OK. What I'm dealing with is a hierarchy of problems. *First, focus/content, second, order/structure, third, language/voice* . . . OK. Now, let's see. I need to ah, need to put that word, hierarchy in here somewhere. Well, that may get into the second paragraph so put an arrow down there (draws arrow from hierarchy to second

> paragraph), then see what we can do about the title if we need to. Think of things like "first problems first" (a mini-plan which he immediately rejects). It won't make sense that title, unless you've read the piece. Ah well, come up with a new title.

Here we can observe the anatomy of a planning episode with a number of goals and subgoals generated, considered, and consolidated at lightning speed: "OK. What I'm dealing with is a hierarchy of problems." . . . "I need to ah, need to put that word, hierarchy in here somewhere." ". . . so put an arrow down there, then see what we can do about the title . . ." ". . . 'first problems first.' It won't make sense that title . . . Ah well, come up with a new title." We can also see the writer's process of discovery at work as he left his draft for a brief period and returned having identified a single meaning-laden word. This word gave Murray an inkling of the structure he wanted for the article—a listing of the problems writers face before they can accomplish clear, effective revision. In this case, a short period of incubation was followed by a period of intense and highly concentrated planning when Murray realized the direction he wanted the article to take.

INTROSPECTION

One of the most helpful sources in this project was the testimony of the writer as he paused between or during composing episodes. Instead of falling silent, he analyzed his processes, providing information I might have otherwise missed. The following segments from the protocols will demonstrate the kinds of insights subjects can give when not constrained by time. At the time of the first, Mr. Murray had completed the tenth list of titles he had made between June 26 and July 23 while working on the revision of his article for *College Composition and Communication*. Frequently, these lists were made recursively, the writer flipping back in his daybook to previous lists he had composed:

> I think I have to go back to titles. *Hearing the student's other self*. Hold my place and go back and see if I have any that hit me in the past. *Teaching the reader and the writer. Teaching the reader in the writer. Encouraging the internal dialogue*. I skipped something in my mind that I did not put down. *Make your students talk to themselves. Teaching the writer to read.*

At this point he stopped to evaluate his process:

> All that I'm doing is compressing, ah, compressing is, ah, why I do a title . . . it compresses a draft for the whole thing. Title gives me a point of view, gets the tone, the difference between teaching and teach. A lot of time on that, that's all right.

The following morning the writer reported, "While I was shaving, I thought of another title. *Teaching the other self: the writer's first reader.* I started to think of it as soon as I got up." This became the final title for the article and led to the planning of a new lead.

Later that day, after he had dictated three pages of the fourth of eight drafts, he analyzed what he had accomplished:

> Well, I'm going to comment on what's happened here . . . this is a very complicated text. One of the things I'm considering, of course, is incorporating what I did in Dallas in here . . . ah, the text is breaking down in a constructive way, um, it's complex material and I'm having trouble with it . . . very much aware of pace of proportion; how much can you give to the reader in one part, and still keep them moving on to the next part. I have to give a little bit of head to teaching. . . . As a theatrical thing I am going to have to put some phrases in that indicate that I'm proposing or speculating, speculating as I revise this . . .

This last summation gave us important information on the writer's global and local evaluation of text as well as on his rhetorical and stylistic plans. It is unique because it shows Murray engaged in composing and introspecting at the same time. Generally speaking, subjects giving protocols are not asked to add the demands of introspection to the task of writing. But, in fact, as Murray demonstrated, writers *do* monitor and introspect about their writing simultaneously.

SUMMARY

Some of the more provocative findings of this study concern the subprocesses of planning and revising that have not been observed in conventional protocols (such as those taken by Flower and Hayes) because of the time limitations under which they have been given. When coding the protocols, we noted that Mr. Murray developed intricate style goals:

> It worries me a little bit that the title is too imperative.

> When I first wrote, most of my articles were like this; they pound on the table, do this, do that. I want this to be a little more reflective.

He also evaluated his thinking plans (i.e., his procedures in planning): "Ah, reading through, ah, hmm . . . I'm just scanning it so I really can't read it. If I read it, it will be an entirely different thing."

Most important, the writer's protocols shed new light on the great and small decisions and revisions that form planning. These decisions and revisions form an elaborate network of steps as the writer moves back and forth between planning, drafting, editing, and reviewing.[24] This recursive process was demonstrated time after time as the writer worked on the two articles and the editorial, often discarding his drafts as he reconceived a major rhetorical goal, and returned to the daybook to plan again. Further, given his characteristic habit of working from daybook to dictation, then back to daybook, we were able to observe that Donald Murray composes at the reflexive and extensive poles described by Janet Emig. When working from material he had "rehearsed" in recent workshops, material with which he was thoroughly familiar, he was able to dictate virtually off the top of his head. At other times he was unable to continue dictating as he attempted to hold too much in suspension in short-term memory. On these occasions the writer returned to the daybook and spent considerable time planning before dictating another draft.

One final observation: although it may be impolitic for the researcher to contradict the writer, Mr. Murray's activity over the summer while he was thinking aloud suggests that he is wrong in his assertion that writers only consider their audiences when doing external revision, i.e., editing and polishing. To the contrary, his most substantive changes, what he calls "internal revision," occurred as he turned his thoughts toward his audience. According to Murray, internal revision includes

> everything writers do to discover and develop what they have to say, beginning with the reading of a completed first draft. They read to discover where their content, form, language, and voice have led them. They use language, structure, and information to find out what they have to say or hope to say. The audience is one person: the writer.[25]

The writer, however, does not speak in a vacuum. Only when he begins to discern what his readers do not yet know can he shape his language, structure, and information to fit the needs of those readers. It is also natural that a writer like Murray would not be aware of how significant a role his sense of audience played in his thoughts. After years of journalistic writing, his consideration of audience had become more automatic than deliberate. The value of thinking-aloud protocols is that they allow the researcher to eavesdrop at the workplace of the writer, catching the flow of thought that would remain otherwise unarticulated.

However, *how* the writer functions when working in the setting to which he or she is accustomed differs considerably from how that writer will function in an unfamiliar setting, given an unfamiliar task, and constrained by a time period over which he or she has no control. For this reason, I sought to combine the methodology of protocol analysis with the techniques of naturalistic inquiry.

This project has been a first venture in what may be a new direction. Research on single subjects is new in our discipline; we need to bear in mind that each writer has his or her own idiosyncrasies. The researcher must make a trade-off, foregoing generalizability for the richness of the data and the qualitative insights to be gained from it. We need to replicate naturalistic studies of skilled and unskilled writers before we can begin to infer patterns that will allow us to understand the writing process in all of its complexity.

NOTES

1. Janet Emig, "Inquiry Paradigms and Writing," *College Composition and Communication*, 33 (February, 1982), p. 55.
2. Emig, "Inquiry Paradigms and Writing," p. 67.
3. Donald Graves, "What Children Show Us About Revision," *Language Arts*, 56 (March, 1979), 312–319; Susan Sowers, "A Six-Year-Old's Writing Process: The First Half of the First Grade," *Language Arts*, 56 (October, 1979), 829–835; Lucy M. Calkins, "Children Learn the Writer's Craft," *Language Arts*, 57 (February, 1980), 207–213.
4. Janet Emig, *The Composing Processes of Twelfth-Graders* (Urbana, IL: National Council of Teachers of English, 1971), pp. 8–11; Linda Flower and John R. Hayes, "A Cognitive Process Theory of Writing," *College Composition and Communication*, 32 (December, 1981), 368.
5. See Janet Emig, *The Composing Processes of Twelfth-Graders*, p. 30; Sondra Perl, "Five Writers Writing: Case Studies of the Composing Processes of Unskilled College Writers," Diss. New York University, 1978, pp. 48, 387–391; "The Composing Processes of Unskilled College Writers," *Research in the Teaching of English*, 13

(December, 1979), 318; Nancy I. Sommers, "Revision Strategies of Student Writers and Experienced Adult Writers," paper delivered at the Annual Meeting of the Modern Language Association, New York, 28 December 1978. A slightly revised version was published in *College Composition and Communication*, 32 (December, 1980), 378–388.

6. See Linda Flower and John R. Hayes, "Identifying the Organization of Writing Processes," in *Cognitive Processes in Writing*, ed. Lee W. Gregg and Erwin R. Steinberg (Hillsdale, NJ: Lawrence Erlbaum Associates, 1981), p. 4; "The Cognition of Discovery: Defining a Rhetorical Problem," *College Composition and Communication*, 32 (February, 1980) 23; "The Pregnant Pause: An Inquiry into the Nature of Planning," *Research in the Teaching of English*, 19 (October, 1981), 233; "A Cognitive Process Theory of Writing," 368; Carol Berkenkotter, "Understanding a Writer's Awareness of Audience," *College Composition and Communication*, 32 (December, 1981), 389.

7. Perl, "Five Writers Writing: Case Studies of the Composing Processes of Unskilled College Writers," p. 1.

8. Evaluations of text were either global or local. An example of global evaluation is when the writer says, "There's a lack of fullness in the piece." When the writer was evaluating locally he would comment, ". . . and the ending seems weak."

9. Emig, *The Composing Processes of Twelfth-Graders*, p. 4.

10. *Ibid.* See also "Eye, Hand, and Brain," in *Research on Composing: Points of Departure*, ed. Charles R. Cooper and Lee Odell (Urbana, IL: National Council of Teachers of English), p. 70. Emig raises the question, "What if it is the case that classical and contemporary rhetorical terms such as . . . extensive and reflexive may represent centuries old understandings that the mind deals differentially with different speaking and writing tasks. To put the matter declaratively, if hypothetically, modes of discourse may represent measurably different profiles of brain activity."

11. Janet Emig, observing her subject's writing processes, noted that "the *nature of the stimulus*" did not necessarily determine the response. Emig's students gave extensive responses to a reflexive task (*The Composing Processes of Twelfth-Graders*, pp. 30–31, 33). Similarly, Murray gave a reflexive response to an extensive task. Such a response is not unusual when we consider what the writer himself has observed: "The deeper we get into the writing process the more we may discover how affective concerns govern the cognitive, for writing is an intellectual activity carried on in an emotional environment, a precisely engineered sailboat trying to hold course in a vast and stormy Atlantic" ("Teaching the Other Self: The Writer's First Reader," *College Composition and Communication*, 33 [May, 1982], 142). For a writer as deeply engaged in his work as Murray, drafting a conceptual piece was as personal and subjective as describing a closely felt experience.

12. Lester Faigley and Stephen Witte, "Analyzing Revision," *College Composition and Communication,* 32 (December, 1981), 410–411.
13. Faigley and Witte, 411.
14. These three pieces of discourse were chosen because their results are representative of the writer's activities.
15. Linda Flower and John R. Hayes describe "process goals" as "instructions and plans the writer gives herself for directing her own composing process." See "The Pregnant Pause: An Inquiry Into the Nature of Planning," 242. However, this definition is not always agreed upon by cognitive psychologists studying problem-solvers in other fields. On one hand, Allen Newell, Herbert A. Simon, and John R. Hayes distinguish between the goals and plans of a problem-solver, considering a goal as an end to be achieved and a plan as one kind of method for reaching that end. See John R. Hayes, *Cognitive Psychology* (Homewood, IL: The Dorsey Press, 1978), p. 192; Allen Newell and Herbert A. Simon, *Human Problem Solving* (Englewood Cliffs, NJ: Prentice-Hall, Inc. 1972), pp. 88–92, 428–29. On the other hand, George Miller, Eugene Galanter, and Karl H. Pribram use the term "plan" inclusively, suggesting that a plan is "any hierarchical process in the organism that can control the order in which a sequence of operations is to be performed." See *Plans and the Structure of Human Behavior* (New York: Holt, Rinehart, and Winston, 1960), p. 16.
16. Flower and Hayes use these terms interchangeably, as have I. "Thinking plans" are plans for text that precede drafting and occur during drafting. Thinking plans occur before the movements of a writer's hand. Because of the complexity of the composing process, it is difficult to separate thinking plans from "process goals." It is possible, however, to distinguish between *rhetorical goals* and *rhetorical plans.* Murray was setting a goal when he remarked, "The biggest thing is to ... what I've got to get to satisfy the reader ... is that point of what do we hear the other self saying and how does it help?" He followed this goal with a plan to "probe into the other self. What is the other self? How does it function?"
17. Sommers, "Revision Strategies," pp. 385, 387. (See note 5, above.)
18. The material italicized in the excerpts from these transcripts is text the subject is writing. The material italicized and underlined is text the subject is reading that has already been written.
19. Flower and Hayes, "A Cognitive Process Theory of Writing," 365–387.
20. Berkenkotter, "Understanding a Writer's Awareness of Audience," 392, 395.
21. Faigley and Witte, 406–410.
22. Michael Polanyi, *Personal Knowledge: Toward a Post-Critical Philosophy,* (Chicago: The University of Chicago Press, 1958), p. 122.
23. Graham Wallas, *The Art of Thought* (New York: Jonathan Cape, 1926), pp. 85–88; Alex Osborn, *Applied Imagination: Principles and*

Procedures of Creative Problem-Solving, 3rd rev. ed. (New York: Charles F. Scribner and Sons), pp. 314–325.

24. For a description of the development of a writer's goal structure, see Flower and Hayes, "A Cognitive Process Theory of Writing."
25. Donald M. Murray, "Internal Revision: A Process of Discovery," *Research on Composing: Points of Departure* (see note 10), p. 91.

response of a laboratory rat— or, being protocoled

DONALD M. MURRAY

1.

First a note on self-exposure, a misdemeanor in most communities. I have long felt the academic world is too closed. We have an ethical obligation to write and to reveal our writing to our students if we are asking them to share their writing with us. I have felt writers should, instead of public readings, give public workshops in which they write in public, allowing the search for meaning to be seen. I've done this and found the process insightful—and fun.

I have also been fascinated by protocol analysis research. It did seem a fruitful way (a way, there is no one way) to study the writing process. I was, however, critical of the assignments I had seen given, the concentration on inexperienced students as subjects, and the unrealistic laboratory conditions and time limitations.

And, in the absence of more proper academic resources, I have made a career of studying myself while writing. I was already without shame. When Carol Berkenkotter asked me to run in her maze I gulped, but I did not think I could refuse.

2.

The one-hour protocol was far worse than I had expected. If I had done that first there would have been no other protocols. I have rarely felt so completely trapped and so inadequate. I have gone through other research experiences, but in this case I felt stronger than I ever had the need to perform. That was nothing that the researcher did. It was a matter of the conditions. I had a desperate desire to please. I thought of that laboratory experiment where subjects would push a button to cause pain to other people. I would have blown up Manhattan to get out of that room. To find equivalent feelings from my past I would have to go back to combat or to public school. I have developed an enormous compassion and respect for those who have performed for Masters and Johnson.

3.

The process of a naturalistic study we have evolved (Can a rat be a colleague? Since a colleague can be a rat, I don't see why not) soon became a natural process. I do not assume, and neither did my researcher, that what I said reflected all that was taking place. It did reflect what I was conscious of doing, and a bit more. My articulation was an accurate reflection of the kind of talking I do to myself while planning to write, while writing, and while revising. At no time did it seem awkward or unnatural. My talking aloud was merely a question of turning up the volume knob on the muttering I do under my breath as I write.

I feel that if there was any self-consciousness in the process it was helpful. I was, after all, practicing a craft, not performing magic. Writing is an intellectual activity, and I do not agree with the romantics who feel that the act of writing and the act of thinking are separate.

Having this researcher, who had earned my trust, waiting to see what I wrote was a motivating factor. While the experiment was going on she was appropriately chilly and doctoral. But I still knew someone was listening, and I suspect that got me to the writing desk some days.

It is certainly true that debriefing by the researcher at some distance from the time of writing was virtually useless. I could not remember why I had done what. In fact, the researcher knows the text better than I do. I am concentrating almost entirely on the daily evolving text, and yesterday's page seems like last year's. I intend to try some teaching experiments in the future that make it possible for me to be on the scene when my students are writing. I'm a bit more suspicious now than I had been about the accounts that are reconstructed in a conference days after writing. They are helpful, the best teaching point I know, but I want to find out what happens if we can bring the composing and the teaching closer together.

4.

I certainly agree with what my researcher calls introspection. I am disappointed, however, that she hasn't included the term that I overheard the coders use. Rats aren't all that dumb, and I think there should be further research into those moments when I left the desk and came back with a new insight. They called them: "Bathroom epiphanies."

5.

I was surprised by:

1. The percentage of my time devoted to planning. I had realized the pendulum was swinging in that direction, but I had no idea how far it had swung. I suspect that when we begin to write in a new genre we have to do a great deal of revision, but that as we become familiar with a genre we can solve more writing problems in advance of a completed text. This varies according to the writer but I have already changed some of my teaching to take this finding into account by allowing my students much more planning time and introducing many more planning techniques.
2. The length of incubation time. I now realize that articles that I thought took a year in fact have taken three, four, or five years.
3. The amount of revision that is essentially planning, what the researcher calls "reconceiving." I was trying to get at that in my chapter, "Internal Revision: A Process of Discovery," published in *Research on Composing: Points of Departure*, edited by Charles R. Cooper and Lee Odell. I now understand this process far better, and much of my revision is certainly a planning or prewriting activity.

6.

I agree with my researcher (what rat wouldn't?) that affective conditions are important in writing. I do think the affective often controls the cognitive, and I feel strongly that much more research has to be done, difficult as it may be, into those conditions, internal and external, that make effective writing possible or impossible.

7.

I was far more aware of audience than I thought I was during some of the writing. My sense of audience is so strong that I have to suppress my conscious awareness of audience to hear what the text demands.

Related to this is the fact that I do need a few readers. The important role of my prepublication readers was clear when my revisions were studied. No surprise here. I think we need more study of the two, or three, or four readers professional writers choose for their work in process. It would be helpful for us as teachers to know the qualities of these people and what they do for the writer. I know I choose people who make me want to write when I leave them.

8.

I worry a bit about the patterns that this research revealed have been laid down in my long-term memory. The more helpful they are the more I worry about them. I fear that what I discover when I write is what I have discovered before and forgotten, and that rather than doing the writing that must be done I merely follow the stereotypes of the past. In other words, I worry that the experienced writer can become too glib, too slick, too professional, too polished—can, in effect, write too well.

9.

The description of working back and forth from the global to the particular during the subprocesses of planning and revising seems accurate to me.

There is a great deal of interesting research and speculation about this process, but we need much more. I find it very difficult to make my students aware of the layers of concern through which the writing writer must oscillate at such a speed that it appears the concerns are dealt with instantaneously.

Too often in my teaching and my publishing I have given the false impression that we do one thing, then another, when in fact we do many things simultaneously. And the interaction between these things is what we call writing. This project reaffirmed what I had known, that there are many simultaneous levels of concern that bear on every line.

10.

I realize how eccentric my work habits appear. I am aware of how fortunate I am to be able to work with my wife. The process of dictation of nonfiction allows a flow, intensity, and productivity that is quite unusual. It allows me to spend a great deal of time planning, because I know that once the planning is done I can produce copy in short bursts. It is not my problem but the researcher's, however, to put my eccentric habits into context.

If I am the first writer to be naked, then it is up to those other writers who do not think they look the same to take off their clothes. I hope they do not appear as I do; I would be most depressed if I am the model for other writers. I hope, and I believe, that there must be a glorious diversity among writers. What I think we have done, as rat and ratee, is to demonstrate that there is a process through which experienced writers can be studied under normal working conditions on typical writing projects. I think my contribution is not to reveal my own writing habits but to show a way that we can study writers who are far better writers than I.

11.

Finally, I started this process with a researcher and have ended it with a colleague. I am grateful for the humane way the research was conducted. I have learned a great deal about research and about what we have researched. It has helped me in my thinking, my teaching, and my writing. I am grateful to Dr. Carol Berkenkotter for this opportunity.

AFTERWORD

Each day I go to my writing desk to find out what I have to say. I have learned how to encourage the unexpected and follow it toward its own meaning. I have learned how to delight in such play, the daily condition of my second childhood. I hope you will be so lucky.

Sit in a chair with your own daybook on your knee or sit before your computer screen. Lower your standards. Do not strive but receive, accept, allow the flow of language in its own time, in its own way.

Do not work at language, but allow language; then read what you have written, not yet critically but playfully, to hear what you do not expect to hear. Follow the music of language where it takes you; allow words to reveal how much you know.

And then, having experienced the gift of reception, pass it on to your students by giving them the time, the environment, the response that will allow them to expect the unexpected.

If you are able to learn how to expect the unexpected on your own pages, you may be able to help your students discover what they have to say—and how to say it.